A Free Range Childhood

Self Regulation
at
Summerhill School

A Free Range

Summerhill School is a large, red brick building supplemented by various rather dilapidated outbuildings and assorted caravans. *[Photo by Matthew Appleton.]*

Childhood

Self Regulation
at
Summerhill School

by Matthew Appleton

THE FOUNDATION FOR EDUCATIONAL RENEWAL, INC.
A Solomon Press Book

Free Range Childhood: Self Regulation at Summerhill School
by Matthew Appleton

The Foundation for Educational Renewal, Inc.
P.O. Box 328
Brandon, VT 05733
phone: 800-639-4122
http://www.PathsOfLearning.net

Front cover photo by Tomo Usuada.

This book was designed by Sidney Solomon and Raymond Solomon
and typeset by Eve Brant
in Baskerville Old Face, Lucida Handwriting, and Eras Medium fonts

First printing June, 2000   ISBN: 1-885580-02-9

Contents

This book is dedicated to Akira

Acknowledgments

I would like to acknowledge the help, advice, and encouragement of the following people, without whom this book would not have been possible:

To Drs. Dorothea and Manfred Fuckert for their support and the essential role they have played in my education and growth.

To Dr. Ron Miller for his support of this book.

To Sidney Solomon for his belief in this book.

To Sidney and Raymond Solomon for their superb design. And to Eve Brant for her help in copyediting.

To Tomo Usuada for his engaging photographs.

To Jenni Meyer and Catriona Neill for their advice and patience in editing the text.

To Sam Doust and Justin Baron for their computer wizardry when I didn't have a clue.

To Dr. Rosie Bailey for believing in my writing capabilities before I did.

To Casilda Rodriganez for her kind donation that enabled me to buy the word processor on which this book was originally written.

To Gunn Saltvedt for patience and space when this book was being written, and to Eva Saltvedt-Appleton for inspiration.

To Dr. Giuseppe Cammarella, Maureen Chard, James DeMeo, Montse Durban, Nana Hatzi, Bronwen Jones, Albert and Popsy Lamb, Ena Neill, Zoë Readhead, Penny Rimbaud, Peter Robbins, Patricia Staines, and Ric Staines, all of whom have added something to this book by their encouragement or presence.

Thanks also to A.S. Neill and Wilhelm Reich, who I did not know, but whose pioneering work paved the way.

Special thanks to the kids of Summerhill, who shared so much of themselves and taught me so much.

—*Matthew Appleton*
March, 2000

Introduction

The popular image of Summerhill has always been a controversial one. In the media it is often depicted as the "school for scandal," the "do-as-you-like school," the "school with no rules." The idea of children regulating their own lives free from adult interference is foreign to most people and is easily dismissed as a "trendy" or "cranky" irrelevance, especially when the language of the media is the only language by which the majority of people get to hear of Summerhill. The many journalists and film crews who visit the school have their own agenda. Usually it centers around the three S's—sex, swearing, and smoking—underscored by anxieties about academic progress in an environment where children do not have to go to class. But serious attempts to come to terms with the deeper processes of Summerhill life, or what they might have to tell us about child nature, are few and far between.

The same is true in academic circles. Following the success of A.S. Neill's *Summerhill* book in the 1960's, a book entitled *Summerhill: For and Against* was published in America. It is a compilation of essays by various educationalists, psychologists, social critics, and others, each giving his or her own opinion on Summerhill. The first writer declares, "I would as soon enroll a child of mine in a brothel as in Summerhill." The second, a clergyman, describes Summerhill as "a holy place." So the lines of philosophical battle, which persist throughout the book, are drawn. Each of these

1

essays reflects the academic and theoretical ideas of the author, his or her own prejudices and longings, the particular area of "expertise" in which the author is grounded. Reading them from the perspective of someone who has lived at Summerhill, where I worked as a houseparent for nine years, I am struck by how little they have to do with real Summerhill life, whether they are for or against the idea of it.

Such books are intellectually entertaining, but they inevitably miss the point. They are not drawn from experience, but from opinion and opinion alone. It is true that many of the authors have experience with children, but not with children in a Summerhill setting. Would we expect a zookeeper to be able to hold forth on the natural behavior of animals in the wild without studying it first? The conclusion we might reach in the case of a tiger, for example, is that in its natural state it spends its day pacing listlessly up and down and is unable to fend for itself. Expertise in one field does not justify judgment in another. We must first gain experience of and familiarity with the new field before we can comment with authority on its content. As such, the world of the "free range" or self-regulated child lies outside of the auspices of any academic institution or tradition, be it psychological, sociological, or educational. Until such time as these disciplines embrace this world seriously and practically it remains the province of those who have; namely the handful of parents, educators, physicians, and others who have had hands-on experience, and the children themselves.

Because of the misconceptions that abound, and also because of my own relationship to the subject, I have made this book primarily a descriptive and anecdotal one, dealing with everyday life at Summerhill, rather than concerning myself with abstract theory. (There is, in fact, no great theory that shapes Summerhill; it shapes itself around the practical and emotional needs of the children and adults who live there at any one time. The only premise, as such, is a trust that children will learn in their own time and do not need to be "pushed" and "molded" by anxious adults to become "decent citizens.") Although I draw conclusions from this experience and make comparisons with other approaches to children, I intend these to be taken as observations that in turn challenge our more widely held ideas about child nature. But this is not an instruction manual on how to bring up children. Such an approach cannot be methodically learned or applied mechanically. It is an approach to life that has to be felt and trusted in. Besides which, every situation has its own milieu that has to be accounted for.

The most detailed accounts of Summerhill have been those in the books of A.S. Neill. These span from the nineteen twenties when he founded the school through to the early seventies when he died. To date, besides Neill, this is the only lengthy first-hand account of Summerhill life to appear. It has not been written because I believe Neill to be old-fashioned, or out of date, but on the contrary, because his insights into childhood and adolescence hold as true today as they did then. Indeed, they belong more to the future than the past.

So what is the particular relevance of this book? To some degree, in my own way, I will inevitably reiterate some of what Neill wrote. This is unavoidable because we are dealing with the same subject matter. Nevertheless, I am not simply regurgitating Neill's philosophy, or spouting "the party line," I am writing from my own experiences and bringing in my own questions and observations. I began to feel the need to write such a book after talking with visitors to the school, and from giving lectures. It was clear from the questions people asked that there was still a lot that people didn't understand about Summerhill, and wanted to know. It was around these questions and the misunderstandings that arose in people's minds that this book began to grow. It also grew out of a certain frustration I felt after showing visiting journalists and filmmakers around the school. The ensuing articles and films that appeared were usually cliché-ridden disappointments that of life. It is the medium through which the newborn experiences the world most immediately. How we are touched in those first few hours, days, weeks, and months tells us who we are; whether we are people who are loved and wanted, or incomprehensible strangers to life. Our relationships with the world begin to form. Is it a place in which our needs are met, or does it impose its own rules, mechanically and without warmth? When we cried out for contact with another, were we held and soothed, or were we left to cry, unheard, unheeded, until we exhausted ourselves and gave up? These experiences shape us. When we reached for the breast, was the nipple warm, moist, and vibrant as it interacted with the sensitive membranes of our mouths? Or was it hard, cold, and contracted? Or did we just taste the cold rubber of a baby bottle? Did it feel as if something was lacking? When we looked into our mothers' eyes, what did we see? Was it warmth and love, or was it ambiguity, or even hate? How shall we know ourselves?

The young child does not rationalize. Everything is happening in the moment, and if the moment is unbearable the child withdraws from it, closing its eyes to it, holding its breath against it, and contracting its muscles against it. Equally, if the child's needs are met, it expands out to the world, looking it in the eye, breathing it deep into the center of its being, languishing in it and in the pleasure of its own bodily sensations. Maybe the child is satisfied in some respects and not in others. If it protests how are its protests met? With indifference? Anger? Understanding? What does this tell us about what we can expect from life? The child does not think this out, but its own responses become the patterns of its expectations: don't feel too deeply—it hurts; don't bother trying—it's not worth it; you have to fight for what you want out of life; life provides, it's good.

Throughout infancy and early childhood these patterns may be reinforced, or undermined, by new experiences. How are we made to feel about our bodies? Should we be proud of who we are, or ashamed? What reactions did we get when we paraded naked around the house, or when we discovered pleasure in our genitals? Were we forced into regular toilet habits before our bowels were ready for it? Did we have to push down hard on command, or produce something to please Mummy, or did it come of its own accord, in its own natural time? Did we feel that we had to fight against our bodies, that they betrayed us, that they no longer belonged to us, but were there to please others? Did we hold on out of spite? Did we soil ourselves for revenge? Or was it no big deal, just something that occurred naturally, a source of satisfaction and pleasure?

Self-regulation can only develop when there is a capacity on the part of the parents to be able to follow the natural development of the child and meet its needs, without inflicting unnecessary adult constructs such as letting the baby "cry it out," timetable feeding, over-zealous toilet training, or negative reactions to masturbation and nudity. By its very nature, self-regulation is not a "method" that can be applied, but depends on a deep emotional contact between the parents, especially the mother, and the child. Because the child does not have words, the parents need to be able to follow its expressions and interpret them. Later they will need to step back and allow their child more independence.

The way in which older children, or indeed adults, are able to regulate their own needs depends to a great degree on how their needs were met when they were younger. This is something I have seen clearly in the children at Summerhill, and which is touched upon throughout this book. The degree to which someone is able to regulate his or her life, free of anxiety and frustration, is variable but not absolute—at least in our society, and even at Summerhill. My experience is that Summerhill kids are, on the whole, more able to regulate their own lives, both socially and emotionally, than most kids who are subjected to ten years or so of compulsory education. But to understand this more fully as it operates in the life of the individual, I feel it important not to lose sight of the early influences on a child's life and of self-regulation as a more unified process from birth through adolescence.

This book does not represent Summerhill in any formal capacity. That is to say, what I have written cannot be taken as "the party line" or "official policy" of Summerhill School. What it does represent is my experience of Summerhill, which was drawn from nine years of living and working as a houseparent. In basics there is no contradiction between what I have written and how the school portrays itself more generally, but this does not mean that all the conclusions that I reach, or emphasis that I put on particular areas of community life, are shared by everyone else in the community or by Zoë Readhead, as the principal. The experience of Summerhill is much broader and diverse than just one person's viewpoint. However, I do not want to give the impression that this book is mere opinion. It has been arrived at by years of patient observation and hard work, digging to get at what is beneath the surface, both within Summerhill and within myself, as I have reacted to it.

It has now been two years since I left Summerhill. This book was written while I was at the school, and re-reading it now I have felt little need to make alterations. Although here and there my views may have changed a little, I prefer to leave the text as it is, so that it speaks with the authentic voice of the moment. From the perspective I have now of viewing Summerhill from the outside in, instead of from the inside out, I am quite happy to stand by what I have written and feel more than ever that society at large needs to move more in the direction of the Summerhill approach, rather than the other way around. Since I wrote this book there have been some structural changes in the buildings and in the way that the staff is organized and, as is the nature of self-government, the school rules are in a state of constant flux. Essentially, though, they are fairly much the same and only differ in minor details. I have heard many ex-Summerhillians, sometimes returning after thirty or forty years, say how little the atmosphere has changed since their time at the school, and it is this essence that I am trying to capture in the book.

On a more personal level there are small, but poignant, details within the book that are no longer true, but I prefer to leave intact. I describe Ena Neill's (A.S. Neill's wife) giving out pocket money. Shortly after I left Summerhill Ena died. As anyone who met Ena knows, she was a very strong personality and during most of the time I was at Summerhill she was a powerful presence in the community. As she became older and more frail she found it more difficult to get out and about, but, for as long as she could, she struggled over to the meetings, so that she could keep her finger on the pulse of school life. Most of the colleagues and kids that people this book have left. I still know a lot of the older kids at Summerhill, but, other than Zoë, there is only one member of the staff still there with whom I worked. This illustrates the high turnover of staff that I have written about in the text. I have visited several times in the two years since I left, and it feels odd to return to a place that was home for so long and to find it inhabited with strange faces. Yet the ease and acceptance with which both new kids and staff begin to interact with me, and the familiar sense of entering into an environment where things flow a little easier, reassures me that the essence of Summerhill, as I have tried to capture it in this book, continues to animate those who live there now.

Conflict with the Department of Education

The strongest motivation for writing this book has been the thought that perhaps one day Summerhill will be forced to close down. My fear was that in such an event, whatever the real reason for Summerhill's having to close, it would almost inevitably go down in the history books as an experiment that failed. I hoped that by creating a document that showed

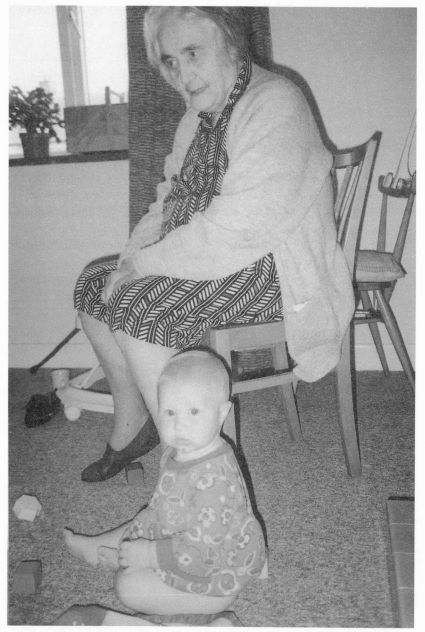

Ena Neill with Eva, Matthew Appleton's daughter. *(Photo by Matthew Appleton.)*

otherwise, I could do something to allay such misconceptions. It is particularly poignant, then, that at the time of writing this introduction Summerhill is facing the threat of closure, following a damning report from the Office for Standards in Education (OFSTED). Summerhill has always had a difficult relationship with government inspectors. In a private document written in 1972, just before he died, Neill wrote; "The Inspector's Report by John Blackie is the only proof that at least one man [within the] H.M.I.* had any inkling of what Summerhill was doing."

During the past ten years the school has been inspected on an almost annual basis, with four official reports being released. Neill described Summerhill as "possibly the happiest school in the world." I would couple this with the claim that Summerhill is also possibly the most inspected school in the world. The inspectors have been as uncomprehending of Summerhill as they have been relentless in their drive to fit it into a neat little bureaucratic box. Neill's daughter Zoë, who now runs Summerhill, commented after one inspection, "Sending Her Majesty's Inspectors into Summerhill is like sending atheists in to inspect a church." My own impression, from my experience of showing around inspectors when I was living at Summerhill, was that it felt like taking someone who was color blind on a tour of an art gallery and trying to convey the vivid colors of a Van Gogh or a Jackson Pollock. I remember one particular scene especially: two of the inspectors had wandered into the swimming-pool area. It was a hot summer afternoon. They stood stiffly, dressed in gray, clasping their clipboards, in stark contrast to the glistening, suntanned kids who darted around them, leaping into the water, splashing and laughing. It was as if they had arrived from another world and could not come to terms with where they had landed. Expressive emotional people do not tend to become bureaucrats, so how then are bureaucrats able to

* Her Majesty's Inspectors, which were replaced in the mid-1990s by OFSTED as the government's inspectors of schools.

Summerhill and are now friends. I cannot think of one of them who is not upset and angry about the way Summerhill is being judged and condemned. Far from seeing it as a place that let them down educationally, they see it as a place that supported and respected them in their growth as individual human beings and as members of a caring community. For many who have lived at Summerhill the threat of closure signifies a great personal loss. For society at large it also signifies a loss, for if we, as a society, cannot tolerate one small school, which draws fewer than eighty children from around the world, doing things a little differently, then it is a sad reflection on the culture of mass conformity that has overtaken us.

If you want to find out more about the current state of affairs at Summerhill you can write to the school at Summerhill School, Westward Ho, Leiston, Suffolk, IP16 4HY, England. Website: http://www.s-hill.demon.co.uk

1

Discovering Summerhill

The first I ever heard of Summerhill was from Bron, a friend of mine whose son was at the school. She lived then at Dial House, a beautiful old house in the Essex countryside, a few miles outside of Epping. Twelve or so other people shared the house, and they lived together as a small, informal community. Most of them were members of Crass, a band around which the anarcho-punk counter-culture of the time centered. It was through meeting the band at gigs that I became friendly with several of the people who lived at Dial House, and I often went out to visit them. This was around the mid-eighties. Living in South London at the time, I enjoyed the rural calm after the constant chaotic roar of city life. There were always people popping in at the house, some on brief visits, some on longer stays. The house, mainly through the band, seemed to attract all sorts of people with all sorts of interests, and I usually left with my head buzzing from new ideas that I had picked up during my stay there. The subject of Summerhill often cropped up in the conversations that seemed to be permanently in progress, either around the kitchen table or in the small, adjoining library.

It was not a subject that immediately drew my attention. Summerhill was a school, and neither schools, nor education,

were topics that I had much interest in. I had turned my back
on all that the day I left school some years earlier, in 1977,
after taking my A-levels.* I walked out through the gateway of
the large Bristol comprehensive school, where I had been a
pupil, and did not look back. This place of concrete and glass,
tarmac and wire, had no nostalgic allure for me. It spat me out
like an anonymous pip. My years there felt wasted, miserable,
frightening, and dull.

What joy there was to be had there was to be had despite
the school, not because of it. These joys were to be found in
the small knots of friendship that developed out of over a
thousand kids being thrown together, and the moments of
comradely mischief that occurred behind the teachers' backs,
the flashes of excitement that were snatched from the dull
monotony of the timetable, which to this day remain my only
happy memories of that time.

My parents had persuaded me to stay on for two extra
years to gain my A-levels. They convinced me that without
these qualifications I would be lost in life, and this fear bound
me to the school, even though I hated its dullness and
brutality. Academically, I was not slow or dim-witted, and I
gained good grades in most of my qualifications, but I found
the work stupefying. It was boring, repetitive, and did not
engage my imagination or awareness in any meaningful way.
Those two extra years were just two more years of drudgery,
and even now I look back on them as a waste of time.

A State Education

There was an air of impending violence that permeated
the school, and with it that awful sensation of apprehension
and fear that so many schoolchildren come to accept as

---

* In England's education system, A-levels, or advanced level exams, are taken at
the age of eighteen, before a student goes on to university.

normal. During my first couple of years at the school I suffered acutely from this atmosphere. Bullying was rife, threats and humiliation were ritual. Violence was an everyday event.

On one occasion my upper jaw was cracked and my teeth loosened for weeks after a larger boy pushed me to the ground and sat astride me, pummeling my face with punches. This happened outside of school, but as an extension of school life and its dynamics. I had nightmares about this incident for years afterwards. Like many children I suffered such things in silence. There is an unspoken rule among schoolchildren not to "tell teacher," nor parents, in case they go to the school and "make a scene." Because of the power structure of the school, the adult is always, to some degree, the mutual enemy, and to put such matters in adult (enemy) hands is to have them taken out of your own, so that once the ball is set rolling you can only sit back helplessly and watch. The fear of unleashing such power, and the subsequent peer estrangement, is often worse than the fear of the bully.

Teachers are not always sympathetic or sensitive to such things anyway. I remember in my primary school there was a girl I was made to sit next to who would pinch my bare legs under the table. When I jumped the teacher would tell me off for making noise. This went on for days, for weeks, and the teacher would not believe my excuses, but was won over by the protests of innocence from my wide-eyed, curly-haired neighbor. Eventually, something snapped in me and I turned on her, biting her neck and drawing blood. The teacher was outraged and I was sent to the headmistress, who was equally outraged. I think I was regarded as something of a budding vampire and was severely scolded for my behavior.

The teachers at the comprehensive were not above bullying tactics themselves. They often had particular kids they liked to see squirm in class, and would pick on them again and again, humiliating them in front of their classmates. We were all afraid of our maths teacher, a one-eyed Scotsman who hated children: he bragged of the fear he inspired in us. His favorite story was of a boy he had once accompanied to hospital after an accident. The boy, suffering from a concussion, was delirious and kept repeating, "Please, no, Mr. Mullen, please don't, Mr. Mullen." Mr. Mullen was proud that in his delirium this boy's fear of him broke through with such clarity.

If anyone was not paying attention in his class Mr. Mullen would hurl wooden blackboard erasers at them. As a recipient of more than one of these attacks, I can guarantee that they hurt. Another of his sadistic pleasures was to return our homework to us by shouting, "Rubbish!" and throwing all the books in the air. He would then select a victim (we all fought for the seats at the back of the class) to pick them up, and then step on the victim's hand as he was doing so, grinding it with the sole of his shoe.

Our P.E. and games teacher was another such sadist. One of his tricks, when he was in a bad mood, was to cram us all in the shower after P.E. and turn the water from hot to cold. I later saw this being done by a teacher in the film *Kes*, (based on the novel by Barry Hines), which is an excellent portrayal of comprehensive school life. I wondered, and still do, if that was where my teacher had got the idea, or whether this was fairly common practice among P.E. teachers that was reflected in the film. The fact that strikes me so strongly now, is that these were qualified men entrusted with the care of children, and yet their personal qualities were so obviously opposed to our well-being. Perhaps this is why I have always been more impressed by what people say and do, rather than the number of qualification they have.

So this was my experience of education. I would like to be able to think it was a rare one, but unfortunately such experiences are not uncommon. They may not always be so overtly unpleasant as some of the scenarios I have described, but most children have their own tales of anguish to tell. Children are very adaptable and each survives in his or her own way. Some have hardened themselves long ago against an unfriendly world, others have resigned, accepting passively whatever comes their way. Some feel a restlessness, an anguish they do not understand. Not all do survive, though, and every now and again our newspapers report another schoolchild's suicide, usually as a result of bullying or academic pressure. Our schooling system is not often questioned, in fundamentals at least, by children or adults, as it is all they know. But it takes its toll in ways that are considered acceptable, as if there could be no other way. This can be as obvious as the everyday misery with which so many children endure school, which they articulate clearly in their complaints. Or it can be deciphered in many of the symptoms of psychosomatic illness that so many schoolchildren suffer from. By the time we are adults we tend to rationalize our experience of school, to put it behind us.

Sitting in the peaceful Essex countryside, it was certainly something I did not want to be reminded of. Yet there was a contradiction in my feelings. The subject of school left me cold, but childhood fascinated me. I loved to read about other people's childhood experiences, and something of my own childhood seemed to linger within me—a deep longing for life, a yearning to live as fully as possible. There was a sense of vitality and aliveness that I associated with childhood, which I had never quite been prepared to surrender. School was the antithesis of this feeling: it was dull and oppressive. It did not enhance this vitality, but smothered it. It did not inspire aliveness, but killed it. It took the vivid colors of childhood and cloaked them in gray. The feeling that the word "school" inspired in me was not so much one of disinterest, but of wrongness and wretchedness.

In time I began to realize that Summerhill was no ordinary school. I heard the term "free school" used to describe it. I did not really know what a "free school" was meant to be, but it sounded archaic to me, a relic left over from the sixties that had buried its head in the sands of time. It did not evoke any great interest on my part. Occasionally, in my travels, I had come across concepts such as "children's rights" and "libertarian education," but they seemed to consist largely of adult polemics and did not touch upon the emotional issues that seemed so important to me as a child. The anti-academics were often more academic in their arguments than the academics were, and seemed to be missing the point somehow.

My own experience had led me to put freedom and childhood into two separate camps, and I had never really questioned the gap between them. On the few occasions that I had witnessed "free" children I had not been impressed. Once I remember sitting in a pub garden watching a little boy who could have been barely four years old, his face full of spite, attacking people's legs with a stick as his parents looked wistfully on. If this was an example of freedom for children it was not an attractive one.

Another occasion that comes to mind is when I was living in a shared house in Islington. One of the women I shared with was continually holding forth about having raised her child in freedom. The boy, a pale, withdrawn twelve-year-old, stayed in his room most of the time, shutting his door on the world and often not appearing for days on end. I gradually got to know him, and would sometimes go and sit with him for a few hours in the evening. His main activity was assembling and painting model soldiers and tanks. He was obsessed by the military and entered into long monologues in praise of the virtues of discipline. (He later joined the army.) He had no friends, and would sometimes not see his mother, or anyone else, for days. His mother often went out partying for several days on end, and when she came back would make a great show of what "good friends" they were. He would stiffen and draw away as she grabbed him and showered him with self-conscious kisses. If this was freedom, it was a sad sort of freedom. Insensitivity and neglect were words that came more readily to mind.

A School to Fit the Child

These were the sort of reference points I had, then, when I first heard of this "free school," Summerhill. Slowly, though, I began to learn more about the school. It had been founded by A.S. Neill, a Scotsman, as long ago as 1921, so it was not merely a fluke survivor of the nineteen sixties, but was almost seventy years old. It appeared that the children did not have to go to lessons if they did not want to, but as they grew older they began to naturally gravitate towards the classroom and more formal instruction. The laws, by which everyone in the school lived, were not made by the adults only, but by the whole community at weekly meetings. Everyone, adult and child alike, had a vote at these meetings. People could dress as they liked, say what they liked—there was no ban on swearing—and there was no form of moral or religious instruction from the adults. The school was international in its mix of pupils, with a large number coming from Japan at that time.

One of the men from Dial House had spent the last two summers helping to supervise the outdoor swimming pool at Summerhill. It seemed that in the summer term much of the school life centered around the pool. Many of the children and adults bathed naked, apparently with little or no inhibition. It sounded idyllic. While most the nation's children spent long, hot days bent over books in stuffy classrooms, the children at Summerhill were outside splashing around in the swimming pool, riding around the grounds on their bikes, building tree huts in the woods, or playing games in and around the main building. Something inside me began to stir, an inkling of interest, but also a sense of unease, for this tempting scenario began to throw a new light on my own school days.

That part of my life that I had put behind me began to rear up before me once more. I had accepted school as an inevitability, a fate shared by all children. Its inevitability had somehow made it an easier burden to bear. If it was an evil, it was a necessary one. Yet here were children whose parents did not consider it necessary. Here were children who escaped the common fate. I felt resentment and tried to rationalize it. They must be the spoiled kids of the idle rich, I told myself. But then, Bron was not rich; indeed, she worked very hard to raise the money for her son to go to Summerhill. She made this task a priority in her life at the expense of other comforts. Nor was her son that particular mix of over-indulgence and unhappiness that we call "spoiled." In fact I always found him to be a very calm, pleasant, and straightforward person. I was also struck by his self-confidence. Once, when he was about fifteen, we traveled together to the continent. On the way out from Dover we were taken to one side by some officials and questioned at great length as to where we were going and why. Whereas this imposition by authority had my nerves jangling, he was not at all intimidated or resentful, but took it all in stride.

Bron suggested to me on several occasions that I might

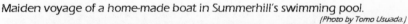

Maiden voyage of a home-made boat in Summerhill's swimming pool.
(Photo by Tomo Usuada.)

enjoy reading A.S. Neill's book about the school, entitled simply *Summerhill*. I put off doing so for some time. In retrospect, I can see this was because I was evading the strong emotions that the subject aroused in me. On many occasions when talking to people about Summerhill since, I have seen this same evasion taking place in others. This turning away from facts and taking refuge in prejudice is understandable given the way that most of us were brought up. When I did eventually pick up one of Neill's books, it was not *Summerhill*, but a collection of letters entitled *All the Best, Neill: Letters from Summerhill*. Neill's insight into childhood touched me deeply. He was not talking in academic abstractions like so many people do, but with a deep instinctive knowledge that he not only preached, but practiced. The letters were sometimes passionate, sometimes pessimistic. They spoke of hopes, and of fears. They painted a picture of a man deeply committed to children and their struggles.

I decided I wanted to read more. Altogether Neill had written twenty books, including *Summerhill*, which was a compilation of four of the others. There was also another volume of letters, consisting of the correspondence between Neill and Wilhelm Reich, as well as numerous books written about Neill and Summerhill. Many of these were out of print and difficult to find, but I scanned the second-hand bookshops and soon I had a small collection. As I read I began to form a clearer picture of this man and his work. Although in many ways his message was a simple one, he was certainly not a simple man in the negative sense of the word, nor was he naive as his detractors have sometimes made out.

Neill had founded Summerhill with the view to creating a school that would "fit the child," as opposed to other schools, which demanded that the child fit the school. He believed that children were born good, and not bad, as was widely believed at the time. He argued that it was society that warped this original goodness by its methods of child rearing, thereby creating conflicts within the child that later expressed them-

selves in anti-social and neurotic behavior. By creating a
school that removed these conflicts from the children's lives
and allowed them the greatest possible freedom, he sought to
demonstrate to the world that his belief in child nature was
correct. He ran Summerhill from 1923 until 1973, when he
died, putting these principles into practice, and in those fifty
years his faith in children did not waver.

He was quick, though, to distinguish between what he
called "freedom" and "license." Freedom was doing what you
liked, as long as it did not harm anyone else, or indeed,
yourself. License was doing what you liked with no regard to
how it interfered with other people's freedom. He gave the
example of children not attending lessons. That was their own
business and they were free not to go. It caused no harm to
anyone. On the other hand, playing a trumpet late at night
interfered with other people's freedom to sleep. That was
license. So, the small boy in the pub garden would not have
been permitted to act in such a way at Summerhill. Such
anti-social behavior was dealt with in the weekly meetings,
again by the community as a whole. Neill saw license as
arising partly as a result of the natural course of children
learning to live with others and discovering where the boundaries lay, and partly as a secondary form of behavior arising
from the conflicts that society had imposed on the child. In
these children he perceived a neurotic, compulsive, and often
hateful form of license. To "cure" them of these conflicts,
which were at the root of their anti-social activities, he would
sometimes reward them for their crimes, or join them on
their escapades. Such acts, along with the free and accepting
atmosphere of Summerhill, helped these children to overcome their unhappiness, and in time they became happy,
socially minded members of the Summerhill community.

After his death Neill's wife Ena took charge of the school.
Then, in 1985, when she decided to retire, their daughter,
Zoë, (now Zoë Readhead) became the principal. The school
thrived, still retaining the principles of freedom and self-

government with which Summerhill had been founded and had functioned for over fifty years.

Visiting Summerhill

Having read so much about Summerhill, I was eager to visit the school. I asked Bron if, the next time she went to visit her son, I might come along too. My chance came quickly. It was summer half-term in a couple of weeks, a time when parents were invited to come along and join in the school's activities. Some parents came just for the day, others would camp for several days on the large field adjacent to the main school building. On this occasion Bron was just going for the day and was happy to give me a lift. As we drove through the flat Suffolk countryside heading towards Leiston, where Summerhill is situated, I felt excited and nervous. Neill's books were moving and inspiring, but would the real thing live up to the promise of the printed page? How would I respond to the children there? How would they respond to me? Neill had written about the difficulties caused by so many visitors to the school. At one time the meeting had banned visitors, which disappointed Neill, as he considered it important for Summerhill to demonstrate to the world how children could live together if allowed to. I wondered if the children would regard me as an intruder into their private world, as a nosy tourist. Would my presence be resented? What did I want from this visit anyway?

Soon we were turning into the front drive, past the words "SUMMERHILL SCHOOL" daubed in white paint onto a low brick wall, past the primitive statuette of a figure with a large ball resting in its lap, down past the tall trees and tangle of bushes that edge onto the drive. I had seen all these things in photographs in various books and magazines, and they seemed very familiar to me. We pulled up outside the school's main building, and got out. It was a lovely day. The sky was a deep blue, with little wisps of white cloud. It stretched out in a great expanse, so vast compared with the miserly glimpses between rooftops that London life allows. Bron went off in search of her son. There were various people wandering around, adults and children. I felt a little awkward. Everyone seemed to know everyone else, and they were busy getting on with their lives, so I decided I would just scout around awhile and get a feel of the place.

The school itself consisted of a large red brick building, supplemented by various rather dilapidated outbuildings and assorted caravans. I stuck to exploring around the outside of the main building. Children's voices echoed from within, and every now and then a band of small children would race in or out of one of the doors, or come skidding around the corner on their bikes, zooming past, oblivious to this adult stranger who was invading their territory. Occasional groups of two or three older children wandered past, nonchalantly nodding and saying "hi" as they passed me. They seemed equally indifferent to my presence. I was beginning to enjoy my anonymity. My attention was caught by the array of names carved into the brickwork, where generations of Summerhill kids had left their mark. For a moment a different image flickered through my mind, that of a war memorial, with its regimented list of names and dates. But these walls had a different message. These clumsy carvings did not speak of sacrifice, death, and war, but of happiness, childhood, and life. That this image should occur to me now summed up the antithesis between what I sensed to be the direction that Summerhill was working in, and the direction our society at large was constantly finding itself headed.

During the afternoon various activities got underway. Stalls were set up just in front of the school. These included several table-top games with prizes, a jumble sale, and plenty of homemade arts and crafts for sale. Bron had caught up with me by now and introduced me to various members of the staff, parents, and kids. They were all very warm and friendly to me, but also busy with their own things to do. Later, there were games on the "hockey field," but by then it was time for us to leave. I felt elated as we traveled back to London. It's difficult to say what it was about the school that had left such an impression on me. It was something in the atmosphere of the place. I still remember a small girl gliding around the school grounds on her bike, quite alone, not at all perturbed by what anyone else was doing. She radiated an air of self-possession and quiet poise that struck me as quite beautiful. There was an unhindered naturalness to Summerhill that I had never really experienced before. It expressed itself in small, almost imperceptible ways, yet it was very potent. I knew that in such a brief visit I could only scratch the surface of this small, seemingly Utopian world. But I also knew that whatever contradictions might lurk beneath the surface, I had still caught a glimpse of something very real and alive.

At the same time that I was discovering Neill and Summerhill I was also studying for a certificate in Anatomy, Physiology, and Massage with the International Therapy Examination Council and attending regular seminars and training sessions. For the first time since that period in my life that had preceded school, I was discovering again that learning could be enjoyable and exciting. (Although I had studied Humanities at Polytechnic, I found that potentially interesting material was generally presented in a dry, academic way by lecturers who had little real interest in what they were teaching.) The people in the massage course were a friendly bunch and we socialized together quite a lot after classes. I often talked about my interest in Summerhill, and we had some very lively discussions with people opening up about their own childhood experiences, remembering incidents and feelings that had long been filed away and forgotten in the "necessary evil" section. There were some fascinating stories (as there usually are if people choose to tell them), and I was amazed by the deep interest that the subject generated.

Some time after the course had finished, a woman I had met in the class wrote to me, including in her letter an advertisement for a "houseparent" at Summerhill, which she had found in her newspaper one morning. I was in two minds as to whether I should apply. On one hand, I was very happy with my life in London. On the other, it was like having a gauntlet thrown at my feet. It was a challenge. It was a chance to act rather than just talk, to discover for myself the truth behind the idea. A voice inside me kept repeating "Put your money where your mouth is!" I was twenty-eight years old, single, and not sure if I wanted to take on the responsibility of being a parent-by-proxy for twenty or so kids. I had some experience working with children, but not much. I had done some playscheme work with younger children, and some work with mentally handicapped youngsters. For a while I had worked in a hostel for young homeless people, but they were older adolescents and above. For several years I had worked in a hospital as an orthopedic plaster technician and was used to dealing with children in that job. I was also used to plenty of informal interaction with children within the circle of friends that I had in London, which gave rise to a great deal of mutual enjoyment. But to live with children twenty four hours a day, nine months a year...that was something else.

In recent years I had been actively involved in music and performance art. My more recent concerns were in health and nutrition—for a while I had made money as a freelance cook, supplying food based on the Bristol Cancer Diet. Now I had my ITEC Massage certificate and was interested in developing work in that area. A lot of my spare time was used up training in Aikido, a Japanese martial art. I always came off the mat feeling relaxed and full of life. I also had many friends in London who were very important to me. It would be a lot to give up.

Yet my brief glimpse of Summerhill and the books by Neill that I had read had a magnetic appeal to me. It had already occurred to me that one day I might consider working at Summerhill, but I had assigned such a notion to the distant future. I did not know if I had the patience or maturity for such a task—as yet, anyway. But the voice continued to nag me, "Put your money where your mouth is...put your money where your mouth is."

So I applied—and heard nothing. Every morning I sifted through the post expectantly. I wrote a second letter. Weeks passed, and still I heard nothing. My feelings hovered somewhere between disappointment and relief. It seemed as if the gauntlet had been withdrawn. Then one day it arrived—a scribbled postcard, signed simply "Zoë," with a telephone number and a request to call to make an appointment. I did so, and arranged to visit the school a couple of days later. I learned later that my original letter had got mislaid under a pile of papers in the school office, and by the time my second letter arrived the interviews were in full swing. It was only when all the other applicants had been deemed unsuitable that I was finally contacted.

The "Gangster Age"

An interview at Summerhill is not like a conventional job interview, as I was soon to find out. But then I had no idea what to expect, and was still unsure as to whether I wanted the job or not. The train journey from London Liverpool Street to Saxmundham Station takes about two hours. From Saxmundham, a small market town, it takes another ten minutes by taxi to reach Summerhill. Soon I was turning into that familiar driveway for a second time, my heart booming in my chest. There were a couple of small children playing just in front of the school, and I asked them if they knew where Zoë was. They escorted me into the house where we found her with her baby son, Neillie, in her arms, looking at a notice board on which various scrawled messages and requests were pinned. The small children scampered off with a chirpy "bye" to continue their game. Zoë greeted me with a friendly handshake and smile. I suddenly found myself feeling very much at ease. We strolled along the corridor together, and back out into the sunshine at the front of the house.

There were two houseparenting jobs going, she explained, one with the very small kids, and the other with the middle-range age group, the "gangster age," as her father used to call them. These children, known as the "House Kids" because they boarded in the large house that was the school's main building, were aged, roughly, between ten and thirteen years old. Neill had nicknamed them "the gangsters" because this was the age at which they tended to be most exuberant in their "breaking out" of old inhibitions and, in doing so, bombarding the school with those aspects of their personalities that had hitherto been considered too unsavory for public taste. This inevitably involved a certain amount of law breaking. The "gangster" tag also referred to the sort of games that these children seemed to enjoy most. These generally involved much fantasy, supplemented by cap guns, wooden swords, bows and arrows, and the like. Although these activities were mainly the domain of the boys, the girls by no means played second fiddle, and were every bit as loud and boisterous as the boys.

Zoë explained that she thought the job with the House Kids would be more appropriate for me. She thought the younger children had more need of a motherly presence, where the House Kids could relate better to a big brother or big sister figure. She warned me, though, that it was sometimes tempting for new staff to identify totally with the kids who were "breaking out" and being anti-social, at the expense of the needs of the wider community. Whereas it was appropriate for the children to let off whatever steam they had to let off in such ways, it was no use to anyone if the staff threw caution to the wind and joined them. The role of the adult was to protect and support the children's needs, to ensure their well being, and create a safe environment in which they could live out their childhood as fully as possible. Summerhill was not there to cater to adults who wanted to live out the childhood that they had never had. She explained all this to me in a friendly but serious manner, looking me straight in the eye, to see if what she was saying registered.

I nodded my assent. I could tell that she was talking, not in moral or theoretical terms, but from experience. I liked her straightforwardness. Some time earlier I had applied for a summer job in a play scheme in South London. I had been asked by a very intense panel of three what I would do if a child made a sexist or racist remark. I replied that I would probably befriend the child. I knew it was the wrong thing to say. The interviewers stiffened in their seats, and I hesitated. I could have gone on to say that I believed the child who felt loved and accepted was far more likely to accept others than the child who felt simply censored and criticized. But I knew there was no point in trying to explain. The whole tone of the interview was that of an exercise in "political correctness," rather than an interest in children. I couldn't be bothered with it. It had all the superficiality of the "Thou Shalt Not" variety of moralism—judgement and censorship, with no attempt to get to grips with the underlying dynamics from which prejudice and hatred spring. Listening to Zoë talk was a whole different experience. We were talking the same language; children, not politics.

Another member of staff, the present House houseparent, was passing on his way to the laundry room. Zoë asked him if he would show me around the school. He was willing, and Zoë departed with a cheery wave. He introduced himself as Paul, and led me to the "Beeston," as the laundry room is called. The name apparently came from the name of some ancient washing machine that had once been housed there. He began sorting out an ominously large and somewhat smelly pile of dirty clothes. In the background various washing machines chugged and groaned as they ploughed their way through the House Kids' laundry. Paul started to explain to me, in great detail, how the weekly laundry routine worked. Every houseparent had one washday a week, which would inevitably end with a ritual chorus of complaints about shrunken garments, odd color changes and mysteriously disappearing socks. As a job candidate these details were of little interest, but after having done the job myself for some time, I can understand his need to get it off his chest. The neverending saga of the lost sock is ingrained into my weekly routine and, I will add here, that nine times out of ten, the absent sock turns up stuffed in the corner under the complainant's bed.

As he talked and sorted the dirty clothes into piles, Paul puffed and wheezed, wiping the sweat from his brow, and breaking into long, anguished coughing fits. He had dark rings under his eyes and an unhealthy pallor. He looked totally exhausted. I began to wonder anew if I really wanted this job. When he told me that this was just his first term at Summerhill my doubts increased. He went on to explain that as much as he liked the House Kids he was going to change to the job of Cottage houseparent. The Cottage Kids were the next age group down. They bridged the gap between the House Kids and the youngest kids. Their title derived from the long-distant past when they lived in "the Cottage," where Ena Neill now lived. They were situated in the House these days, just along the corridor from the House Kids. He felt more drawn to the Cottage Kids, he said. In fact, he never returned the following term, but disappeared without a word. To this day no one knows what became of him.

During the rest of the day I was passed on from one member of the staff to another. I sat around in various staff bedrooms, chatting and drinking tea. In each of these rooms there was a constant procession of kids wandering in and out. Some would just pop their heads around the door and disappear again. Others would settle, sometimes engaging one of the adults in conversation or retiring to a corner to involve themselves in a game of some sort. Some made a point of making contact with me, perhaps to suss me out, or to try out a joke on me that had become a bit threadbare with everyone else. But none of the kids showed any great interest in this possible houseparent-to-be. They filled me in on a few of their own requirements such as, "You've got to buy us sweets everyday, ha, ha," but I got the feeling that they were not terribly concerned whether I got the job, or the next guy did.

As I was shunted around the school I picked up little snippets of information about the place as I went. I discovered, for example, that the House Kids had been without a long-standing houseparent for some time. The last few houseparents had lasted only a term or two at a time. On a couple of occasions the school had received phone calls just days before term started to announce that the houseparent was not returning. The job with the younger children was beginning to sound far more attractive. I began to wish that I was a bit more motherly.

As the day progressed, though, despite the doubts that my mind kept churning up, I found myself irresistibly expanding out to the place. As when I had visited the school before, there was an almost intangible quality to the life here that could not be reduced to a single element, but was manifest throughout. The children had a zest about them and a directness that felt natural and relaxed. There was a liveliness in people's interactions that meandered freely, without all the stumbling blocks of strained manners or unspoken tensions that are so common to our culture. Yes, I wanted to be a part of this.

At four o'clock a tea bell rang and I was ushered into the dining room to drink tea with the small crowd of children that gathered there, cups ready. The adults retired to the staff room. They emerged half an hour later and I was informed that the job was mine. I was to be the new House houseparent!

"Oh God," I thought to myself, even as my senses danced

with exhilaration, "I've gone and done it now."

Traveling back to London in the train, I wondered what challenges working at Summerhill would bring, and what disappointments. What would the reality of Summerhill be like on a twenty-four hour basis, day after day, week after week? The day's events skipped around my mind. Snippets of conversation. A flurry of faces slipping in and out of focus. Faces that I would learn to know, that would fit into my life like pieces of a jig-saw puzzle. I wondered how time would fit those pieces together, and what shape the overall picture would take.

As it happened I slipped into my first term with unexpected ease. There were things to be learned, people to be met, mistakes to be made, crises to be borne, but I felt at home. I felt a sense of belonging. The House Kids were not the horrors that I had begun to suspect during my interview, or maybe I have just coped better than I thought I would! Given the choice now, I would certainly not swap my job for that of the youngest kids' houseparent. Not that either is the better job; all of the posts at Summerhill have their own particular pros and cons, but I think my temperament suits the House job better. Nor was washday quite the terrible ordeal that Paul had seemed to find it. With a little self-management it took on more reasonable dimensions. All in all I remember my first term as passing in a whirl of pleasure and excitement. There were ups and downs of course, but none of the downs were very long standing.

Now, seven years later, I am still House houseparent, though to a different bunch of kids. The "gangsters" of my first term are now the big kids. It's they who hold the community together, who are the driving force behind the school's self-government. I still have strong ties with them, and at the risk of sounding sentimental, I am very proud of them. I haven't just watched them grow up, but I have grown up with them, as I will do with the kids who are in the House now. It is not that I regard the House Kids as the raw material and the older kids as the finished product, far from it. Each age group has its own charm. But I love to see the changes, the developments, the struggles that each individual brings. When new children arrive, they arrive having lived according to adult expectations, often at the loss of their own. In time they begin to drop their façades, the false faces with which they have learned to meet the adult world, and begin to reveal something of their lives that has never been allowed to surface before. It is like the peeling of an onion. Layers of superficiality, frustration, and resentment are expressed and abandoned as the children begin to trust in their deeper, more vulnerable feelings. It is a sort of emotional archaeology, except that the past is not dug up, but thrown off.

2

The Adult/Child Relationship

When the school is full, there are between sixty and seventy children at Summerhill. Among this number there are a handful of "day" children, but most are boarders. There are twelve or so staff members, the majority of whom live at the school, and a daily domestic staff, that takes care of most of the cooking and cleaning. The live-in staff includes houseparents and teachers. At the moment there are four houseparents, one for the youngest children, myself, one for the older girls, and one for the older boys. Among the teachers there are two "primary" teachers who teach a broad range of basic skills to the younger and middle-range children. The other teachers specialize in various subjects, which are taught up to GCSE standard.*

Zoë and her husband, Tony, with the help of Sarah, the school secretary, deal with the administrative aspects of school life, such as finances, repairs, maintenance, and dealing with outside bodies. They do not live at Summerhill, but on a farm

* GCSE, or General Certificate of Secondary Education exams, are normally taken at age sixteen. They used to be called O-levels, and they precede A-levels, which are taken at age eighteen.

a couple of miles away, which Tony runs. Zoë comes in most days, but she is also busy with her family and horses, which she regularly displays at horse shows, and for which she has won many prizes. Although as principal her role is central to maintaining the Summerhill way of life, because she does not live in the community her presence is relatively peripheral.

The children are aged mainly between eight and seventeen. There are a few younger children, but they are usually either day kids or the children of staff. Children come to Summerhill from many different backgrounds and cultures. In the seven years that I have been here we have had children from France, Spain, Greece, Germany, Switzerland, Austria, Poland, the United States, Mexico, Brazil, Africa, Taiwan, Korea, Japan, Indonesia, and Malaysia, as well as from Britain. During my first couple of years almost a third of the kids were Japanese, but more recently the school has filled up with German, other European, and English kids.

My room is at the end of a short corridor on the first floor of the main building. The corridor is lined by five bedrooms, which altogether house around twenty children, and one teacher's bedroom. I live here as an equal member of the community, a fellow citizen with the children whom I am houseparent for. Being an adult does not give me authority over anyone, so I am not in the position of telling anyone else

Various animals are adopted by the kids at Summerhill. *(Photo by Matthew Appleton.)*

what to do. But I do have equal rights, and recourse to enforcing those rights in the same manner as the children, namely by taking any concerns or personal infringements to the weekly meetings. So, if anyone keeps me awake at night, or won't leave my room when I ask them to, I have the weight of the rest of the community to back me up. The other side of the coin is if I keep any of the children awake, or won't leave their rooms when they ask me to, then I can have a case brought against me in the meeting as well. In seven years I have been fined around a dozen times for various small misdemeanors.

Living together in such a way has a deep effect on the quality of the relationship between adult and child. Artificial barriers are soon dropped, allowing for more honest, direct communication. Everyone is able to be more themselves and to be relaxed with each other. The adults do not strive to set examples for the children. We go about our business naturally, unhindered by stances of stiff dignity or condescending paternalism. We do not bark orders or bristle with moral indignation, but nor are we timid and ever suffering. Each of us defines our own boundaries in our own way and becomes involved in community life at our own level. The way that we live together with the children is functional, defined by personal choices and needs, rather than abstract morality and conformity to unnatural norms.

For their part, the children do not fear the adults, nor do they see us as "the enemy," though elements of these attitudes often come in with new kids and take some time to dissolve. The children talk honestly and openly about their interests in life, asking questions of the adults without embarrassment. I wonder how many teachers and other adult dignitaries realize how children really view them? Like the little boy who saw through the Emperor's new clothes, children are quick to see through adult pretensions. As a child I often imagined what my teachers would look like sitting on the toilet with their pants around their ankles. Later, as a teenager, I tried to picture them masturbating, or in a sexual embrace. Children and teenagers are fascinated by these things, and the more they are swept under the carpet and masked by false dignity, the more the imagination becomes fixed on them. The more guarded the secret the greater the interest.

At Summerhill such things are not shrouded in secrecy. Not all the adults may choose to talk openly about their private habits and relationships, but the children are never made to feel that their interest in such things is "wrong" or "dirty." As a ten-year-old I once drew a picture of one of my male teachers chasing one of the female teachers. My knowledge of adult anatomy at the time was somewhat limited, so I imagine the picture was lacking in some of the finer details, but I remember that both of them were naked, and he had large erection bobbing around in front of him. A friend of mine, inspired by a sense of mischief, put the picture in the female teacher's desk. She was furious and demanded to know who had drawn it. Scared out of my wits by the ferocity I had unleashed with this innocent drawing, I admitted to it. She hauled me up in front of the class shaking me and screaming at me, calling me a "dirty-minded little boy." I was devastated and totally miserable for weeks after.

That evening I was scared to go home, as she had threatened to phone and tell my parents. So I wandered around the local park trembling and crying for what seemed an eternity, before finally setting off homewards. As it turned out the phone call had not come, and when my mother learned what was wrong with me she took my side, comforting me and marching down to the school the next day to berate this teacher for her prudishness.

Children should not be put in the care of such people. The utter misery that they inflict upon children is incalculable. Anyone who has dealt with children in a relaxed, uninhibited atmosphere will be in no doubt that sexual matters and other bodily functions, which polite society deems unsavory, are of great fascination to them. To squash this interest, to turn it into a sin, into something unspeakable and unpleasant, is an assault upon the integrity of the child. Such emotional battering belongs to the category of child abuse every bit as much as physical battering. The problem is the irrationality and inhibitions of the adult, not the interests of the child. At Summerhill the adults too have their own personal inhibitions and irrationalities, but we do not try to alleviate them by foisting them on the children. We talk about life in a straightforward and honest manner, or where we feel the need for privacy we simply state it. The children are never made to feel bad about their natural curiosity.

As houseparent I am responsible for the health and welfare of the children in my care. There are lots of trivial, everyday things that need to be done, such as clearing blocked toilets, making beds, and washing clothes. Some of these jobs are shared with the domestic staff, others are the sole responsibility of the houseparent. Sick kids have to be nursed, medical records need to be kept up to date, grazed knees and elbows have to be cleaned and patched up. When necessary, trips to the doctor or dentist are arranged.

Most of the children keep their valuables in the safekeeping of their houseparent and I have several locked drawers and cupboards where purses, wallets, and bags of food are kept, as well as a locked medicine cupboard. The children have their own locked spaces too, but many prefer the extra security of keeping their belongings in the houseparent's custody. Visitors are often surprised at the number of locks, and locked doors, around Summerhill. It is something that I took a while to get used to myself. There was a certain irony that here I was in probably the freest school in the world, carrying around a bunch of keys that would be the envy of the average prison officer. It was also an inconvenience to have to be constantly locking and unlocking things, and I found it a relief in the holidays to be able to discard my bunch of keys.

It is not that the kids at Summerhill are an especially immoral bunch that necessitates this profusion of locks, nor is it an authoritative whim on the part of the community. It is simply a practical measure, for where there is an absence of fear there will always be kids who will steal. In some cases this will be compulsive, a substitute for freely given love. In others, it will be merely a matter of temptation winning out. Not all kids steal, but many do at some time, and in a situation where there are continually new kids coming in, kids who have always had their anti-social impulses curbed by fear and authority, it would be foolishness to expect anything other than a testing of the limits. The fact that I would be happy to trust any of our big kids with my keys has proved to me that the practical way works. I have seen new kids come to us term after term and shrug off their façades of virtue, allowing the sneaky thief in them to emerge. The moralistic way is a superficial one that does not turn out honest citizens, but fearful ones. I have yet to be convinced by those teachers who say they have no fear in their schools, but the children still do not steal. Their heads are in the clouds. It is far better to have a lock on a cupboard than to chain a child in insincere virtue.

The Role of Adults

Like any kind of parenting, houseparenting differs very much from individual to individual. Different people handle situations in different ways, and beyond the range of responsibilities that are inherent in the job there is great scope for developing and sustaining a rich level of contact with the kids. To some kids the houseparent may be a valued confidant, to others an occasional adult playmate. Some may prefer the company of one of the other houseparents or teachers and it is the kids' choice who they hang out with. New kids often transfer old resentments onto their houseparents, so that we are at the receiving end of all that they have wanted to say and do to their parents, but have never dared to. The personal

dynamics of such situations can be difficult at times as boundaries are drawn and feelings are aired. But it is also very
pleasurable when distrust and animosity begin to give way to
affection and warmth.

An eleven-year-old Japanese boy spent his first term
spitting at me, pushing or hitting me whenever he passed me.
His eyes glittered with resentment, and he was furtive and
distrustful around adults. Depending on the situation, and my
own mood, I would sometimes express annoyance, and sometimes playfully engage in a face pulling competition with him.
The notion that adults have always to be consistent with
children totally denies the emotional element of our interactions. Children are quite able to follow the expansion and
contraction of personal boundaries that go with mood
changes, and as long as sudden and unwarranted outbursts are
not the response, it is far healthier for all concerned to be
flexible, rather than live in a state of static falsehood.

For some weeks this boy continued to treat me in this
manner. One day as I was walking along the corridor I saw
him coming the other way and prepared myself for the usual
response. However, as he approached, instead of his by-now
standard grimace, he looked up at me with a broad grin and
clear, sparkling eyes.

"I like you," he announced, as he threw his arms around
my waist. These were the first words of English I heard him
speak. It was a lovely moment and I glowed with happiness
for the rest of the day. I do not know what brought about this
change of heart, but I have seen it happen many times here;
an unexpected shifting as old anger melts away, with spontaneous shows of affection and tenderness taking its place. It is
often just a question of patience, of waiting and trusting that in
time the need to be unpleasant and abusive will fade as the
child feels more fully accepted for who he or she really is.

We are often asked by visitors what training Summerhill
staff have before coming here. The answer is that there is no
specific training that can ever prepare anyone for living at

Summerhill. It is a unique situation and whatever skills and life experiences we may have, we all have to start learning anew when we first arrive. A degree in psychology or ten years in teaching mean nothing if you cannot relate to a child as an equal. It takes new staff some time to really understand how Summerhill works, to follow its processes and see them unfold.

Even then there are always new questions, the answers to which are usually grasped intuitively, through experience, rather than academically. It is practice, not theory, that provides the deepest insights. I have made many blunders and sometimes handled situations very badly over the years. But I have learned better ways of dealing with things and a deeper trust in the way that Summerhill functions, as well as its limitations.

One lesson that new staff quickly learn is that adults take on far less importance in a community of children who are empowered in their own lives than they do in a situation where the adults have all the authority. The popular expectation is that children need constant guidance and supervision to feel secure. What I see happening at Summerhill is that the more children are trusted, the more they trust in themselves. The continual adult interference that occurs in most children's lives, in fact, creates deep insecurities in the shape of a lack of self-trust and an expectation that things will go wrong unless there is someone to supervise. This inevitably becomes a self-fulfilling prophecy. The children at Summerhill are generally much more busily involved with their peers than with the adults. At times I can feel quite superfluous.

Nor do adult opinions hold the same weight that they do in more adult-oriented environments. When I talked to a boy a year or so later about an interaction that I had with him in my first term, in which I very much over-reacted, he shrugged and said, "I don't remember that." Yet I felt I had done him a great injustice. This is not to say that children are not sometimes deeply affected by the things that adults say, or that the relationships between the staff and the kids are not important. Indeed, there are very real and deep bonds that develop here. But all this happens in the context of a community in which no one group is all-powerful, in which as much time as is wanted can be spent playing or hanging out with peers. In the meetings I have often seen kids grow far more serious and thoughtful when scolded by their peer group than by a member of staff. Being an adult is simply not such a big deal at Summerhill.

This is an aspect of Summerhill life that newcomers and onlookers often have difficulty with. Recently, when I asked a visitor who had stayed at the school for three weeks what her impression was, she told me it was just as she had expected, her only surprise being that the adults had "no interest" in the children. I was surprised by her remark. Of course the adults at Summerhill are interested in the children. But we do not live removed from them in the same way that most adult groups do. The adults and kids are continually interacting on many different levels all the time. So the adults do not stand back and regard the kids as another species to be manipulated and interfered with. The children are able to go through their own processes, without adults constantly stepping in and telling them what is best for them. In fact, many of the children found this visitor intrusive and insensitive. She interacted with the kids with the best will in the world, but was simply not able to let go of the culturally ingrained role of the adult as an ever-interfering guardian angel.

Her misconception was also partly due to a problem we often have with visitors who stay in the community. They think they are part of the community, and do not grasp the deeper dynamics of everyday life from which they are excluded. They grasp an aspect and think it the whole. In this case, our visitor was often invited along to participate in small adult social gatherings, in which the adults wanted a little time and space away from the kids. She was rarely actually involved in the almost constant interaction those adults might have with children throughout the rest of the day. I tried to put this to her, but she would not budge in her opinion.

Another element of the relationship between adults and children at Summerhill that visitors often find it hard to comprehend is that there is no "hidden agenda." We do not suffer from the "in order syndrome" that so many child/adult relationships suffer from. This involves doing one thing in order to bring about another, instead of doing things for their own sake. Interactions between adults and children are a minefield of such hidden motives. So, for example, at Summerhill, we do not take children for walks in order that they should learn to appreciate nature. If we go for a walk it is to get from A to B or to stretch our legs, and if the children do or do not appreciate nature that is their business. We do not organize games in order to tire the children out so that they will go to bed quietly. If an adult organizes a game it is because she or he enjoys the game. We do not talk about our ideas and beliefs in order to raise the consciousness of the child, but because we enjoy talking about our ideas and beliefs. This lack of connivance puts both adult and child at ease. Each feels the others' integrity and there is a sense of working together, rather than at odds with each other.

Unlike the children, each of the adults has a specific role at Summerhill that is his or her reason for being here. Each of these roles has its own particular stresses and strains, and each has its own pleasures and rewards. The teachers do not have the option not to attend lessons as the children do, but are expected to be available to teach at the appropriate times. Outside of lesson times the teachers are fairly much free to come and go as they like, although most teachers participate actively in other aspects of community life as well. Some teachers live in caravans slightly apart from the main building, which enables them to live a more peaceful and private life. Most teachers have spent some time living in the main building, and then move into a caravan when one becomes available. This usually works on the basis of the teachers who have been here the longest having the first option. Although this move is often accompanied by a sigh of relief after the noise of the House, it is sometimes tinged with an element of regret at no longer being in the thick of it all.

The houseparenting roles are generally less structured than those of the teachers, though the houseparents are often more intimately involved in the lives of the children. The houseparent for the youngest children (known as the "San Kids," as they were once housed in an outbuilding originally intended to be a sanitarium, but which Neill found to be of no real use as there was never enough sickness in the school to justify it), has the most built-in structure, in that the children require more routine assistance in matters such as trimming toenails, bathing, hairwashing, preparing for bedtime, etc. At the same time, an earlier bedtime and a smaller number of children helps to lighten the load.

The houseparents for the older kids have the most undefined roles, as the kids in their care are the most independent. At this age there is one houseparent for the girls and one for the boys. The reason for this is a geographical one, in that the older boys and girls are not housed in the same building. This older group consists of the "Shack Kids" and the "Carriage Kids." When kids leave the House they move up to the Shack. The name came from the wooden shack in which the boys were originally housed. The need for a Girls' Shack did not come until later, as the Shack was originally created to absorb a plethora of boys around this age. When it later became appropriate to create a similar group for the girls they were also called Shack Kids, even though they were originally situated in the House. Later still, when the San Kids moved up into the main building, the Shack Girls moved to the old San, where they are at present.

If this sounds complicated, it does at least reveal something of the way in which the school is continually adapting to best meet the needs of the community at any one time. Unlike the younger kids, the Shack Kids have electrical sockets in their rooms, which enables them to have their own music systems, computers, and televisions if they wish. Such things would not last five minutes in the San or the House, but would soon be broken in the general excitement of daily life.

The Carriage Kids are the very oldest kids, the elders of the community. Yet again a little semantic detective work uncovers another chapter in Summerhill's history. The Carriage Kids used to be housed in a pair of old railway carriages, which was the cheapest and most effective way Neill could find to accommodate them. The carriages have long since gone, but in line with Summerhill terminology, the name has stuck. Now the Carriage Kids are housed in a couple of long wooden outbuildings. Unlike any of the other kids in the community, Carriage Kids each have their own room.

Although houseparenting for the older kids does not have as many restrictions built in, it can also pose its own difficulties and challenges. These roles are far more nebulous than the others, and the individual houseparents are very much thrown back on their own resources to find an identity within the community, and in particular with their own group of kids. To some extent this is true of everyone at Summerhill, kids and adults alike, but it is often more difficult for adults, who have had many more years of being told what to do and how to do it, and have lost the capacity for adaptation and self-regulation. For some staff this evokes feelings of guilt and failure whenever they are not actively involved with community life. Others may feel resentment that they are being overworked, when, in fact, it is their own inability to define boundaries with the kids, or find outlets for their own needs, that is causing them grief. Some swing between the two. It often takes new staff some time to find a happy balance in their lives.

My own houseparenting role lies somewhere between those of the houseparents for the youngest and the oldest kids. The kids in my care do not need as much attention as

(Photo by Tomo Usuada.)

the youngest kids. They wash their own hair and organize their own baths themselves. They are generally more independent. But they like to know that their houseparent is around and will often pop into my room to hang out for a while, or talk over something that is bothering them. Outside of my houseparenting role I have also found plenty of opportunities to integrate my own interests into the life of the community.

I have helped run a café, produced a termly magazine, taught massage and aikido, sung in a band of teenage musicians, and recorded with them at a local recording studio, written and produced cabaret sketches and a play, and organized an information center for visitors. Other teachers and houseparents bring in their own interests. One teacher formed a choir and staged a musical, which was performed over three nights to an invited audience from the town and around. Another took time off to rehearse with an operatic society, and returned along with the cast and orchestra to give a performance. An American friend of mine who researches unidentified flying objects and was writing a book about an incident at a local air-force base gave several talks on the subject, which really caught the kids' imagination. Michel Odent, the author of several books on childbirth, presented a lecture on his work. A professional storyteller and a traveling poet visited. People have come in to give workshops in pottery, computer graphics, dance, singing, playing the didgeridoo, and eye improvement exercises, among many others, all of which were organized by various staff.

Summerhill is not a place to sit back and wait for things to happen, it is a place to make things happen. This is true for staff and kids alike. It relies on the creative impulse, rather than compulsive principles of conventional education and, indeed, most jobs.

New Kids and Homesickness

A lot of my time and energy is spent helping new kids settle in and building up relationships with them. Most new kids come first into either the San or the House. (Between the San and the House there used to be the "Cottage," but this became integrated into the San and House shortly after I arrived.)

New kids do not usually go straight into the Shack, as we rarely take kids over the age of twelve, and when we do we nearly always try to give them a term in the House. This gives them some sense of what it is like to live in the main building. The reason we do not generally take children over the age of twelve is that it is often more difficult for them to adapt to the freedoms and responsibilities of community life. They tend to come with more resentments and it would be unfair on both the older kids, who have already sorted these conflicts out in themselves, and on the younger kids to have lots of big kids in

the community running around stealing things, bullying people, and keeping people awake at night.

Almost every term there are at least one or two new kids.
Some settle in very quickly, making friends and grasping the
essentials of community life almost overnight. Others find it
more difficult. They are more used to being guided by the
constellations of adult approval and disapproval than navigat-
ing their lives by the currents of their own emotions and
interests. They often cling to the nearest adult for support and
it sometimes takes weeks or even months to wean them off.
But after a while these kids too are off on their own, playing
with friends, asserting themselves in the meetings, and won-
dering why they felt so unsure of themselves to begin with.

I have sometimes heard it said that Summerhill is all very
well for kids who are outgoing and extrovert, but not so
suitable for the timid child. Yet I have often witnessed children lose their timidity here and begin to reveal a previously
unexpressed aggressive side to their nature. I can only conclude that the original timidity was a defense against an adult
environment in which the child's natural aggression was
squashed. I use the term "natural aggression" to describe the
capacity of someone to stand their own ground, to be self-
assertive and expansive. I do not use the word "natural"
flippantly here, but to distinguish this primary form of aggression from the more bristly and sadistic aggression of the bully,
which develops only as a secondary characteristic when the
primary personality has been chronically undermined. I am
not the first person to make such a distinction, but that such a
distinction is valid has certainly been borne out by my experience with the kids at Summerhill.

Adults who find assertiveness threatening in a child tend
to find timidity endearing. So the child's capacity for natural
aggression becomes diminished in the face of the overwhelming need to feel approved of, finding its expression instead in
small, spiteful sidelines. One boy clung to me for nearly two
terms, in a state of almost continual apprehension, especially

in situations of great excitement where there were other kids leaping around and play-fighting. Yet he was forever provoking the other kids by sabotaging their fun and calling them names. Then he would run back to me, with big, pleading eyes, in an attempt to manipulate me into taking his side. The picture he painted was of himself as helpless victim and the other children as cruel aggressors. No doubt he was used to indignant adults rushing to his defense, thus satisfying his own latent sadism, while justifying his helpless impotence. In such a way he could express his hate without taking responsibility for it or being punished for it.

In time, at Summerhill, he learned to express his natural aggression more directly, without fearing adult reprisals or resorting to sadistic pleasure as consolation. I remember one evening, as I sat in my room, overhearing him confront a much larger boy in the next room. He stated in a clear and confident tone to the bigger boy, who was well known as a bully, "If you don't leave me alone I'm going to bring you up in the meeting."*

It is often in such situations that new staff are tempted to rush in and play the guardian angel. That children, when empowered by their environment, are actually quite capable of working out their own difficulties is something that many adults find hard to swallow. In such instances adult interference hinders, rather than helps.

There are occasionally exceptions, when children find themselves out of their depths, but it is a question of being sensitive to these, instead of acting the omnipotent adult to all the dramas of childhood. I experienced this myself as a new staff in my first term, when a rather loud and forceful teacher took it upon herself to tell the kids when and where to stop bothering me. It did not seem to occur to her that if they were bothering me I was quite capable of setting my own limits with them. Despite my asking her not to, she continued in this

---

* "Bringing someone up" means you will raise a formal complaint about them at the community meeting.

annoying habit until she left. It occurred to me that actually the kids were far more receptive to the setting of personal boundaries than she was.

What I have seen of how Summerhill kids respond to new kids has also made me realize that children are generally far more sensitive to insincerity than adults. There are some new kids who are forever trying to impress. These are children who have never really been accepted for themselves, but have always had to live up to other peoples' standards. They are self-conscious without being self-aware. They spout ideas that they have no feeling for. They are more interested in making an impression than in genuine contact with another person.

Children have a keen eye where adults are often blind in such matters. Many adults want to be impressed. Maybe it is because it makes them feel impressive themselves when someone makes so much effort to seek their approval. I have several times seen new kids shunned by the other kids in their first few weeks, as they parade around the school reciting their repertoire of impressive qualities and daring deeds. Yet I have met few children who have not got over this and finally found their place in the community, free of this façade.

Mostly, though, it has been a surprise to me just how easily new kids do settle in. There is very little homesickness at Summerhill. I was surprised recently when a boy announced to me that he was feeling homesick.

"But it's almost end of term," I replied. "You'll be back home in a few days."

"That's what I mean," he sighed. "I'm feeling sick because I have to go home."

When kids genuinely do pine for home, it is not necessarily because they were happier at home. The home that they sicken for is often an idealized one, a fantasy. One young girl talked incessantly about how much she missed home, how happy she was there. In reality her parents had no time for her, and she was cared for by childminders throughout the holidays. One day she was droning on about how much she loved her family and asked me if I loved mine.

"Ugh, no!" I cried in mock disgust. "I hate them! They're horrible!"

"Oh, that's terrible!" she exclaimed, with feigned indignation, her eyes brightening, and a broad grin spreading across her face.

When things are going wrong at home children often feel they ought to be there. Perhaps one day they will stumble across the magic words that will make Mummy and Daddy love them. Or they will find a way to get Mummy and Daddy to love each other again. They may feel guilty that they are enjoying themselves and a moment of "homesickness" overwhelms them. After all, Mummy and Daddy are miserable back at home.

A girl plays happily with her friends. She has been contentedly going about her business for days. The phone rings; it's her mother. She grabs the receiver and in seconds is in floods of tears, telling her mother how unhappy she is, how she wishes she was back at home. A few minutes later she thrusts the receiver into my hand.

"Mum wants a word with you," she announces and rushes off again to play happily with her friends. For the next ten minutes I try to reassure the distraught parent that actually everything is all right and her daughter is, really, quite happy. This is a scenario I am quite familiar with. It is as if the children feel the parent's expectation that they will be unhappy away from home. The shedding of tears has a dutiful quality to it, as if the children do not want the parents to feel rejected. Children often have a deeper sense of what is happening in their parents than the parents do themselves.

Sickening for home can also be a way of evading issues that arise in day-to-day life at the school. A twelve-year-old boy calls his parents every other day throughout his first term begging them to take him away. He is pompous and condescending with the other kids and they do not like him. He comes into my room crying and complaining that he will never fit in. I encourage him to be patient and to commit himself, instead of looking to home as a way out every time things became difficult.

The root of his problem is not that he prefers being at home, but that he has a huge inferiority complex, which he covers up by trying to be cleverer and better than everyone else. He has never really got on with his peers, but at home he can sit in front of the television or play the computer and hide away from his problems. I tell him that if he sticks it out at Summerhill he will learn to like himself, and will find that the other kids like him for who he really is. I tell him that he only shows off because he doesn't really think he's good enough, and if he doesn't take this opportunity to find out that people really can like him, he will never feel that he is good enough. I point out a few kids who are now happy and popular members of the community, and tell how they once felt like he did. He feels relieved after expressing his anguish, but my words are of little comfort. These are adult concepts. Children live for today, not for tomorrow.

His parents try to persuade him to stick it out. They remind him how unhappy he was at home, but to no avail. They have always bowed down to his wishes before, but now, after much deliberation, they tell him he must stay at Summerhill for at least a year. Over the next couple of weeks he seems more settled and at ease with himself. When he returns for his second term he sheds a few tears to begin with, but soon gets into the swing of things. Now, in his third term, he is totally integrated into his peer group. He doesn't show off half as much as he used to, and is never homesick.

"The only thing I hate," he told his parents, "is that you were right and I was wrong."

It had been a difficult decision for the parents to make the choice for him that he had to stick it out at Summerhill. They felt they were being authoritarian. Yet they also felt that in this instance they knew best. They knew what lay in front of him if he was to go through the conventional school system, and saw already the negative effect it was having on him. Ironically, in taking this choice out of his hands, they were also freeing him to deal with his difficulties. As long as he could run away from his problems by thinking life would be easier somewhere else, he would never be free to be himself.

Often children will ask to be taken out of a situation because they are facing some difficulty. But it has to be the parents' responsibility to weigh up the long-term pros and cons. Children do not take the long-term view. I have seen too many children made unhappy by their parents' delegating this responsibility to them. The girl I mentioned who often complained of homesickness has been with us for three years now, but has never really settled in. As soon as things become difficult she phones her mother and asks to be taken home. The mother takes her out for a week or two, leaving her with childminders, as she is too busy to look after her. Almost every term this girl decides she is going to leave and has her mother looking around for new schools for her. She then decides that maybe she will stay after all. Her mother succumbs to her every whim. The result is that the girl has made few friends, and lacks a sense of stability in the community.

Homesickness, then, can have many qualities to it. It can be sickening for a home that never was. It can be dutiful. It can be evasive. It can also be simply a process of grieving, of letting go. One young boy spent his first two weeks at the school crying his eyes out. He refused to mix with the other kids and clung relentlessly to his houseparent. His parents phoned him every day and his father, a homeopath, sent him remedies to help him. The boy would hang around the phone for hours waiting for his parents to call. He was misery personified. I had never seen such a severe case of homesickness, and was concerned that if it went on for much longer he would soon become so isolated from the other kids it would become even more difficult for him to break out of it and make any friends.

I wrote to the parents, who were also friends of mine, telling them that I thought they were undermining his settling in by phoning so often and sending remedies. Perhaps there was an element of truth in this, but I recognize now there was also an element of dogmatism on my part. The parents were annoyed by my remarks and continued to phone. They felt strongly that their child needed their support in this period of transition. As it turned out, soon afterwards, of his own doing, the boy began to miss being there when his parents phoned, as he slowly began to play with the other children, losing himself in the excitement of the games. Not long afterwards he told his mother on the phone, "I don't want you to call so often." His grieving was over and he felt free to play. My criticisms of his parents were ones that had often proved correct in other situations, but I had misread the quality of this boy's homesickness. An insight in one instance can easily become a dogma in another. It is something I have been very careful about since.

Children Away from Their Parents

There are three terms a year, each eleven weeks long. The question of whether it is damaging for children to be away from home for such long periods is one that I have given a great deal of thought to. The boarding school ethic, which has only ever been a middle- and upper-class concern anyway, has drastically declined in the past few decades, with more and more emphasis being put on the family as the ideal setting for children to grow up in. Boarding schools in general are something that I find repugnant, with their emphasis on character building, discipline, academic high-mindedness, sexual repression, and snobbery. Although technically speaking Summerhill is labeled a boarding school, it is in reality a totally different phenomenon, and is not comparable to other boarding schools in either function or fashion. I prefer to use terms such as "an international children's community" or a "self-governing children's community" to describe Summerhill. These are far more to the point than the "boarding school" label, which often has unhappy connotations.

In the time I have been at Summerhill I can think of very few children who have not become happier people, more at ease with themselves, more relaxed and expansive. And in each of these instances there have been very obvious conflicts between the school and home that have prevented the children from settling in. Of the vast majority who do enjoy their lives at Summerhill, many come from quite happy homes in which they know they are loved and their integrity is respected. By the integrity of the child I mean something very specific. I mean the integrated wholeness of the child, the various elements that make up the integral being of the child—natural liveliness, emotional interaction with the world, the biological sensations of life, the curiosity of life with its own natural functions and the urge to love and make contact. The child with integrity is the child who is unified in his or her own nature and with nature as a whole.

The parents of two boys in Germany became deeply concerned when their eldest boy, who was almost eight, began to grow irritable and morose. He was clearly being affected badly by the school he was at. They had brought him up to express himself without fear, without anxiety about his body or his sexuality. At school he was picked on by the teachers, who could not tolerate his lively manner and directness. He felt at odds with his peers who were contemptuous of and embarrassed by their bodies, who were sneaky and scared around adults. This in turn began to affect his relationship with his parents, as more than anything he wanted to be one of the gang, not an outsider. There were few places to play in or around the house, so both he and his four-year-old brother spent much of their time in front of the television, with which they frequently became bored and frustrated.

School was compulsory, so the parents could not keep the elder boy at home. They also recognized that he needed to mix with children of his own age, that it would not be healthy for him to be stuck at home with them all day long. They had heard of Summerhill many years ago, but thought it had closed when Neill died. It came to their attention that the school was still going, and they decided to visit with a view to moving to England so that both their children could attend as day kids. They were both doctors with established practices in Germany, so this would be quite a move for them. But they hated the idea of their children being away from home.

When I first met them I was rather worried that maybe they were being a bit idealistic about Summerhill. I was anxious that they would uproot themselves only to be disappointed. After all, I pointed out, not all the children at Summerhill had been raised as they had raised their children. Lots of kids when they first came to us had negative feelings about their bodies and were resentful towards adults. The parents stayed several days and asked lots of questions. By the end of the visit they were determined that their children should come here. For all its limitations they felt Summerhill had a liveliness and honesty to it that made a strong impression upon them.

Over the next year the mother tried unsuccessfully to find a suitable home in England, while the father continued to work in Germany. It was a hard time for them, full of frustrations and disappointments. Everything that could go wrong did go wrong. Eventually, after much heartache, they came to the conclusion that it was not feasible for them to move to England, but decided instead to send the elder boy as a boarder, with a view to sending the younger boy over later. The older boy has been at Summerhill as a boarder for over a year now, and despite the pain of being apart, his parents are happy with the changes they have seen in him. They see a return of his zest for life, which had begun to ebb away when he first attended school in Germany. He is more open and soft in his expressions than he dared to be with his German friends. He had not wanted to be away from home at first and had grieved deeply, but now he tells his parents, "I'm glad to be at Summerhill. I would prefer to be at home and have Summerhill too, but as I can't I would rather be at Summerhill than be at home and have to go to the German school."

A few years ago the mother of a Spanish boy at Summerhill organized a series of lectures for me in Spain. I was always deeply impressed by the warm bond between the mother and her son, and her respect for his individuality. She had arranged things so that I should fly back to England with him for the beginning of the new term. At the airport she hugged him goodbye, her eyes brimming with tears.

"It always hurts when he goes," she told me. "I need him more than he needs me. I hate it when he's gone, but I know he's happy at Summerhill. I see it in his face and that makes it all worthwhile."

When we were on the plane I asked him if he felt sad about leaving his home behind.

"Of course not," he said, looking genuinely puzzled. "All my friends are at Summerhill."

I use these two examples to illustrate my own thinking on the question of whether it is damaging for children to spend so much time away from home. Like these parents I have wrestled deeply with this issue, and like them I have come to the conclusion that, even though it may be temporarily painful, it is not damaging, but extremely beneficial, at least in an environment such as Summerhill. The two above examples are of homes in which the children feel secure and wanted, yet the parents have still felt that Summerhill could provide better for their children's needs. We also have children from homes in which the children do not feel loved and relaxed; homes in which the parents are forever quarreling, or tolerating each other in silent misery; homes in which the parents have split up and use the child to get at each other, leaving the child feeling torn between the two. There are endless variations on the theme, all of which the child involved feels acutely and anxiously in his or her own way.

It is inevitable that children with painful home lives will have chips on their shoulders. They may feel that they have been dumped at Summerhill. They may feel a sense of abandonment. The crux of the matter is this: those children who feel a sense of abandonment felt abandoned even when they were at home. It is not the physical distance that sets the tone, but the emotional distance. Summerhill cannot fully recompense for this loss, but I have seen children begin to heal these wounds, to feel accepted and cared for sometimes in a way that they have never felt before. They are able to live their everyday lives happily, finding companionship and a sense of belonging among their peers in a way that they could never have found in the conflict and tension-ridden atmosphere of home.

To understand this is to understand that for the children who live at Summerhill, whatever their home situation, Summerhill becomes home to them as well. It is not so much their school as their community. It is their larger family. It is a place in which they feel they have a voice and can truly be themselves. They are approved of for who they are, without being measured against anyone else's abstract idealism. We belong where we long to be, and for the kids at Summerhill the beginning of term is something to look forward to. So the boy who defined homesickness as feeling sick because he was going home was not just being flippant. He was expressing something deeper than wit.

Our society puts all its eggs in one filial basket. Children are expected to get most of the emotional nourishment they need from their parents, and their parents are expected to be able to provide it. It is an impossible task, yet it is the measure that every family sets itself up against. To be unhappy or unsatisfied is to throw the whole picture into disarray. It brings into question everyone else's role. "Am I such a bad mother?" "Am I such a terrible son?" Discomfort becomes dissent. The family is larger than the individual and it makes its larger entity felt in such common phrases as, "Why must you always spoil things?" "Why are you always so awkward?" "What have we done wrong?" "What did we do to deserve this?" "We've always done our best for you haven't we?" "Your brother never complains." Questions of individual happiness unwittingly become questions of collective guilt and blame. We soon find ourselves in a no-win situation where no one dare move. Emotional stalemate.

Something we have come to underestimate greatly is the need that children have to belong to a larger peer group. Children need other children to play with, to fight with, to break rules with, to fall in and out of love with, to grow with and find their place in the world with. Parents cannot do all these things with their children. Summerhill is a children's community. It is a space where the parents step back and let their kids live their own lives, in their own way, without interfering. Sometimes it is hard for the parents. At the beginning of every term I watch as the cars draw up outside the school. The kids rush out and off to play with their friends again. Within minutes their parents are forgotten, left to wave wistfully into the distance.

Children have always led much of their lives out of sight and earshot of adults. Meeting other children in the local streets and parks they have created their own worlds, with their own intrigues and dramas. Worlds full of fantasy, where the landscapes of the imagination reign supreme. Worlds in which the body becomes a blur of life; laughing, panting, leaping, tumbling, running into the wind. Friends are won and lost here, bonds are strong and powerful while they last and painful when they are broken.

These meeting places have diminished greatly over the past few decades. The streets have become busy roads. The parks have become places of fear and anxiety, where parents worry that strangers may molest and abduct their children.

More and more children have been driven back into the home to sit in front of the television, the video, the computer game, designated to the care of childminders, of parents who are exhausted from work and not enough space for themselves. More and more children are having to succumb to an adult environment, in which their own worlds are never really allowed to develop, and the turning on of the television becomes the only respite from boredom. Beyond this there is only the school, a world of timetables and activities again supervised by adults. This is not the world of children, but the world of children as adults think they should be. Here the accent is on childhood as a preparation for adult life, not as a state of being valid in its own right.

The children at Summerhill are not supervised by the adults, except in a few specific situations, such as in lessons, the swimming pool, or when using tools that might potentially be dangerous. Mostly they are free to roam as they like within the eleven or so acres of ground that belong to the school. If they want to play in the woods all day they do not have to ask anyone's permission, they can simply do so. If they want to go to lessons, or would rather sit in their rooms talking to friends, that is their business. If they want to go into the village, as long as they go at the times and in the groups decided in the meetings, they can go. The world of childhood is a disappearing one. It is one that many people will never really know, except as a dull, claustrophobic existence that they were happy to escape from. Today, Summerhill is one of the few places where children are able to live their lives unsupervised by adults, where they can live their lives according to their own desires and motives, rather than those of adults. As one Summerhill parent said, "I'm not sending my children away. I'm letting them go."

This was echoed by a nine-year-old German boy at the beginning of his first term. His parents had just driven away after an emotional farewell. "Now," he announced with a sigh of relief, "I can begin to live my own life."

A Children's Culture

ommunity life at Summerhill has two basic elements to it. On one hand there is a certain structure, which runs throughout the days and weeks. On the other, there are the spontaneous moods and crazes that seize the community every now and then. Both these elements weave in and out of each other, creating a pattern that is both static and yet ever changing. The spontaneous aspect develops out of the chemistry created by whichever kids and adults are active in the community at that time.

It may be that a particular game suddenly catches the popular imagination of the school. Or someone makes a wooden sword in the woodwork and overnight the school is transformed into a medieval battleground. A new cap gun has everyone rushing to the toy shop and the corridors become lined with cops and robbers hiding in shadowy doorways. It is a boiling hot afternoon and suddenly there are water bombs and buckets of water flying in all directions. Everyone is mending their bikes, building sledges, making tree huts. In reality, of course, not everyone is doing any one thing. There are always small groups getting on with their own thing regardless of whatever everyone else is doing. But every now

Games at Summerhill spontaneously spring up and evolve with the children's imaginations—in this case, the kids play medieval battle. *(Photo by Tomo Usuada.)*

and again a certain activity will seize the imagination, sweeping through the community like a wave, peaking and subsiding again.

It may also be that a certain bunch of kids begin to dominate the concerns of the community. Perhaps a small gang is making a nuisance of itself, flouting the community laws and disrupting other people in what they're doing. There may be "Special Meetings" called, and other activities are abandoned for a while as the community comes together to sort out whatever problem has arisen. At other times life goes on with no such disruptions for many terms running.

Throughout the ebb and flow of such happenings, the static aspect of daily life provides a skeletal structure. This begins at eight o'clock with the "wake up" bell. There are usually some kids who are up and about before this, and always some who sleep through it. At fifteen minutes past eight the bell is rung again announcing that breakfast is being served. Those who want breakfast go down to the kitchen where they are served cereal by one of the teachers. This is eaten in the dining room, where tea and toast are also available. At forty-five minutes past eight the kitchen hatch is closed and breakfast is over.

At nine o'clock the Beddies Officers go around to tell everyone who is still in bed that they have half an hour in which to get up. There are two different Beddies Officers every day, who are elected by the community to enforce the laws concerning bedtimes and getting up in the morning, which have been decided upon in the meeting. Although occasionally a staff member will run for Beddies Officer, they are mostly either Shack or Carriage Kids. At nine thirty they go around again to make sure everyone is up. Anyone who refuses to get out of bed can then be fined by the Beddies Officer unless, of course, they are ill.

Lessons begin at nine thirty. These continue until twelve thirty for the two "primary" classes, and until one fifteen for the older children who are doing courses in specific subjects.

To some children lessons are a distant realm into which they rarely, or sometimes never, venture. To others they are an integral part of their lives at Summerhill, which they rush off to eagerly every day. The choice is theirs, and no adult tries to influence them one way or another.

The woodwork is open in the mornings as an informal, drop-in space, and it is usually a hive of activity. Anyone can go in and make whatever they want, and the teacher is just there to offer practical advice, and to oversee the use of tools and equipment. Recently when I popped in to see what was happening there were mostly older kids at work. One was making a litter bin, another a tripod for his camera. A home-made bed base was being put together. A chair was beginning to take shape. In the corner a half-finished table was awaiting its owner's return. There was an air of deep concentration about the place. On other occasions I have seen the woodwork full of smaller kids, hacking away at bits of wood to make bowls, boxes, bows and arrows, shields, swords, machine guns, or whatever had taken their fancy. It is rare to find the woodwork empty. At times the art room has also functioned as an open space similar to that of the woodwork. The present art teacher, though, has chosen to concentrate on more formal lessons. If any of the children objected they could take the issue to the meeting and push to have the art room available on a more informal basis.

I often go out during lesson times or shut myself in my room for some undisturbed reading. The teachers are generally available during these times if anyone needs some first aid or anything else in an emergency. When I first came to Summerhill I made myself available all day long, but soon found I needed more time to myself to catch up on my own needs and interests. I have seen many staff come and go, leaving after only a year or so, feeling totally burned out. To survive on a long-term basis as an adult at Summerhill requires a strong sense of identity and personal boundaries. It is a question of mastering the balance between personal need and the needs of the community. Living in a community of children can be very taxing. There is always somebody who needs something. There is always noise. The intensity and energy of children free of adult constraints is more than many adults can tolerate.

At ten minutes to eleven there is a twenty-minute break. Orange juice, tea, and biscuits are served in the dining room. It is one of my favorite moments of the day. There is a chaotic clamor for cups. Children and adults of all different ages and sizes wind their way around each other as they queue for the teapot and biscuits, or just wander around to see what's happening.

The room is full of chatter as people exchange friendly greetings, or thrust and parry good-humored insults. One day we were visited by a state school teacher, who became so anxious by all this unregulated activity that she could barely restrain herself from wading in and attempting to enforce quiet and order. The sight of all these children rushing around carrying hot mugs of tea went completely against the grain of all she had been taught at teacher training college. Visions of severely scalded children flashed before her eyes. She was quite pale and shaken by the time break was over. I've seen a lot of tea spilled at break, but I've yet to see anyone scald themselves.

The younger children have lunch at twelve thirty. When they turn thirteen they go to second lunch at a quarter past one. Most of the staff go to second lunch, which is usually more sedate than first lunch. There is a law at the moment that nobody in second lunch can cadge food from the first lunchers. This came about after a few of the older kids started to get peckish early and began hanging around the first lunch queue, asking the younger kids if they wanted their chips or their puddings. They were not being threatening, but it was obvious that some of the little kids were finding it difficult to say no.

There is also a law saying that first lunch kids can't come

into second lunch. This was passed after several incidents of smaller kids coming into the dining room and playing around, making lots of noise and disturbing people who were trying to eat in peace. Generally, though, no one makes an issue out of small kids coming in, unless they are disturbing someone.

There are no lessons after lunch until four thirty. Sometimes a group of kids will organize themselves for a game of football, rounders, netball, volleyball, or the like. A popular game at the moment is Tork, which is a game played with two teams and a Frisbee. (The name comes from the first two letters of Tomo, one of the kids, and the last two letters of Mark, a teacher, who both introduced the game to the school.) Some kids will saunter downtown, usually to buy sweets and drinks. Others wander about complaining of boredom until they stumble upon something that fires their imagination. All around the school small clusters of friends sit around chatting, listening to music, playing games, climbing trees, and thinking of things to do. During the summer term the swimming pool is open most of the time. This depends largely on the weather, as the pool is unheated. But when it is open it is usually full of yelling, splashing kids. A lot of tennis is played in the summer too, with tournaments being organized throughout the term.

At four o'clock the bell is rung again and tea and biscuits are served from the kitchen. The adults retire to the staff room for this break. Throughout the afternoon many of the staff will have been involved with kids in various activities, or in jobs that have needed doing around the school. It is the first time during the day in which the adults get together as a group separate from the rest of the community. People sit around chatting about things that have happened to them during the day, sharing stories, or making arrangements for this, that, and the other. The staff room is no more formal in its atmosphere than the rest of the school.

At four thirty lessons begin again. At around four twenty-five there is usually a clamor of kids at the door eager to remind their teachers that it is lesson time and demanding that they hurry up. This is a far cry from my experience of school when the whole class sat hoping that the teacher would be late, hanging on to every last minute of freedom, savoring its sweetness, praying for a little while longer. The experience of being taught compulsively and the experience of learning voluntarily are not the same. This is something that needs to be remembered by those who say, "If I hadn't been forced to go to lessons I would never have learned anything." Lessons continue until five thirty for the younger kids and six fifteen for the subject courses. The older children studying specific subjects will not necessarily be in class throughout the times when these subjects are being taught, but only for the periods that are relevant to their particular courses. So someone could have lessons for five periods one day and only two the next.

At five thirty the younger kids have their supper, at six fifteen the older kids and staff have theirs. For this meal the staff eat in the staff room. Those staff who want to go out in the evening let the others know, so that there will always be enough adults on the premises. The houseparents have specific evenings off. The San houseparent and I each have two evenings off a week. The houseparents for the older kids have only one formal evening off each week, but have more freedom to go out for a few hours at any time. The teachers organize among themselves who will be in or out at any one time. Some will go down to the local pub, or to evening classes, or to visit friends outside the school. Others will sit around talking with kids or other adults in their rooms and caravans, or maybe become involved in some specific activity with the kids. One teacher organized a singing group last term, another built a sweat lodge based on those used by the North American Indians and arranged regular evening sessions. Some terms certain adults will be more actively involved in such projects, other terms it will be someone else. It changes all the time, but there's always something happening.

The Social Life of the Children

The vast majority of activity, outside of lessons, is not organized by the adults, but by the kids. Four evenings a week there is music in the lounge. This is known as "Gram," harking back to the days when the community's music was provided by a gramophone. Today it is a more sophisticated affair with twin record decks, a CD player, powerful speakers, and colored lights. The "Gram Committee" plays the music from the "gram box," a small semi-enclosed wooden platform on legs, high up in the corner of the lounge. The Gram Committee is elected through the meetings, so that not everyone can play the expensive and delicate equipment, which would otherwise quickly get wrecked. As it stands at the moment, no one under the age of twelve is allowed to run for the Gram Committee.

As well as being the school's disc jockeys, the Gram Committee members are also responsible for looking after and maintaining the equipment. Any new records or bits of equipment that have to be replaced are paid for out of the community fund. This is a pool of money that has been raised through "bars" and money fines that have accumulated from the meetings. Bars are where an elected group of kids prepare and sell food to make money for special events, such as half-term, end-of-term, Guy Fawkes night, and Halloween. They are known as "Bar Committees," with the name of the respective event tagged on, such as the End-of-Term Bar Committee. The money they raise goes towards financing the parties that celebrate these events, but what is left over goes into the community fund. When the Gram Committee wants some money from the community fund, it asks for funding in the meeting, and a vote is taken as to whether it should have the money. If the Gram Committee buys new records a piece of paper is put up on the notice board and people can write down the names of records they would like.

At various times there has been a Social Committee

elected by the community to organize games and entertainment during the afternoons and evenings. This committee comes and goes as the need arises. Otherwise, one or two kids may spontaneously decide to organize a game after supper and run around gathering people together to play. There are lots of little social scenes dotted around in various staff's and kid's rooms—people talking about this or that, listening to music, playing chess, reading comics and magazines, play-fighting. Small expeditions set out to explore the woods, with all the enthusiasm of Dr. Livingstone as he set off into the interior of Africa. Fires are a popular focal point for small social gatherings. There are certain laws about lighting fires. They always have to be overseen by an older kid or member of staff. The present laws regarding matches and lighters read, "No matches and lighters [to be used] inside," and "Only Shack [Kids] and over are allowed matches and lighters."

One evening I was invited to spend a couple of hours with three boys in their homemade hut in the woods. They had spent the last few days building the hut out of assorted old doors, bits of wood, pieces of rope and scaffolding poles. This rather odd-looking construction rested over a deep dip that had been hollowed out of the ground by some previous generation of Summerhillians. We climbed down the somewhat slippery slope that served as stairs, and I was offered a seat. One of the boys slid away a section of roof, as the others lit a fire in the carefully constructed fireplace below. The wood was soon ablaze, lighting up the mud walls of this subterranean den with a warm glow. There was a chair, a table, a set of homemade shelves propped up in one corner, and a plank of wood resting on some bricks that served as a bench.

It felt very pleasurable to be there. I felt much more privileged and at home to be invited into this secret alcove of childhood than I ever would if I had been invited to tea at Buckingham Palace or 10 Downing Street. As the fire crackled away, sausages and marshmallows were produced and roasted on the end of sharpened sticks. Up above us the stars glimmered through the chinks in the roof. The gentle patter of rain and the swishing of treetops drummed and whispered around us. Occasionally the wind would change direction, sending swirls of stinging smoke into our eyes and causing us to crease up in fits of convulsive coughing. But, somehow, this was all part of the fun.

Some evenings there is a café above the woodwork. For a couple of years I helped run the Orange Peel Café with a group of kids. The name "Orange Peel" came from the title of Neill's autobiography *Neill, Neill, Orange Peel.* We raised quite a lot of money and were able to replace the harsh strip lights in the café with spotlights, to buy a table football game,

Roasting marshmallows in the woods. *[Photo by Matthew Appleton.]*

Relaxing in the Jazz Café. *(Photo by Tomo Usuada.)*

and stock the café with new comics every week. I quit, feeling very fed up, after a couple of terms when the café kept getting broken into. A group of kids tried to keep it going for a while, but it did not last long. It was a very young school at the time with no big kids to take the responsibility of running and safeguarding such a project.

After the Orange Peel Café collapsed the space was turned into a homemade casino called the Silver Bullet, but known affectionately in the community as the Silver Swipe. Later a new café opened called the Jazz Café run by a couple of the big kids. It continues today, a far more sophisticated affair than the Orange Peel Café, which was very much a younger kids' café with its chocolates, sweets, lemonade, and comics. The Jazz Café serves salad sandwiches, teas, and coffees, and often has live piano music tinkling away in the corner.

Going Into Town

Groups of kids will go downtown throughout the evening to the chip shop, the Chinese takeaway, the "little shop" (a small sweet shop that opens only for a few hours in the evening), or the cinema. Again, there are specific laws that govern the hours that kids can go downtown, the groups they must be in, and how they behave. They seem to me a complex affair and I have never been able to fully digest them, but the kids seem to come to terms with them quickly. If I ever want to know one of the downtown laws I just ask one of the kids and he or she is usually able to tell me without having to think too hard about it. There are always small changes being made in the downtown laws, as they are discussed and voted upon in the meetings, especially regarding the times that people can go downtown in the evening. As the evenings get darker in the autumn, the times when people have to be back in school are usually brought forward. In the summer the downtown laws are as follows:

Anyone can go downtown from 5:00 a.m. to 9:30 a.m., and 12:00 noon to 6:15 p.m. On weekends these hours change to between 5:00 a.m. and 6:15 p.m. In the evenings, after they have had supper, House Kids have to be back by eight o'clock, and Shack and Carriage Kids have to be back by ten o'clock. However, the Shack and Carriage Kids have to go in mixed sex groups of four or over after eight o'clock. This came about after a couple of incidents when some of our older boys were harassed by some local louts. It was felt that a group of boys and girls together was less likely to get picked on than a group of boys only. It seemed to work and there have been no problems since.

Even in the daytime, though, not everyone can go downtown on their own. Anyone under eight years old has to go with someone who is sixteen or over. A twelve-year-old can go alone. A nine-year-old can go with a ten-year-old. An eight-year-old can go with a thirteen-year-old. Two twelve-year-olds can go on bikes. One thirteen-year-old can go by bike. A fourteen-year-old can take two eleven-year-olds on bikes. My mind begins to boggle as I try to unravel all these different combinations, but they seem to make perfect sense to the kids. It is a good job that the kids willingly bring cases against each other for breaking the downtown laws as I, at least, rarely know who should be downtown with whom, or when.

The laws continue. First-lunch kids are not allowed downtown before 1:00 p.m. This law was passed after quite a few first-lunch kids started to miss lunch, rushing down to the shops to stuff themselves with chocolate instead. Two fourteen-year-olds can go to a radius of fifty miles. A sixteen-year-old can go to a radius of one hundred miles. The younger kids are not allowed beyond the boundaries of Leiston unless accompanied by an adult. However, anyone can propose he or she is made an exception to these limitations if there is a good reason. No one can take sheath knives downtown, or behave in a rowdy manner, including swearing. No one should wear very dirty clothes. No one is allowed on the railway track. Only sixteen-year-olds and older can smoke downtown. Staff and parents can take anyone downtown after dark. The local farm, where Zoë lives (about a mile from Summerhill), is an annex to the school until 8:00 p.m. Anyone going to the cinema can stay out until 9:30 p.m. It makes me smile when I hear Summerhill described in the media as the school with no laws!

The majority of these laws are concerned with creating safe limitations for appropriate age groups. Others are concerned with defining what is a suitable way of behaving downtown. For example, no one turns a hair if anyone swears in Summerhill, but in the village it may cause offense. The kids understand and accept this. When a case is brought against someone in the meeting for behaving in an obnoxious manner downtown, the other kids are quick to point out that they do not want the whole of Summerhill to get a bad reputation just because one person doesn't know where to draw the line. They are aware that people often want to see the worst in what they do not understand, and that the concept of kids running their own community is certainly a foreign one to the majority of people. They are also quick to distinguish between what is natural, spontaneous behavior and what is showing off in front of others. So a new kid who starts swaggering and swearing downtown is soon told to stop being such a fool.

Some evenings there are organized trips to the local cinema and on Sunday evenings, except in the summer when our own pool is open, trips to the local swimming pool. Otherwise there is not much in the way of organized trips. There is an annual outing to a local theme park, and occasional trips to the coast, to wildlife parks, and other local attractions, but mostly the kids are so involved in the life of the community they have little interest in such distractions.

There are several televisions and computers around the school, and although the kids enjoy these at times they don't tend to spend as much time in front of them as many children do when they are stuck at home with nowhere else to go. The only law about watching television or playing computer games is that they should not be done during lesson times. Computer games and graphics are especially enjoyed by certain children, and they may become quite immersed in them for a while.

Some kids also resort to switching on the television when they're bored. But with lots of other kids around, there is always something more exciting that comes along and grabs their attention after a short while. Given the choice, most of the kids do not spend hours on end sitting passively in the glow of the computer or television screen. Instead they are out playing or chatting with friends. When I see the kids running around, making lots of noise, and playing with all their energy, I sometimes think of a quote from book by a Sioux medicine man called Lame Deer. He writes, "We have a new joke on the reservation: 'What is cultural deprivation?' Answer: 'Being an upper-middle-class white kid living in a split-level suburban home with a color TV.'"

Certainly many of the kids complain that there isn't much to do in the holidays except watch television. But for most children who do not have the freedom to roam and play as they like as Summerhill kids do, this is a reality they have to contend with all the time.

There is even less interest in expensive toys. Sometimes one of the kids will arrive at the beginning of term with a brand new radio-controlled car, or a bleeping, flashing space gun. They play with them enthusiastically for a while, but they soon tire of them, or abandon them with indifference when they get broken. Often someone will give me a toy to look after at the beginning of term and it will remain locked away in my box throughout, forgotten about until end of term when I remind them about it. Their interests seem to lie more with the inventions of their own minds and the expression of their own excitement than the expensive gadgetry of the advertisers.

Bedtimes

The Summerhill day ends (in principle at least) with each age group having its own bedtime and lights out. There is a general silence hour throughout the school at 10:00 p.m. This does not mean that everyone has to literally be silent, but that they should start to quiet down so that those who want to wind down at the end of the day, or to sleep, can do so. Throughout the evening the two Beddies Officers of the day wander around putting people to bed at the various bedtimes that the meeting has decided upon. Bedtime is a time when people have to be in the area of the school where they sleep. This is followed by lights out, when they have to be in their rooms with the light out and really be quiet, so that people can sleep. On Friday and Saturday nights everyone has a later bedtime, though this can be withdrawn as a fine if a room is brought up in the meeting for being consistently noisy throughout the week.

The bedtimes at present are 8:00 to 9:00 p.m. for the San Kids, 10:00 to 10:30 for the House Kids, 10:30 to 11:00 for the Shack Kids, and 11:30 to 12:00 for the Carriage Kids. The Shack Kids can keep their own personal lamps on for half an hour after their lights out, and the Carriage Kids, although they have to be in their own rooms after midnight, can keep their lights on as late as they like. Everyone has bedtime half an hour later on "late nights." Staff do not have an actual bedtime or lights out, but can be fined for disturbing anyone who is trying to sleep, or for breaking any of the bedtime laws with kids.

At ten o'clock my room begins to fill with kids, some of whom I have hardly seen all day. Someone may need to have a bandage changed, or to take some medicine. If it is cold there are hot water bottles to be filled. A can of hot chocolate and a bottle of orange juice are put out for anyone who wants a drink before they go to bed. The San Kids also get fruit and biscuits at bedtime, whereas for the rest of the school cereal is served in the dining room between 9:30 and 9:50, which has been christened "evening breakfast." Despite the silence hour, House bedtime is usually noisy. It is as if the kids are trying to squeeze every last possibility to have fun out of the day before going to bed. Sometimes I read or make up a short story to a small group of kids in the corner, but mostly they prefer to race in and out engaged in some last-minute horseplay.

Then the Beddies Officers tell everyone it is lights out and they go around making sure everyone is in their room, turning the lights out as they go, and telling people to keep their noise down. The Beddies Officers have the power to fine people who break the bedtime laws. This can be a "pudding fine," which means you lose your dessert the next day at lunch, or a half-hour "work fine." This consists of having to work for half an hour on behalf of the community the next day. It's usually a matter of doing some weeding, or picking up litter. Anyone who objects to being fined can appeal it in the next meeting and be compensated by the community in some way if it is felt that the fine was unfair. In this way the Beddies Officers are always accountable to the community at large. If people are disturbed after their lights out they can go and get the Beddies Officer to tell the person who is making noise to be quiet, or they can ask the next day to have the culprit fined. It is usually enough just to say, "If you don't shut up, I'll get the Beddies Officer."

Sometimes it can be quite noisy after lights out and the Beddies Officers have to come back several times to get people to quiet down. The first few weeks of this last term were particularly noisy. By and large this was due to the fact that there were five new kids in the House who couldn't see the point of having a bedtime. Wanting some peace and quiet at the end of the day, I had to keep going out to complain. Whereas the kids who had been here a while simply apologized and agreed to keep their noise down, the new kids scattered whenever my door opened, only to re-emerge minutes later as noisy as ever. It is always this way with new kids. They are always less reasonable and think of adults as an authority to run away from, rather than people to respond to.

Parents, Visitors, and New Staff

On weekends there are no lessons. People can stay in bed as long as they like. On Saturday mornings a lot of the young kids like to watch children's programs on television. Sometimes parents arrive to take their kids and some of their friends out for a few hours. It can occasionally be a problem if parents come too often, in that it prevents their children from really settling into community life. It can also be very fragmenting, breaking bonds formed during the week and dividing the community temporarily into those who are going out with someone's parent and those who are left behind. For the first term, or often only the first few weeks, kids are pleased to see their parents regularly, but this usually dies off and it is not uncommon to hear someone say, "Oh no, my parents are coming this weekend." It is not because they don't want to see their parents, only that they don't want their life at Summerhill to be interrupted. Most kids are happy to be visited only once or twice a term, although the older kids usually shun any parental contact in term time. Those who look forward to seeing their parents most are often those who feel most insecure about their home lives, and after their parents have gone anticipation quickly turns to disappointment and depression as the reassurance that they had longed for fails to materialize.

Parents sometimes find this letting go difficult. But it also has its own rewards. As the mother of one boy put it, "Summerhill has taught me to let go, to let him live his own life without interfering all the time. It was hard at first, but our relationship is so much better now. We get far more out of being with each other in the holidays than we ever did when we were always under each others' feet. He's so much more confident now. So much happier. It's a great relief." I hear such things from parents all the time.

It is also true that there are sometimes conflicts between the school and parents, but this is usually when the parents are not ready to relinquish power over their children. They want to interfere all the time. Perhaps they have undue anxieties about how their children will cope without them. Usually the children are doing fine and the real issue is around the parents' need to feel needed, not the well being of the child. Some parents wish they had come to Summerhill themselves and try to live out their own childhood through their kids, instead of standing back and letting their children get on with it in their own way.

There are also times when the parents have split up and each wants to win the child from the other. The child ends up tugged one way, then another, and is little more than a pawn in the battle between the parents. In all these instances the parents may resent the independence and happiness of the child and, in small ways that they are not even conscious of, try to undermine it.

In 1926 Neill wrote a book entitled *The Problem Child*, but several years later followed it with another one called *The Problem Parent*. The first line of the latter book reads, "There is never a problem child, there is only a problem parent." To fully understand what Neill was getting at it is important to place his ideas in the context of the times. With his knowledge of child psychology he was challenging the idea that children were born in a state of "original sin." He recognized that what was called "badness" was in fact unhappiness, arising not out of some inherent trait, but out of the conflict between the nature of the child and a hostile environment—in particular as presented in the primary relationship with the parents. This earned him the reputation of being "anti-parent," a reputation that Summerhill still lives with to some degree.

When Neill founded Summerhill he stated unequivocally that he was founding a school that would be "on the side of the child" and this is as true of the school today as it was then. If to be "on the side of the child" is to be "anti-parent," then it is a sad state of affairs. The unfortunate truth is that not all parents do have their children's best interest at heart. If to be on the side of the child means having to face this uncomfortable fact, there is nothing that can be done; it has to be faced. Happily, though, the majority of Summerhill parents feel that in being on the side of their children Summerhill is also on their side.

But to return to my description of the Summerhill weekend. After second lunch the bell rings for "poc." This is when pocket money is given out in the dining room by Ena Neill, now in her eighties. Although Ena retired from running the school in 1985, she still comes over from her cottage every Saturday to hand out poc, and on most days of the week to visit the domestic staff in the kitchen. Sitting next to Ena is the Fines Officer. The Fines Officer is elected by the community to keep a record of and collect money from people who have been fined during the week. At the Saturday evening meeting she or he gives a report of who still owes money to "the fines," and how much the fines has. If there has been a bar that week the Bar Committee will also be at poc to collect money. There is a system that they operate called "pay on poc," whereby people can buy food on credit during the week. There is also a law that says Bar Committees can not let San Kids run up more than half their poc on pay on poc. Otherwise many a disappointed San Kid would leave poc empty-handed. The younger kids are not very adept at handling their money. The temptation of the moment quickly overshadows the concerns of tomorrow.

After they have collected their poc, nearly the whole school goes downtown. The village shops are used to this weekly invasion and the relationship between the shopkeepers and the kids is a very friendly one. The overall relationship between the school and the people of Leiston is friendly and courteous. We have been neighbors for over seventy years, and people have got used to this peculiar school on their doorstep. Many of the local traders and workmen have been doing business with the school throughout, carrying on the relationship from one generation to the next. There is still, occasionally, the odd rumor that lingers here and there. I once heard someone refer to us as "that school for delinquents." An adolescent boy in a nearby village asked one of our girls if it was true that "the boys and girls all have sex together in the swimming pool." A taxi driver bringing a radio journalist to the school told her that we were "a queer lot," and if she needed help all she had to do was get to a phone and he would be there in minutes. But these sorts of notions are very rare these days.

On Saturday evening there is the meeting, then Gram. The school is very quiet on Sunday morning, having had two late nights. Lots of people stay in bed until quite late. But not the little kids. The little kids are up early every morning, running around and making noise to a chorus of sleepy voices calling out for them to shut up. Each Sunday a member of staff cooks lunch with a small group of kids who get paid a couple of pounds for helping out. The kids usually really enjoy this and put a lot of effort into making it a nice meal. There is also a rotation of older kids and staff to do the washing up, as no domestic staff comes in on Sundays. During the afternoon some of the little kids may get bored. The pace of the rest of the school has slowed down and they don't know what to do with themselves. Sometimes someone will organize something for them to do, or maybe they will be left kicking their feet and complaining until they eventually come up with something that has them charging around again in a flurry of bright-eyed excitement. In the evening there is a trip to the local swimming pool, which is always a favorite with the little kids.

There are two or three days a term that are devoted to visitors. These are days on which anyone who wishes to visit the school is invited to come along. They are shown around by staff or kids, and in the afternoon there is a question-and-answer session held in the dining room. These have proved to be quite successful. We used to have a much more open policy towards visitors, where anyone wanting to visit could just drop in. But this often meant that the visitor was just left to wander, as everyone was busy getting on with things and had no time to show people around or answer questions. It became a problem as sometimes there would be visitors almost every day, sometimes for weeks on end. People began to feel uncomfortable with these strangers wandering around, often prying into what they were doing and demanding to have their questions answered.

The visitors' days are much more enjoyable. We are prepared for strangers poking around and asking questions. No one feels resentful. On the whole, the kids tend to ignore visitors day and get on with what they're doing. Many of the staff, though, like to talk about the school and to meet other people who are interested. It is easy, when living in a community such as Summerhill, to take for granted what after all is just daily life to us.

I remember in my first term being constantly thrilled by the meetings and amazed by the confident and articulate manner in which the kids argued their cases and made their decisions. A couple of years later, after attending a meeting that I found very boring and frustrating, a visitor who had sat quietly throughout wrote to me saying, "That was one of the most wonderful experiences of my life." He went on to describe all the elements of the meeting that had once inspired me, whereas I was looking no further than my own proposals, which the meeting had dropped. For a moment I had quite forgotten that it was just this possibility for kids to challenge and throw out adult ideas that had attracted me to Summerhill in the first place. I think all the adults have days like this sometimes.

There is quite a large turnover of staff. If a visitor to Summerhill were to make a return visit five years later there would be many new faces, and only a few familiar ones. Of these, most would be among the older kids, though they will have changed a lot in five years, from scruffy, dirt-streaked House Kids, running around doing their own thing, to well-groomed, sociable adolescents. There would be some familiar faces among the staff, but these would be outweighed by the new ones, some enthusiastic and eager to talk about their fresh experience of Summerhill, others more reserved as they ponder their own emotional reactions to the place.

With people coming and going all the time the school is always in flux. In my first term this was especially so. A group of the older kids had just left, and there was a large intake of new kids. At the same time almost half the staff were new that term too. Of the returning staff, many had only been there a few terms themselves and there were many conflicting opinions in the staff room about how best to handle this or that situation. Yet the community seemed to go about its business with an inner coherence that was not disturbed by the differences of opinion that ricocheted around the staff room.

If I felt I had any concerns about one of the kids, or maybe the way I had dealt with something, I would usually go to Zoë and discuss them with her. Although she did not actually live in the community, she had grown up in it and her understanding of its ways ran deep. I usually found her advice helpful and reassuring. But apart from Zoë, my main source of coming to grips with and understanding Summerhill came from talking to the older kids. This is something that I have seen many new staff struggle with. They find it difficult to let go of the idea that adults should know best, or at least be seen to know best. It turns their sense of hard-earned "professionalism" on its head, and appears to them topsy turvy. It is a shame when they are not able to make the leap, as there is a lot to be learned from the older kids. But at a time when many teachers are being told they should not smile in the first six months of working at a school because the kids need to be sure of who is boss before such informalities are introduced, it is not surprising that some teachers, fresh out of training college, find it hard to trust in children.

The Older Kids As Community Elders

Although there are adults who take active and powerful roles in the community, by and large the guiding light of community life comes from the older kids. They are, so to speak, the elders of the community. Many of them will have been at Summerhill longer than most of the staff, and have a much deeper understanding of its processes. The big kids are very powerful in the school's self-government. They have strong voices in the meetings, drawn from their years of growing up through the school and an understanding of the younger kids, who may be going through phases that they went through themselves not long before. They also take on many of the more structured roles within the community, such as chairing the meeting, Fines Officer, Beddies Officer and Ombudsman, who sort out problems that arise between people throughout the week.

The various committees are made up largely of big kids. As well as the committees I have already mentioned, such as the Gram Committee, Social Committee, and the committees that organize bars and parties, there have been many other committees that have come and gone as the need has arisen. There was a Table Tennis Committee to ensure that the table-tennis equipment was looked after and kept in repair. A Bike Committee helped the younger kids keep their bikes in good repair. A Food Committee helped the kitchen devise menus for a short while after there were lots of complaints about the food. A Swindling Committee made sure that the little kids were not being cheated by some of the more devious characters in the community when swapping or buying things. A Visitors Committee took visitors on guided tours of the school. These are just the handful of committees that come to mind as I think back over the time I have been at Summerhill. No doubt there are other more obscure ones that I have forgotten.

On any of these committees there may be an occasional staff or a handful of younger kids working alongside the big kids. But it is the big kids who are most active in organizing things and passing on certain ways of doing things that have developed within the community to its newer and younger members. This is true of both the self-government and socially. Summerhill has been described elsewhere as "the bare minimum of a school."

This description is a valid one in the sense that Summerhill has been designed to accommodate the needs of the children, rather than to impose unnecessary restrictions and adult ideology on them. But this lack of adult imposition does not mean that the children live in a vacuum. Summerhill has its own culture and built-in traditions that have evolved through the generations, passed on from one group of big kids to the next.

Many of the games that are played, such as Kick the Can, Touch Prisoners, British Bulldog, and Villains in the Dark have also been picked up by one generation from another. Zoë recalls playing these games when she was a child at Summerhill in the 'fifties and 'sixties. Sometimes some of the big kids will organize The Murder Game. This was a game that was devised by a couple of big kids shortly before I came. Usually most of the school will sign up for it. It consists of various people being murderers, private investigators (P.I.s), and undercover private investigators. Everyone else is "normal." No one knows who the undercover P.I.s are except for the P.I.s and no one knows who the murderers are. The murderers have to kill people by touching the bottoms of their feet, but mustn't get caught by the P.I.s or they can be killed themselves. They must carry a "murder list" with them at all times, with the names of all the people playing the game, and can be searched by the P.I.s if they are acting suspiciously or have been seen killing someone. The game sometimes goes on for days and becomes deeply interwoven into ordinary, everyday life.

In my first term one of the teachers called me into the bathroom to have a look at something. The next minute he was grabbing my leg. My first thought was that he had gone mad. It was only when he tapped the sole of my foot and hissed a triumphant "dead" at me that I remembered the Murder Game. During a later game a teacher had to take a girl to the doctor. When the doctor asked her to climb up on the couch, she pointed wildly at the teacher and cried, "Keep him away. I'm sure he's a murderer!" The teacher hastily reassured the doctor it was only a game.

More recently another big kid, who was interested in international politics, devised a variation on the theme, called The Cold War Game. In this, the players were split into two teams with various people playing the roles of generals, lieutenants, sergeants, privates, spies, and military police. The object of the game is to find out who the other side's general is and kill them. The inventors of both these games have now left Summerhill, but the games continue to be played by kids who have mostly never known the kids who devised them. It is their legacy to the community.

Throughout the year occasions such as Halloween, Guy Fawkes Day, St. Valentine's Day, and end of term are celebrated in their own traditional way. At the stroke of midnight on the eve of St. Valentine's Day a large group of kids runs around the school kissing whoever they can find. Even though the bedtime laws are being broken, the Beddies Officers take no notice as it is an accepted, albeit unspoken, exception to the bedtime laws. During the week before, the art room will have been busy with people making Valentine cards, which are then left on a table in the lounge for people to collect at the party. The Valentine's Committee are very productive at this time, making sure that everyone in the community has at least one card.

At summer half-term there is a walk to the local beach, about two and a half miles from the school. It is called The Midnight Walk, though everyone is usually back in school long before midnight. This is organized by the Half Term Committee, who arrange wood for a fire, soup, marshmallows to roast, and transport for the smaller kids who are too tired to walk back.

The single most important event of any term is the end-of-term party. The lounge is closed about a week before end of term and decorated by the End of Term Picture Committee. They decide among themselves on a theme and the walls are covered in paper and painted to depict that theme. In recent years the themes have included madness, black and white, Disney, Batman, popular music, the Jungle Book, cities, a street carnival, a haunted house, and inside the waste bowl (the bowl into which leftovers are emptied at mealtimes). One of my favorite themes was the school meet-

An end-of-term play. *[Photo by Tomo Usuada.]*

ing, in which life- size cutouts were painted of everyone in the
community and stuck around the walls, as if it were a real
meeting in progress. Nobody other than the Committee and
the staff, who have to pass through the lounge to get to the
Staff Room, are allowed to know what the theme is until the
party begins and the lounge is opened again.

The end-of-term party is an emotional affair, not only
because everyone is preparing to go home and will not see
each other for several weeks, but also because it is when the
community says goodbye to those who are leaving and not
coming back. At midnight everyone links hands and gathers
in a circle around the people leaving. The Gram begins to
play "Auld Lang Syne" and everyone sings along. When the
music ends the circle breaks up and closes in around those in
the middle. Tears are shed as friends hug each other maybe
for the last time. Many will be returning to countries on the
other side of the world. They are saying goodbye to an
intimacy and way of life they have been a part of and shared,
sometimes for many years. It will not be the same again.

It is difficult to express the emotional intensity of end of term. Any Summerhillian will instantly know what I am talking about. When ex-Summerhillians sometimes return to visit at end of term, their faces still well up with emotion as the Gram churns out "Auld Lang Syne." I feel this myself even at the thought of end of term. I have had to say goodbye to many kids who I have grown close to over the years. It is like a wound that is opened again every time another one goes.

As kids move up through the school from San to House, from Shack to Carriages, each stage has its own sense of being a rite of passage. Standing in the circle is the final stage that everyone must pass through. When I left my school I did not look back. I felt only a relief at being free of it and a slight anxiety as to what the future would hold for me. But kids leaving Summerhill are not just leaving school. They are leaving a way of life they love and have felt a part of. They are leaving home.

The sense of being part of a huge family is a very strong one. For some kids it will be the place they have felt most at home in life. I have often heard older kids talk about their friends being like brothers and sisters. It is a closeness that comes from being able to be yourself and being accepted as yourself by everyone else. As one girl said, "I feel closer to the people I know least well here than I did to my best friend in my old school."

Many of the younger kids feel the loss of the older kids' leaving acutely. In fact, I have seen more emotion generated by big kids' leaving than by many of the staff who have come and gone. This is not because the kids don't form strong relationships with staff, or feel a sense of loss when particular individuals go, but the fact is that many staff do not stay as long as the kids who have gone through the school to become big kids, nor are they necessarily as involved in community life. Sometimes there have been obvious friendships where one of the big kids has taken a younger child under his or her wing. Sometimes the connection is not so obvious. Perhaps the big

Older kids often befriend younger kids and pass on their skills.
(Photo by Tomo Usuada.)

kids said or did something that had a lot of meaning to the younger ones. Maybe they helped them to accomplish a task or deal with a problem. To the younger kids the big ones are cool, powerful people, closer to their own age and immediate future than the staff. To be noticed by a big kid is thrilling and exciting. I remember myself, as a boy, the elation I felt when an older kid paid some attention to me. It really made me feel like I was somebody.

One of the older girls told me once, "When you're a little kid you like the staff, but you don't look up to them. It's the big kids that you look up to. You look at them and think, 'Maybe I can be like that one day.'" This does not necessarily reflect the experience of all kids at Summerhill, but there is certainly some truth in it.

As an adult at Summerhill I find it takes a certain amount of self-discipline to stand back and not try to impose preconceived ideas on the kids. There are other times when it is important to get involved, not as an adult with a capital "A," but as a caring member of the community who just happens to be an adult. Being an adult is not something to be scared of, anymore than it is an elevated status. My own impression is that a core group of adults who are actively engaged in community life at any one time and who understand and care about it is vital. But this does not undermine the role of the big kids in passing on the traditions and the sense of empowerment that they have picked up themselves as they have progressed through the community.

Community
Meetings

There are two weekly meetings: Tribunal on Friday afternoon, and the General Meeting on Saturday evening. Attendance is not compulsory, but a large section of the community usually turn out, reflecting the whole age range of its members. Everyone has one vote, adults and children alike, and all decisions are made according to which proposals get the most votes.

There is a chairperson who is voted in the week before. The chairperson remains neutral in all discussion and has no vote. If s/he has anything to say s/he must stand down, letting someone else chair the meeting for the rest of that case. The chairperson's job is to take hands, count votes, and control the meeting. S/he has the power to fine people for talking when their names have not been called. S/he can wind a business up if it has been going on for a long time and people are beginning to repeat themselves. If people are being continually disruptive the chairperson can throw them out. The chairperson even has the power to close a meeting if it becomes very unruly, though I have only ever seen this happen once.

There are usually a lot of cases to get through, and no one wants to sit around for ages in a noisy meeting. So those who chair the meeting most effectively get voted in most often.

The meetings are held in the lounge, which is a huge room just inside the front door. The walls are lined with wood, and the wooden floorboards are uncarpeted. In one corner is the Gram box. Double doors lead off to the staff room on one wall and on another a single door leads into the library. There is a fire door that opens up onto the bottom corridor and French windows that look out across the grass and onto the woods. A staircase leads up to the top corridor. The lounge is unfurnished, unless the odd chair has made its way there from one of the sitting rooms. When the bell rings people begin wandering in, sitting themselves around the walls, and along the stairs. After a while the chairperson calls out, "Meeting come to order," and everyone quiets down.

Law breaking and disputes between individuals are dealt with in Tribunal. The meetings have something of the atmosphere of a tribal council. People listen carefully to cases, offer opinions and make proposals as to what might be done to resolve a conflict, or curtail a certain activity. Maybe Nick has taken Roger's gun and refuses to give it back. Roger tells Nick, "I'll bring you up at the meeting if you don't give it back." The chances are that the gun will be returned there and then, but if not, Roger brings his case to Tribunal. At every meeting there is someone acting as secretary who keeps the minutes, and anyone wanting a case heard sees the secretary beforehand. The chairperson then tells Roger when it's his case. Roger tells the meeting his side of the story, then Nick has the chance to defend himself. If anyone has anything further to say, perhaps to offer an eye-witness account as to what happened, or to make a proposal, they do so.

A number of proposals may be made. Perhaps an ultimatum to return the gun, maybe with a warning to leave other people's stuff alone. A fine might be proposed, such as a money fine to compensate Roger for the loss of the gun. If the case seems unfounded someone could propose that the case be dropped. The chairperson reads out the proposals and

Everyone has one vote in the meetings—adults and children alike.

(Photo by Tomo Usuada.)

they are voted on. The proposal that is carried is read out again, then the business is closed and it's on to the next business.

There is no systematic procedure for bringing cases to the meeting. People just bring up what is important to them. Cases brought on behalf of the community, rather than between individuals, are perhaps a bit more arbitrary depending on how community-conscious the individual is. But there are always enough people aware of the wider needs of the community to keep the ball rolling. Maybe Dawn has broken a community law by going downtown on her own after dark. Someone saw her coming back and brings her up. She has the chance to offer an explanation, then anyone who has anything to say can add their piece. The proposals are taken. She may receive a strong warning to keep the downtown laws. She may be fined some money, or be issued a social fine, such as picking up litter. The usual fine for breaking a downtown law is to be "gated" for a day or two. This means she cannot leave the school grounds for that period. The community mainly leans on the side of leniency. After all, most of us have been brought up for something or other at some time.

In most situations where adults and children live together all the power and decision-making is in the hands of the adults, and they soon forget how the world looks through the eyes of children. One summer night I was woken up by voices in the room next to mine. I went in, irritated and bleary eyed, to find a roomful of fully dressed kids preparing to sneak out.

"If you're going to sneak out," I told them, "can you be a bit more quiet about it?"

They apologized and quietly filed down the stairs into the grounds outside. I could have, of course, told them that I was going to bring them up for sneaking out after lights out, but as they were being quiet I didn't want to make an issue of it. I returned to bed, but could not get back to sleep. After a while I decided that rather than lie there and become resentful, I would go out and see what they were up to.

It was a beautiful night, well lit by the moon, and I soon traced the little band of nocturnal nomads to the large beech tree that stands at the front of the school grounds, some way from the house. Known as the Big Beech, it has become quite a well-known Summerhill landmark, the focus of many a photograph, and generations of Summerhill kids have swung, Tarzan style, from its lower limbs. Hiding behind some bushes I started to make growling noises. These were echoed by low-pitched nervous whispers and shuffling feet. Then I sprang out from my hiding place and was immediately surrounded by kids overjoyed and relieved that it was only me, and not some hideous monster that had taken up residence in the woods. For the next hour or so I wandered around the grounds with them, exploring the shadows that the night cast, so different from the world of daylight, and charged with the thrill of being against the law.

The next day at Tribunal I was brought up by one of the older kids for being out with a group of kids after their lights out. It's a fact that you can't keep much secret in this community! The kids were each fined their late night and their pudding for the following day. As I didn't have a bedtime and so could not be fined my late night, I was fined two puddings. I have always found such experiences useful reminders as to the child's view of life. When I start getting on my high horse about something one of the kids has done I don't have to cast my mind back quite so far to remember what it's like to be on the other side of the fence.

I have always liked a quote by the Polish educationalist Janus Korczak, from his book *When I am Little Again*, published in 1926. He writes, "You are mistaken if you think we have to lower ourselves to communicate with children. On the contrary, we have to reach up to their feelings, stretch, stand on our tiptoes." This insight paves the way to an understanding of the very reason that self-government functions in a fairer and more competent way than an authority

exercised by adults only. Children understand the emotional
dimensions of each other's actions more readily than most
adults do. They feel an empathy for the law-breaker, even
though they feel s/he should be fined, unlike the adults who
look upon such misdemeanors from an ivory tower of self-
righteousness, feeling that they have left such childish ways far
behind.

Respecting the Rights of Others

The tone of Tribunal is neither moralistic nor psychological. There is no attempt to rise above the issue, only to deal
with it as practically and straightforwardly as possible. Summerhillians are an uncomplicated lot. Antisocial behavior is
accepted, but not indulged. By accepted I do not mean
acceptable. What I mean is this: at Summerhill we look at life
frankly and honestly, and we recognize that almost everyone
has stolen something at some time, lost their temper on
occasion, invaded someone's privacy, or behaved in some
manner that has hurt another person's feelings. So when I say
that we accept anti-social behavior I mean we do not meet it
with shock or outrage, but with down-to-earth practical solu-
tions. We may get fed up and annoyed with each other's
shortcomings at times, but we never get superior about them.

How, it may be asked, if we do not teach morals, will the
children learn right from wrong? But what are right and
wrong, other than artificial distinctions by which we each
define our own way of perceiving the world? To another
person right and wrong might have quite different meanings.
Who am I to say that my way of viewing the world is superior
to another's? Who knows what nightmare may propel another into dark awakening? Who can comprehend the config-
urations of another's anxieties, fears, and loneliness? Who is
to judge? Who is to say that this part of our nature is good and
that part bad? Each of us carries our own stigmata, our own

wounded nature, which we are trying to come to terms with. I can only defend my own right to view the world through my own eyes, to not have it blurred or blotted out by another's reality. That is the right of every human being, no matter how young.

How, it may be asked, can children be expected to understand themselves, if we are not psychological with them? Children understand themselves much more directly if their minds are not cluttered with adult ideas about who they are. *At the root of every spiteful and destructive action there is a natural expansion towards life-affirmative contact that has been thwarted.* The more we concentrate on the symptom, the more we compound it. When we can begin to accept people as a whole, then they can begin to accept themselves. It is then that their defenses can begin to melt and their life-affirmative core nature can expand and extend into the foregrounds of their lives once more. Psychology has its place in the world, but acceptance and self-government are therapeutic in themselves.

It is important, though, to distinguish between acceptance and indulgence, and this is where Summerhill's down-to-earth, practical approach to problems is most effective. Joe is brought up in the meeting for stealing from the Orange Peel Café. He has been trying to buy friendship by giving away free sweets and chocolate. I and the other kids on the Café Committee who have been putting a lot of time and effort into the café feel angry and betrayed by Joe's abuse of his position on the committee. We have been trying to raise money to improve the café, to buy comics and games and make it a more active social center within the school.

At the meeting a lot of strong views are aired by both the Café Committee and those who enjoy the café's facilities. Joe is fined. It is carried that he has to make a bookshelf for the café in woodwork, and clean the café up on the next three occasions it is open. There is no long discussion about his motives. His insecurities are not dragged into the arena of the

meeting. After the meeting no one is hostile to him. The air
has been cleared. He realizes, even if just as a glimmer, that
people accept him for who he is. He does not have to put on
a show to impress people. Friendship does not have to be
stolen, it comes of its own accord. He realizes this because he
has been caught out, but not rejected. The proof of the
pudding is in the attitude of the community, not in long
drawn-out discussions and analysis.

Just as there is an absence of morality and authority, there
is also an absence of resentment on the part of the person
who has been brought up. The conflict is rational and not
based in a power struggle, so the response is also rational.
Skateboarding inside is banned by the meeting, yet the boys
in the room next to mine were constantly rolling up and down
on their skateboards, creating a most disturbing din. After
several requests to stop it, which went unheeded, I told the
chief culprit I was bringing him up. He was fined twenty-five
pence in the meeting, yet afterwards we went downtown
together and he was as friendly and cheerful as ever. The
business was finished and there was no resentment.

Often you will see two kids playing together after a
meeting where one has been fined in a case brought by the
other. Because they have been able to sort out their problem
through their own means, rather than having to rely on the
great bastion of adult authority to step in, no one feels the
odds have been loaded against them. The conflict has not
become confused with power struggles and resentments beyond the immediate event.

Some people may find it difficult to talk at the meeting in
their first few terms, or, if they are from abroad they may have
problems with the language. In either case there will always be
someone to help them, whether it be to bring the case for
them, or to translate. Often an ombudsman will bring a case
on someone else's behalf. When I first came to Summerhill
ombudsmen were elected at the beginning of each term.
They consisted of a group of older kids and occasionally a

member of staff who drew up a rotation where three ombudsmen were available every week to arbitrate in on-the-spot disputes. The names of the ombudsmen for that week would be announced at the beginning of Tribunal, and if anyone was having a dispute with someone that could not be deferred to Friday he or she would call an ombudsman to help sort things out. The same system operates today, except instead of being elected at the beginning of term, volunteers for ombudsman for the next week are called for at every Tribunal.

Perhaps David won't get out of Lizzy's room. So she calls an ombudsmen to uphold the law for her. Or maybe Paul has been calling Adam names. The introduction of the ombudsman brings in a slightly more serious, formal element that prevents the dispute degenerating into a shouting match. If an ombudsman is called, it is expected that everyone concerned take part in what has now become an ombudsman case. The ombudsman asks each person in turn for his or her side of the story, making sure that the other does not interrupt all the time. Usually ombudsman cases are settled there and then, with the ombudsman suggesting some compromise, or telling the people involved to leave each other alone. But if this does not work the ombudsman may take the problem to the meeting. There is a time given to ombudsman cases at every Tribunal. The ombudsmen themselves do not have the power to fine, though they do have the power to confiscate anything that is being used dangerously or in a threatening manner.

If a more serious problem crops up anyone has the power to call a special meeting any time of the day or night. This is done by going to see whoever is acting as chairperson or secretary that week. If the chairperson or secretary feels it is too trivial to warrant a special meeting, he or she can suggest using an ombudsman or waiting for Tribunal, but otherwise a special meeting is called, and everyone stops what they are doing to gather in the lounge. It may be that someone has really been harassing someone else. Perhaps the night before some kids were running around keeping everyone awake. It could be that something has been stolen.

In cases of theft the meeting may spontaneously elect an Investigation Committee. This committee has certain powers. It can search through people's belongings and can question people at length. But in granting these powers the community issues the clear message that these powers should not be abused, and it chooses its investigators very carefully. Investigations are often quite simple. We are a small, intimate community, and the culprits often stand out like sore thumbs. A few terms ago a box was broken into and some money stolen. Two boys, who had a history of breaking into things, had been seen hanging around outside the room where the box was. Their restless and shifty manner was familiar from previous occasions when they had broken into things, and even before the box was broken into several people had commented that they were up to something. Later they were seen returning from downtown with fish and chips, despite the fact they had been complaining they had no money earlier in the evening. It took the investigation committee little more than an hour to talk to both boys separately, plus another boy who had gone downtown with them, before their stories began to fall apart. They were both fined. It was carried they should return the money and repair the box.

Not all investigations are so successful, though. If someone has left his or her wallet lying around and some money goes missing, it is almost impossible for the Investigation Committee to get a lead. Sometimes there is no evidence, but everyone just knows who did it. One day the whole school's pocket money was stolen. Everyone knew who did it simply because there was no one else in the community at that time who would attempt such a thing. But the culprits would not admit to it, and nothing could be done. Over the next few days, though, the boy and girl concerned began to feel the cold shoulder from the rest of the community, who had gone without their pocket money that week. Then, out of the blue, the boy suddenly "found" the money just lying on the floor of the Beeston. Everyone knew he was lying and he knew that everyone knew he was lying, but at least the money was returned and the air was clear again.

If children are able to handle their affairs in such a fair and rational manner, day in, day out, year after year at Summerhill, then why are they not allowed to do so throughout society? Why is it that a community such as Summerhill, which is a demonstrable and observable reality, exists at the edges of society, while a work of fiction, such as William Golding's novel *Lord of the Flies* is popularly upheld as a testament to child nature? In all the schools I ever attended as a child, from the infants through to the comprehensive, whenever there was a fight a large group of kids would gather around, chanting for blood, egging the fighters on, filling the air with hate. I have never witnessed this phenomenon at Summerhill. Rather, I have seen kids step in and try to stop fights, and when this has not been possible run off to get help from an older child or an adult. Why these two opposing experiences of childhood? The answer cannot be found in questioning the innate nature of the child alone, as this underlies both situations. It must then be sought in the experience of the child; whether its needs are met, thus allowing its inherent capacity for rationality to develop without distortion, or whether it is molded into something at once superficially moral and yet conversely brutal and sadistic. It is worth noting that Golding's kids were all boys, the products of a moralistic, authoritarian, sex-negative, public school system. That is, they were chained animals suddenly let off the leash.

Making Laws

On Saturday evenings we have our General Meetings. These always begin with a Tribunal report: a review of who was brought up, what for, and what they were fined. This is then opened up to general comments. Maybe someone went downtown when they were gated, or didn't go to the back of all queues as fined. This may get mentioned, or brought up at the next Tribunal. A question often asked is, "What if someone consistently refuses to do their fines?" All I can do is say I have never known this to happen.

It is generally assumed that, because in most schools kids succumb to punishment for fear of greater punishment, then in a school not governed by fear any sanctions will be disregarded. There are two aspects to this question that I think may account for the willingness to accept fines. The first is that we fine people at Summerhill, but we do not punish them. To punish implies a moral judgment, one that is meted out by goodness above to badness below. Fines, at least in Summerhill, are practical penalties in which everyone has a say, and to which everyone is subject. Secondly, kids want to be part of the community, not apart from it. They feel a sense of belonging, and with it a feeling of commitment, even when they are caught breaking the rules. There is a strong sense of fair play at Summerhill.

At the end of the General Meeting there is time for appeals, when anyone can appeal against any outstanding fine, such as being banned from a certain area of the school, or any previous fine that they think is too harsh. Quite often a fine will be reduced or dropped, for rarely is a fine appealed against unless the person really believes it to be excessive or unjust. Maybe a case was very emotive and a somewhat over-zealous fine was proposed in the heat of the moment. In a few days the air has cleared and everyone is seeing things from a calmer perspective. The appeal is carried. Having said that, there are occasionally one or two kids who will scowlingly appeal almost every fine they get, and their appeals will be repeatedly dropped. But they know they are pushing their luck and after a brief outburst of, "God, this community sucks!" have forgotten their grievances and are contentedly getting on with life.

But the main function of the General Meeting is to formulate the laws by which we live. As with the Tribunal, if you want a case you see the secretary beforehand and your name is called when it's your turn. You are then able to challenge the validity of any law, and propose it is dropped or replaced by a more relevant one. Likewise, you may want to draw up a new law to cover something you think needs to be defined more clearly. There is usually some discussion, then further proposals may be taken. These are then voted on and whichever one is passed becomes law until someone chooses to challenge it. So the school laws are forever in a state of evolution, reflecting the needs of the community at any given time.

Sometimes these cases may drag on for a long time. Whether they become boring or not usually depends on the emotional investment the individual has in them. A few years ago there was a lot of noise upstairs in the House after lights out. Someone proposed there should be a later bedtime. I argued strongly against it. At bedtime, after a long day, I have a solid half-hour of dispensing hot chocolate, clean Band-Aids, and medicines, and generally dealing with the kids' last minute needs of the day. After that I have only an hour or so to wind down before going to bed myself. The debate went on for ages, but because it was an issue of great importance to me it flashed by in what seemed like no time. However, when the next case came up, about skateboarding downtown, it had no emotional content for me and seemed to go on forever. Here again kids are wiser in their understanding of kids than adults are. If Chris has had his toy gun stolen and wants something done about it, it is every bit as important to him as it is to me if the paint work on my car has been scratched. At Summerhill everyone's feelings are taken seriously. Such is the way of self-government.

In the particular case about bedtimes, the vote went my way and the bedtimes remained the same. In fact, many of the kids who had argued for the later bedtime actually voted in my favor after listening to my side of the story. A couple of years later and under different circumstances, the bedtime did get moved to half an hour later, to the time it is now. Self-government involves compromise. There are two types of compromise; with one we give up the core of who we are and live our lives in the periphery, and with the other we live from our cores and are flexible with our peripheries. It is the latter way that we live in Summerhill. In this particular case I was able to find more time in the day to meet my own needs, so did not resent the later bedtime. If I had gone back to the meeting and argued with real feeling to bring back the earlier bedtime, I am sure it would have got passed sooner or later.

At one time I favored the concept of consensus, whereby differences are talked through until a solution agreeable to everyone is reached. Having watched and been part of Summerhill self-government at work, I have changed my mind on this. To begin with, our meetings would go on for days. As it is, it takes a good chairperson to keep things concise. Secondly, a world in which everyone agrees is not one that appeals to me. Ironing out differences also irons out individuality. At Summerhill we learn to live with differences. We are free to dissent and to express our dissent if we wish. No one tries to bully anyone else into resignation with well-articulated, highbrow arguments. One day a case goes in my favor, another day it does not. It is something we all learn to live with, and living with other peoples' points of view can often prove, in reality, just as valid, if not better, than the original opinion that was fought for so passionately in the meeting.

Summerhill is often portrayed in the media as being "the school with no rules." This is a complete fallacy. Summerhill probably has more written laws than any other school in the country. Many of these laws have arisen to clarify situations that, in other schools would not arise. For example, "You can't watch television in lesson time," "No playing with water inside," "No one must harass day staff," "You can't take school furniture into the woods," "No sheath knives downtown," "Kids are not allowed to drink alcohol," "Staff get £5 fine if drunk," "BB guns are banned," "Cross bows and arrows are only allowed on the Hockey Field if no one is around," "No one is allowed to smoke in public," "No wheels (i.e., skateboards, bikes) inside." In most schools children (or staff) would not dream of attempting most of these things, but in Summerhill, where there is so much more freedom, the need to define certain limitations arises spontaneously.

We have something like two hundred or so written laws at the present moment. These are always displayed in the lounge, as are the minutes of the previous week's meetings. They are divided into different sections, covering various aspects of school life. There is a section on San Kids. These are laws that have been specifically made with regard to the youngest kids. There is one that reads, "San Kids go first [in the school Land Rover] to Leiston Swimming Pool." Another says that if San Kids want to buy, sell, or swap anything there should be two Carriage Kids or staff members present to make sure no one gets swindled. There are laws with regard to the meetings. For example, "Visitors may attend the meeting with the community's permission" or "You can only leave the meeting at the end of a business." There are laws with

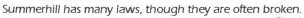

Summerhill has many laws, though they are often broken.

[Photo by Tomo Usuada.]

regard to smoking, use of the Gram equipment, drinking, bedtimes, going downtown, the swimming pool, bike safety, dangerous things (such as knives and catapults), parents and visitors, sitting rooms (i.e., "You can't take cushions out of the sitting room"), meal times ("You cannot save your place in the queue"), and a section of miscellaneous odds and ends.

Most of these laws operate throughout the community, but there are also some that apply to individuals only. Someone may be banned from a particular area. One of the Shack Kids, for example, was recently banned from the top corridor of the House, after being found hanging around up there a lot and intimidating new kids. Another boy, in the House, was banned from another House bedroom, where he was several times caught going through other people's belongings. People can also ask to be exceptions to laws. There is a law that states only twelve-year-olds and older can have sheath knives. An eleven-year-old boy asked to be an exception to this law, and it was passed. It is expected that people should have a good reason as to why they should be made an exception to a law. If they disagree with the law in principle they should try to change it, not simply ask to be an exception. In this case, the boy concerned had lots of experience with knives, as his father had taught him how to throw and handle them safely. In this way the needs of the community and the needs of the individual find their equilibrium.

All laws go through the community meetings except for certain health and safety laws and other laws that are mandatory in the eyes of the law of the land. The meeting could not, for example, decide that adolescent boys and girls could sleep in the same rooms. If it did the school could be closed down. Health and safety issues include things such as not being allowed on the roof, no drinking, drugs, or using BB guns. There are only a handful of these laws, which are in Zoë's hands and not open to the meeting to drop or change. There are also some safety laws that the meeting has the power to change, but not to drop, such as some of the downtown laws.

Decisions about which rooms people sleep in are made by the staff. This is to avoid cliques of popular kids and ghettoes of unpopular kids forming. Instead, the community is a place in which all the kids become integrated. It is ultimately Zoë's decision as to which kids are accepted into the school and if necessary, though thankfully this is a rare event, which kids should be told to leave. She will usually discuss the matter with the staff to get an overview of the situation, but the final decision is ultimately hers and hers alone. Having information about the home, or other relevant background knowledge, which the individual may not want exposed to the whole community, can make all the difference in such a decision. Also in this area, adult experience tends to be the most reliable barometer, as there is more understanding of the issues at large, beyond the immediate concerns of the community. But the feelings of the community as a whole are certainly deeply considered.

The meeting can vote to send someone home for a few weeks, or until the end of term if they are really pushing the community's limits. It can also make the suggestion that someone be asked to leave, though again this is a very rare event. The decision to throw someone out is an especially difficult one and is only taken if the person concerned is putting such a strain on everyone else that the well-being of the wider community has to be put first. It would be even more difficult for the kids to make such a decision about another kid, and it is felt that this would be an unfair weight to put on their shoulders, which is another reason this has become an adult responsibility rather than a meeting one. As a member of staff I have felt deeply unhappy when adding my recommendation that one of the kids should go. Even when someone obviously is having a detrimental effect on others, they have still become part of the community, and people may yet have very warm feelings for them. It would be an awful burden for the kids to have to live with the fact that they had made the decision to send someone away.

There have also been a few occasions when older kids have been told to go for continually flaunting the laws concerning drink or drugs. There has never been a real problem with drugs, only occasional episodes of marijuana being brought into the school, but it is a sensitive issue. The misconception in wider circles that Summerhill is a place where anything goes makes the school particularly self aware in such matters. Such concerns are taken very seriously. The older kids are reminded that not only are they putting themselves at risk, but they are putting the whole community at risk if they bring in illegal substances, or start getting drunk.

There was a short period, just after Zoë took over running the school, when kids were allowed to drink. It was an experiment that did not work. Although it was still against the law to get drunk, this was a hard law to define and the older kids found it difficult to regulate their drinking themselves. I remember myself as a teenager being desperate to experience being drunk. With a large group of teenagers living together the temptation to throw caution to the wind becomes even greater. Alcohol can also become the easy option in trying to deal with the difficult emotions of adolescence. Because of the many problems that it was causing, alcohol was banned again. As it is one of the health and safety laws that isn't open to the meeting it was Zoë's decision to ban alcohol, just as it had been her decision to allow it in the first place. Like many areas of Summerhill life, though, it was through trying something out and discovering why it didn't work that it was rejected, not through dismissing it out of hand. In this way Summerhill has evolved and continues to evolve, out of real experience, rather than rigid, preconceived ideas.

The hiring of staff is also Zoë's decision, though one in which the opinions of the rest of the staff are taken very seriously. The kids are not, on the whole, interested in staff interviews, as I discovered when I came for mine and have seen with other job applicants. Nor are they interested in the adult concerns of what skills and qualifications would be most suitable for this or that job. However, when any of the kids choose to get involved with talking to job applicants their thoughts and feelings are taken seriously. The sacking of staff is also Zoë's responsibility. At the end of the day it is she who is responsible for the school and must answer to any criticisms from parents or the world at large.

Aside from the community meetings, there are also weekly staff meetings. These meetings do not have the power to make wider decisions on behalf of the community, or to change any of the community laws. As well as the sort of issues raised above, such issues as visitor's days, school inspectors, fire drills, the safety of equipment, staff cover, and other internal staff issues are discussed. It is also a time when a member of staff can talk about any child they are worried about, or are having a particular problem with. This may lead to a discussion of how something could be done to improve the situation, such as asking an older child to help out with a younger one who is finding it hard to settle in. It could also be that an adult's own anxiety needs to be aired. Perhaps they do not know at what point to stand back and let things happen and when to get involved. What does it mean to be an adult at Summerhill? The staff as a whole tries to be supportive of new staff and individuals within the staff who are having a hard time, struggling to find their own answers to these questions.

A judge or a politician could learn a lot from a Summerhill meeting.
(Photo by Tomo Usuada.)

The Laws Get Thrown Out

Over the years the community tends to accumulate a lot
of laws. Once in a while the meeting drops the whole lot, with
the exception of the health and safety laws. Every few years a
large bunch of big kids will leave all at once, leaving a very
young school, who feel they have no need for laws. This
happened a few years ago. The school was very young, with
most of the older kids being no more than thirteen or
fourteen. They were more interested in having a wild time
than in self-government. The meetings were ill attended and
lacked stamina. Many of the Beddies Officers, after going
through the motions of putting people to bed, sneaked out
with them an hour or so later, running around the school late
at night and making lots of noise. There were lots of special
meetings, and some of us became irate.

"Who are you doing this for?" we asked. "This is your
community. If you don't want laws, don't have them. If you
don't want bedtimes, get rid of them. But don't pretend you
do when you don't. At least be honest about it. This is
Summerhill; you don't have to pretend. You've got a voice
here, so use it."

They did. The laws and the bedtimes were all dropped.
Yet when I added that the meetings should also be abolished
my proposal was outvoted. ("That's a really stupid proposal!"
announced one small boy, to a chorus of cheers from around
the lounge.) So the meetings remained, allowing anyone to
bring the laws back as and when they wished, and to bring up
anyone who annoyed them. It did not mean, in the community's mind, that just because there were no laws, anyone had
the right to hurt or harass anyone. (Indeed, there have never
actually been laws stating "You cannot hurt, harass, or annoy
anyone.")

That evening things were very chaotic. Kids were skateboarding and cycling up and down the corridors until late in
the night. The Gram was played all evening, instead of being

turned off at the previously required time. Some of the House Kids started smoking. (The law at the time prohibited smoking, though anyone could ask to be an exception and could smoke in certain restricted areas.) Hardly anyone went to bed at the usual time, but wandered around the school looking for some excitement to justify this new turn of events. But that was about the extent of it. There was more mess than usual, with a few upturned bins and the odd bicycle abandoned along the corridors. By the following morning the Gram was no longer in working order, but apart from that things were not so different.

At the next Tribunal there was the usual number of cases, and in the following General Meeting three of the dropped laws were returned. One related to the use of wheels inside. People were fed up with having to dive out the way of bikes and skateboards all the time, and one or two of the adults were concerned about the state of the floors. The second was that only the Gram Committee could use the Gram equipment, which would have to be repaired. The third saw a return of the smoking laws. It was felt that the House Kids who had started smoking were only doing so to show off because the laws were dropped, and if they really wanted to smoke they should ask to be exceptions. Many of the kids felt very strongly about this, and were proved right in that the new smokers did not ask to be exceptions, but discarded their cigarettes.

Over the next few weeks more of the laws began to trickle back, and although the bedtimes were not returned, there were several attempts to introduce silence hours, so that people who wanted to sleep could do so. These proved to be ineffective and it was difficult to get an undisturbed nights' sleep. The atmosphere in the community grew increasingly apathetic and aimless. People were waking up and going to sleep at different times, so at any one time there was always half the community sleeping. Everyone was tired and irritable. With the blurring of boundaries that came with the dropping of laws, an atmosphere of laissez-faire pervaded the school. Those kids who were still very much in the mode of pushing against the limits found they had further to go to find them, and as they wandered around the school late at night looking for things to do, there was a wave of break-ins. The kitchen, the café, the freezer room, the staff room, all were broken into, sometimes for several nights running.

When, just a week before end of term, it was finally carried that bedtimes should return a huge cheer of relief went up in the meeting. Everyone was tired of no bedtimes. By then many of the laws had returned. At the beginning of the next term a lot more laws were voted back in. This was done in one single case called by a member of staff who felt that with the large influx of new kids that we had that term, it would be better to start with a clear idea of what was acceptable or not at Summerhill. The community was happy to vote in most of the laws that he read out.

Personally, I did not enjoy the experience of no laws or bedtimes, and I know that many of the kids felt the same. But by knowing that this was not what they wanted, they discovered what they did want. After all, how many kids ever get to throw out all their school rules? Curiosity was satisfied. The laws that were returned were the laws people knew they wanted. During all that time no one had behaved in any way that was dangerous and no one was hurt. It was more of an anti-climax than a cataclysm. For most of the kids who remember that period it was not a time of great excitement, or wild excess, but of aimless boredom. Last term a bunch of new kids were talking to some of the older kids in my room.

"We don't need laws and bedtimes," said one of the newly arrived-kids. "We ought to throw them all out."

"Yeah!" cheered the other new kids with enthusiasm.

"Oh no," moaned the older kids in unison.

"How did you like it when the laws were dropped before?" I asked them.

"It was horrible," said one.

"It was my worst time in Summerhill," said another.

This is precisely why self-government runs most smoothly when there is a group of big kids who have gone through this phase of pushing against the laws just for the sake of it. They become a strong stabilizing force within the community.

Self-government, then, is a powerful current that guides our lives at Summerhill and gives the community shape and substance. The meetings are not lame affairs overseen by benevolent adults, but are dynamic, animated affairs that put the running of our everyday lives well and truly in the hands of the community. Some time ago a member of staff proposed that all televisions, with the exception of the communal one in the big kids' sitting room, be banned. The staff does not usually vote as a block in the meetings, but is as split on a vote as anyone else. On this occasion, though, it was nearly all staff members who voted for the proposal, and the majority of kids voted against it. So the proposal was dropped. The kids do not look up to the staff in matters of self-government. We are their fellow citizens, not their mentors. They do not naturally follow our opinions, they have their own. Through self-government we are all the time learning to listen to each other while making our own minds up. This applies as much to the adults in the community as the kids.

There is a lot that the judge and the politician could learn from a Summerhill meeting. Watching the Houses of Parliament at work on television, I am amazed at how well-ordered and respectful our meetings are in comparison. Neill recognized long ago that children were able to determine the course of their own lives. He saw his role as a spokesman for children, because the adult world did not know how to listen to them; as a protector of children's rights, because the adult world did not know how to respond to them. Moreover, he founded Summerhill to demonstrate to the adult world that his view of childhood was not merely a theoretical whim, but a practical, livable reality.

Many people put Neill's success down to his personality,

rather than to the validity of his vision. Many thought that when Neill died in 1973 Summerhill would close. But Summerhill continues today, more than twenty five years after Neill's death, not in the shadow of any one personality, but by virtue of its built-in system of self-government. It is a system where adults and children live as equals. No one has the upper hand. There have been many changes in education and child rearing since the days when Summerhill was first founded. Corporal punishment has largely been banished. There have been attempts to make classrooms less formal and lessons more interesting. But if some of these changes can be put down to Neill's influence, the essentials of what he was saying have yet to be understood or assimilated. Children are still not given the approval and respect they deserve as fellow citizens. A confused mixture of authority, bribery, and seduction continues to keep the young under the thumb of the adult world, a world that has lost contact with what it is to be a child.

5

Destructiveness and Unhappiness

During my first year or so at Summerhill many of the meeting cases centered on the activities of three particular boys. As I have already mentioned, a short period or intermittent episodes of law-breaking or general antisocial behavior is something we have come to accept as part of life at Summerhill. Not all children have the same need to go through this sort of stage, but when they do we do not regard, or treat them, as naughty or bad. Instead, their misdemeanors are dealt with practically in the school meetings.

We often see, in new arrivals to the school, a mask of insincerity. There is a quality of falseness that has been fostered over many years, a means to gain acceptance in a society that rates affected social graces of greater value than genuine human qualities. It expresses itself in many ways, such as feigned coyness, false modesty, mechanical politeness, an exaggerated desire to please or impress. It is very self-conscious.

At a deeper level it binds and wards off feelings of anxiety; the anxiety that comes with not feeling approved of, of being rejected or ridiculed. It is this anxiety that governs most children's lives, and by the time we are adults it has become an ingrained element of who we are, underlying all that we do.

But life at Summerhill is not regulated by such values. Children are accepted for who they are, not for who anyone else might expect them to be. They can do as they like as long as they do not interfere with anyone else. It takes time for the new arrival to sense this atmosphere, and to trust in it. It may take just hours, it may take weeks or even months. It can be a sudden realization, or a gradual one, but it is at this stage that the bulk of the child's antisocial feelings will express themselves. If we puncture a pressurized canister it explodes. Children under pressure react very much the same way when the pressure is suddenly removed. The "thank yous" turn to "fuck yous." Tidiness and cleanliness are thrown to the wind. Laws are broken.

Although this period can be very tiresome it is usually brief, lasting only a few terms. It is a time of re-adjustment from a world that is governed by external pressure, to one that is self-regulating. Our older children are by no means saints, nor is this, as some moralists have mistakenly assumed, the aim of a Summerhill upbringing. But they do possess qualities of sincerity and self-confidence that most children have been sadly robbed of by the time they reach adolescence. They are not motivated by anxiety or resentment, but are genuinely self-motivated. At a time in life that is most often characterized by awkwardness, embarrassment, and rebellion, they are emotionally agile, direct, and straightforward in their interactions and as well as running their own lives, are also running their own school.

A Troublesome Trio

The three boys mentioned earlier seemed to be deeply entrenched in a mood of total disruption. Their escapades would either involve all three together, any two of them with the exclusion of the other, one with a small band of temporary followers, or, occasionally, one on his own. Two of the boys had arrived at Summerhill a couple of terms before I did. The third came at the same time as me. They were all ten coming on eleven years old in my first term. As well as being relentless in their pursuit of illicit excitement, they were also very extreme. The two who had been here before me had thrown stones at their houseparent, breaking her windows in the process. During my first few terms they were constantly having cases brought against them in the meeting for bullying, stealing, and general destruction. Yet the meetings seemed to have no effect on them.

One term they stuck a small tree down a manhole, blocking the school's main sewer outlet. This was only discovered a term later when the school was suddenly filled with a very bad smell of an excremental nature. It took one of the teachers and Zoë's husband, Tony, several days and a lot of expensive equipment to set matters right again, during which time we had to resort to the bushes to relieve ourselves. On another occasion they completely wrecked their room, pulling down a large section of the ceiling, tearing the door from its hinges, and throwing most of the furniture out of the window. They later demolished a wall at the rear of Ena's cottage. Their rampages were always accompanied by high-pitched squeals of excitement, so that everyone knew when they were up to something.

I was, however, very drawn to these three kids. They had plenty of endearing qualities too, which made them very likable characters in many ways. Perhaps it was also as Zoë said when I came for my interview, new staff are often drawn to the more anti-social elements of the community. I certainly had a lot of patience, energy, and enthusiasm, and I wanted to understand these kids. What motivated them? What could be done to help them? There is something in most of us, an aspect of ourselves we have never fully expressed, that identifies with the rebel, the outsider, and the underdog. Our films, our novels, and our songs are rich with examples of such identification. This capacity to identify has a lot of scope at Summerhill to engage with the experience of the children, and to understand its underlying emotional quality. But, as Zoë warned, it can also become misplaced, with the adult being drawn into the introverted world of that particular child, rather than drawing the child out into the larger world of the community.

Aware of this danger, I questioned my involvement carefully, for I spent a lot of time with these kids. Sometimes, if I was confused by a certain interaction or event I would talk to Zoë, whose intuitive understanding of children often put things into perspective. As time rolled on, though, there was a lot of talk in the staff room as to whether it was in the community's best interests to keep these three children. As I mentioned in the last chapter, the decision as to whether a child, or for that matter, a member of staff, be thrown out is not in the hands of the school meeting, although the meeting can strongly suggest that this be done. Such a move is ultimately in Zoë's hands. She will usually consult the rest of the staff, and listen carefully to what they have to say, but, at the end of the day it is her decision.

No one is ever asked to leave for being a "bad" person, or for not pulling his or her weight in the community. The point in question is whether their presence in the community is having such a detrimental effect on others that the community can no longer justify keeping them. In this particular case, the whole community was feeling worn down by the constant disruption caused by these three boys, and this was going on term after term. Meetings were sometimes lasting several hours, with case after case being brought against one or more of the three.

There were special meetings about them, sometimes two or three in a week. The community struggled hard to find ways to deal with them, but nothing seemed to work. Patience began to wear thin. There was an air of frustration, and then despondency, especially among the big kids.

Among the staff it was being discussed whether by asking one of the three to leave the others might stand a better chance of settling in. If so, then which of the three should go? Being terribly fond of all three I found myself arguing on the behalf of each of them in the staff room. In retrospect I see that I was being very idealistic. I believed that Summerhill could cure any conflict, no matter how deep. It was just a matter of time. I did not want to give up on these kids. But the growing concern was not whether they benefited or not by staying at Summerhill, but whether everyone else should have to suffer.

Eventually, after much soul-searching, it was decided on which of these boys should go. I had fought for him in the staff room and in conversations with Zoë for several terms, trying to buy him extra time, always hoping he would make it. Eventually even I conceded, and I felt like Judas. I felt I had betrayed the relationship we had built up together and the trust he had developed in me. I felt a great sense of disappointment and defeat, and a deep sadness at the prospect of his leaving.

This particular boy's history had a lot to tell us. He had been conceived in rather bizarre circumstances. The mother had left her boyfriend and had gone off with the boyfriend's father, at which point she became pregnant. Some months into the pregnancy she left the father to return to her boyfriend. This put the baby in the position of being his stepfather's half brother. Throughout the pregnancy the mother deeply resented the growing child within her. When he was born she was disgusted by him. An image that came to my mind time and again, and touched me deeply, was of this newborn baby looking into his mother's eyes and seeing only revulsion and rejection. Was this the first reflection of his existence that he ever encountered?

His parents neglected and abused him. He was often left

hungry and cold. Eventually he was taken into foster care. When his foster mother first met him in the children's home, he was curled up in the corner, withdrawn and uncommunicative. He was afraid of darkness and of getting into water, and sometimes went several weeks without emptying his bowels. After a few weeks at his new foster home he became increasingly destructive, breaking things and throwing furniture out of the window. It put a great strain on his foster family, but they were determined to stand by him. After putting up with this for some years, though, the strain became too much. It was then that his foster parents considered Summerhill, hoping that he could work through some of his problems here.

It is the exception, rather than the rule, to take on such a deeply troubled child, and he was accepted on the understanding that if his behavior proved too difficult for the community to handle, he would have to leave. Neill's experience had been that while such children overcame many of their conflicts by being at Summerhill, it tended to put extra strain on the other children. Towards the end of his life he considered he had erred in keeping persistent bullies at the school, and was quicker to turn such a child out. His great regret was that there was no real help for them elsewhere, that the only other alternatives were schools ruled by fear and harsh discipline.

The question that remains difficult is at what point do we decide that it is no longer appropriate to keep a child on? The atmosphere of Summerhill is more like that of a big family than a school, and a deep bond grows between people who have been here for some time. People have a sense of belonging, of a place where they can be true to themselves. So the decision to ask someone to leave is not taken lightly.

When I first met this boy, he latched on to me and spent a lot of his time hanging around me. He was hungry for adult affection. He had previously latched onto various other members of staff and visitors. He was a good-looking boy, quite well built for his age, with bright, sparkling eyes. But his eyes also had a remote and cut off quality about them, as if a thick layer of glass came between him and the rest of the world. They seemed to brim with life and yet remain unreachable. It was this contradiction between a strong surge of aliveness and a sense of being cut off from human contact that struck me as being at the root of his crisis.

This conflict expressed itself in various ways. He had a deep need for intimate contact with others, but then could not handle it. He often snuggled up to me and took great pleasure in this physical closeness. But after a little while his pleasure turned to anxiety and he would laugh nervously, before gleefully hitting me. It was not difficult to sense the hate beneath this gleeful exterior. The punches hurt. I would gently hold him away from me and tell him to stop, or direct him to hit a pillow instead. But his anger never really surfaced. Instead he stood impassively, his cheeks sagging, his mouth drooping open a little.

The pattern repeated itself again and again, and in doing so, no doubt, mapped out the geography of his earliest experiences in life. Like any baby he would have reached out for pleasurable contact as an innate expectation. But this expectation of pleasure was not fulfilled and so turned to anxiety, a shrinking away from an unfeeling world into an unbearable isolation. The anxiety became rage as the frustrated need for contact reasserted itself, but he had to swallow this rage, to bottle it up, for who knows what retribution his angry screams would have brought down on him. So he learned to deaden himself, to lie impassively, fearful of the terrible anger that his natural demands evoked from this monstrous world he had been born into.

More or less, this would have been his experience. It is easy enough to put the pieces together. Anyone with even a basic understanding of babies and young children knows how terribly they suffer when their needs are not met. I had read his history in the files that Social Services had compiled on him. This pattern of pleasure-anxiety-rage-resignation was simply the same experience being re-enacted again and again, like a stuck record. The shameful truth is that such children are usually condemned as being willfully destructive or "wicked," rather than given the help they need. Their behavior is often contained, at least for a while, by threats of punishment, but they are rarely helped to work through their conflicts.

He was a difficult child to live with. Sometimes he would quietly get on with things for a while, especially spending a lot of time in woodwork, an area in which he showed great skill and concentration. But then he would be off on the rampage again, with one or both of his comrades—I would hesitate to call them friends, for there was little affection between them, just a mutual mania for mayhem. He would get extremely excited at these times, yet was unable to contain his excitement, discharging it instead in various acts of destruction around the school. He was like a ball that once set in motion just keeps bouncing, and there is no stopping it until it is ready to come to rest.

He often seemed totally unconscious of what he was doing. Passing someone in the corridor, he might suddenly trip them or push them over, yet remain totally disengaged from his action, blandly raising his eyebrows and pouting when anyone got angry with him. He reacted in the same way throughout the endless meeting cases there were about him. There was no sense of identification with his actions, no response, no emotion. If something could be broken or pulled apart he would usually be the one to do it. On one occasion he pulled the pipe away from the toilet that was situated just above the Beeston. It was about nine o'clock in the evening, and it had been a particularly hard wash day. The dirty water came through the ceiling, soaking the neat row of clean washing that I had stacked in baskets below. Most of my day's work was ruined, and I was up to three o'clock in the morning catching up. The temptation for murder was strong that night!

There were several incidents that finally convinced me he should go. For example, he began playing with matches. One day I found one of my books lying open on my bed, several pages badly charred. On another occasion he set fire to an underground hut that some of the kids had made in the woods. One evening, he was in my room playing around on my bed with one of the girls. They got quite giggly and cuddly after a while. All at once he slid his hands around her neck and with a look of detached fascination began to squeeze. The girl pushed him off quite easily, grabbing his hair and giving his head a shake for good measure, but it left a deep and worrying impression with me. He was almost twelve, and big for his age. How would he handle the strong sexual excitement of adolescence? Suddenly it all seemed too risky. Perhaps the degree of freedom that Summerhill made possible was more than he could handle. The well being of the other children had to come first.

We contacted his foster mother and made some inquiries as to what other avenues were open to him. I felt strongly that a lot could be done for him in the right environment. He craved adult attention, a degree of attention that neither I nor anyone else could ever give him at Summerhill. He had a strong need to relive those early stages of his life that he had previously missed out on. He expressed this quite clearly himself. He often asked me to carry him "like a baby." He liked to be rocked, or to curl up like a fetus and be gently stroked. After watching Zoë feed a baby goat with a baby bottle one day, he asked for one and sucked it incessantly from then on. He was fascinated with babies. In time, if he was able to regress and catch up on some of this lost experience, I felt sure he could learn to trust in his pleasurable feelings, to handle his anxieties, to express his anger openly, directing it in some safe, inanimate direction. But this would require specialized therapeutic skills, and a great deal of individual commitment.

It was tragic to see how little there was available for kids like this. We only came across one place that operated along these lines, called the Cotswold Community. The fees were quite high to cover the cost of the individual attention that the youngsters received there, and they were very selective in which cases they took on. This was reasonable enough, as they had few places and there was a great need, so they only wanted to take on those individuals who they were sure would benefit. But he was offered a place and the local authorities, after much complaining about the state of their budget, agreed to pay. Eventually, though, his foster mother turned the place down. The Cotswold Community had a policy of distancing the children from their home backgrounds so that they could make a fresh and committed start to their new lives. She was very unhappy about this, and so instead he was sent to a local authority school, which concentrated on teamwork and outdoor activities—a means, I am afraid, of diverting children from their emotions, rather than dealing with them.

His leaving was an emotional affair. Despite the trouble he caused, he was well liked by both adults and children. A small crowd gathered at the front of the school to give him a final hug and wave him off. As one after another embraced him he stood immobile, arms hanging limply at his side, coughing every now and again as if something was stuck in his throat. When I wrapped my arms around him I could feel his whole body trembling. Finally he climbed into the car, complete with a rabbit hutch, which he had made in the woodwork, strapped onto the roof rack, and disappeared up the front drive. The small crowd dispersed, many of us wiping tears from our faces.

We continued to write to each other for a while and once, a year or so later, he came back to visit the school. He was much bigger and more subdued, but he had lost his sparkle. He said that he liked his new school, but his voice was mechanical and toneless. I cast my mind back to the days when his wild whoops echoed around the school as he embarked on yet another of his rampages, and could not help but feel a twinge of regret that nothing of that old zest seemed to illuminate him anymore.

A Conflict Between Parents and School

It was coincidental that the following term we lost another of our terrible trio. His parents had decided not to send him back after the holidays. This followed a period of steadily escalating tension between them and the school. When this boy had first arrived, at the same time as the previous boy, his parents had not indicated that there was any problem with him at all. They kept up this denial, in fact, throughout the whole time he was at Summerhill. Yet he was a deeply unhappy and disturbed child. He existed in a constant state of tension, always on edge. His relationship to both adults and his peers was one of belligerence. He was constantly abusive, and taunted people, goading them until he got a reaction.

He made the smaller children anxious, and unlike his aforementioned companion in crime, he was not generally liked. In the meetings he continually grimaced and pulled faces at people, deriding and mocking them. Yet in any immediate confrontation he was cowardly. Sometimes he did respond to the meetings, and was quiet for a while afterwards, pondering things. But this did not last for long, and he would switch back into his manic mood, throwing insults in all directions, and disrupting whatever pleasures anyone else was peacefully engaged in.

At home he had a younger brother whom his parents were continually doting on, while in the next breath hinting that, unlike his younger sibling, he was not quite what they had hoped for. The sense he had of being at Summerhill was not an optimistic one, but was one of having been dumped. It was not a welcome choice, but a final resort. His parents were quick to assure us that they supported the school, yet they were forever picking away and finding faults in little things. In the holidays they openly criticized the school in front of the boy, and he often came back full of confused questions about aspects of school life. The message that he was getting from the parents was that they did not approve of the school, and therefore, by sending him here, did not approve of him. And he was right.

He regularly received letters from home, but despite the love and kisses at the bottom of the page, they were inevitably disapproving. There was usually at least one reference to the younger brother, in whom they had discovered yet another wonderful quality. Then there was the emotional blackmail. "Granny and Granddad love you very much," read one letter that he showed me, "and what would really make them happy is if you went to lessons."

There is something very dishonest and underhanded in sending a child to the one school in the country where lessons are not compulsory, and then making him feel guilty for not attending them. Here was a boy caught in the crossfire of a whole barrage of conflicting messages. It is little wonder that he was confused. His eyebrows were permanently raised in an expression of puzzlement, as if to ask, "Why am I here? Why am I alive?" (We later learned that when he was three years old his mother had been suffering from a prolonged and severe depression and he had threatened to commit suicide by throwing himself in front of a lorry.) His eyes were sad and full of longing, but his bottom lip was thrust out in a gesture of defiance and he walked around with an exaggerated swagger, like a little lord. Everything about him seemed to be poised between fight and flight, between making a stand and resignation.

His determination to make a stand could sometimes be very laudable. I remember one occasion when his houseparent had accidentally put all of his trousers in the wash at once so that he had no trousers to wear downtown. He had set his heart on going to the local sweet shop and so, undeterred by this turn of events, he simply wrapped himself in his dressing gown and went downtown trouserless. A lesser being would have waited until the next day, or at least asked someone else to get the sweets for him. I took great pleasure in this side of his personality.

I also felt for him when he was unhappy. We went for long strolls in the woods and downtown, and he would ask me searching questions about the world and life. He genuinely grasped for knowledge, but I always felt he was reaching for something deeper than the questions he was asking, something unformulated and obscure; an answer to the riddle of his own unhappy existence.

The question of whether he should attend lessons or not continued to bother him throughout his time at Summerhill. Quite often after receiving a letter from home he would go to class for a few days, but he soon grew bored, and became unfocussed and disruptive. Then his more immediate urges got the better of him again, and he would abandon the classroom for the woods, his friends, and play. But he could never really absorb himself in play as his peers could. His bad conscience caught him every time. It was a vicious circle, and he was trapped. It is little surprise then that he became spiteful, abusive, and disruptive in his behavior.

He was also very careless with his clothing, and this was even more noticeable after he had received a letter from home. Articles of clothing, often quite expensive ones, would disappear. He was genuinely bewildered as to where they had gone, but I am convinced there was an unconscious connection between the arrival of the letter and the disappearance of the clothes. It happened too many times to be a coincidence. On some unconscious level he was rejecting his parents by losing the clothes that they bought for him. I am sure that every time I saw him finally sigh and give up the search, I glimpsed a twinkle of triumph in his eye. So, despite being the son of fairly well off parents, he meandered around Summerhill looking more like a lost street urchin who had wandered out of a Charles Dickens novel.

Several times he came to me for individual reading and writing lessons in the hope that he could placate his parents, but again he found it hard to concentrate. He told me that his parents had taken him to an educational psychologist in the holidays, and "I've got this thing called learning difficulties." During his sessions with me he ended up filling several exercise books with endless repetitions of his name, and "fuck off." He was not stupid. He was making the two most important statements that he had to make.

Whenever the parents visited the school I took the chance to talk to them. I spent many hours trying to point out how the conflicting messages between the school and the home was making it impossible for him to settle down. From our perspective the problem was simple, but the parents were blind to it. They denied there was a conflict. They denied he was unhappy. Instead, they always turned the conversation around to petty criticisms of the school, such as blaming us for losing his clothes. Finally I wrote to them, explaining again that the pressure they were putting on him to attend class was making life unbearable for him and if they could not support his choice not to go to lessons, it would be fairer to send him to a school where classes were compulsory. They chose the latter. I still hear from him every now and again. It seems that he spends a lot of time in detention at his new school.

I was very attached to both these kids and had made it my personal mission to try and make them feel approved of and at ease with themselves. I felt a great sense of defeat and loss when they left. I can see now that I was being naïve and idealistic. I experienced a period of deep disillusionment for a while. But this was not to lead me down the path of cynicism. After all, losing our illusions should not be a negative thing. Instead, it led me to a fuller understanding of both Summerhill and human nature, based not on wishful thinking, but on experience. Far from making me doubt the Summerhill way of treating children, it has qualified my trust in it. But I have learned to recognize the limits.

The first boy had suffered great trauma as a baby. He did not have the capacity to enjoy spontaneous excitement, or loving contact. It made him anxious, which in turn provoked his hate. The freedom and emotional liveliness of Summerhill was too much for him. The problem was not his welfare—indeed he rapidly overcame many of his phobias at Summerhill—but that of the other children. The second boy was caught in a conflict between his life at Summerhill and his home. His parents were not only unsupportive of Summerhill, but actively undermined his attempts to integrate by criticizing the school in front of him and pressuring him to go to lessons. I was cheered, some months later, to hear a story from a Danish ex-Summerhillian, now middle aged, who had left in similar circumstances many years before. He had only been at Summerhill for a few terms, but his experience of that time had remained with him since, and had given him the strength to deal with the difficulties he encountered at various schools afterwards.

From time to time we have taken on other kids with similar difficulties. It's never black and white. It's always a matter of degree. But experience suggests certain conclusions. Summerhill cannot compensate for extreme emotional deprivation in early life, nor, if we have to continually fight against parents, can we ultimately win. This experience has wider implications too. In it we may see something of humanity's struggle for freedom in microcosm. We have a deep longing for freedom. We reach for it through religion, politics, therapy, art, music, literature, philosophy, drugs, the trinkets of consumerism, the intimacies of our sex lives and yet it still seems to evade us. That our capacity for freedom, for the enjoyment of life is diminished in the cot and the classroom cannot be doubted. Instead, our childhoods prepare us only for the emotional impotence that passively accepts authoritarianism, be it the authoritarianism of the politician, the guru, the academic "expert" or the images of the media manipulators.

Freedom and Approval Are Healing

I have said nothing of the third boy in our troublesome trio. He is still with us, though he will soon be ready to spread his wings and leave the nest. I have seen an immense change in him since he came to us six years ago. He was a compulsive thief. Anything not locked up he considered to be his by natural right, and that which was locked away he saw as a challenge. At one time there were a lot of stolen keys circulating around the school, which were being used to break into people's drawers and boxes. In the meeting one of the older kids proposed that anyone carrying keys that did not open locks belonging to them should have the keys confiscated then and there. Our young friend's face turned from disbelief to horror as the proposal was carried. As it dawned on him what was happening he made a dash for the door, but was gently stopped by some of the big kids. Reluctantly he handed over a huge bunch of keys that must have taken him months to accumulate.

He also interfered with whatever anyone else was doing, disrupting it totally. An extremely annoying habit of his was playing with other people's things and then breaking them. "Let me have a go, let me have a go," he would plead, and then after a few minutes of rough handling, ending in a breakage, he would walk off announcing, "Well, they didn't make that very well, did they."

The younger children felt intimidated by him. When he was not indulging in mayhem with the other two, he lurched around the school on his own, imposing himself on whoever would put up with him. He would usually go away when asked to, maybe not the first time, or the second, but after ten minutes of demands for his departure he would eventually lumber off with a shrug. He didn't seem to know how to make friends, and I wondered if he ever would.

He had a gruff voice, and a tic that would send his face into spasms for hours on end. It was as if he had a large wad of invisible chewing gum stuck on his face that he was trying to get rid of. His favorite pronouncement was, "It's not fair!" and it would pepper any interaction with him in which he did not get his own way completely. He seemed genuinely perplexed and distressed at the time, but minutes later would forget all about it.

At the meetings he was full of excuses for whatever he had done. If allowed to, these excuses would go on and on and on, but the chairperson usually told him to get to the point or shut up. He loved the meetings though, and had something to say in nearly every business. It was often irrelevant, but he said it all the same. For a while he always asked to have his name put last on the agenda, just in case he thought of a business during the meeting. When it came to appeals he appealed every fine he had been given, until a limit was put on the number of appeals he could have per meeting.

He lived with his mother and younger sister. There was no father at home, though the mother had occasional boyfriends. She worked hard to bring in the money, and found it difficult to do this and be a mother as well. Her relationship with her son was particularly difficult. Things just seemed to run smoother with the sister. She found it hard to set boundaries with the boy, to know how much she should expect from him in the way of helping with household chores and the like, and how much freedom she should allow him around the house. It would sway one way and then the other as she tried to find the balance between her needs and his, yet a point of mutual understanding never seemed to emerge. It was a constant battle.

An aunt helped put up the money for him to come to Summerhill. The mother was forthright and straightforward about the problems she was having with her son. She knew something had gone wrong between them, and was eager to seek advice from the school as to how things might be improved. Her hope was that he could have his needs met by being at Summerhill, without being constantly frustrated by her, and that she could begin to find some space in her own life without having to battle with him all the time. Maybe if the both of them could find a better balance in their own lives, they would also find a better balance between them.

Over the next couple of years we received many enthusiastic phone calls from her saying how things had improved, and what lovely holidays they were now having. She marveled at his growing maturity, the manner in which he now accepted the necessary limitations of living with other people. He started explaining to her how things were dealt with at Summerhill, and although he was somewhat selective in his explanations at first, they began exploring new ways of relating to each other, incorporating various aspects of his experience of Summerhill. There were the odd hiccups, but they were nothing compared to the storms that had existed before.

After the other two boys had left, he continued to behave at Summerhill very much as he had done from the start. His compulsive stealing was particularly problematic for the community. Then suddenly, a year or so later, it stopped. There was no climax to it, no particular event or events that led up to it. It just stopped. Over the next year or so there were many more changes. He became much more reasonable. I remember on several occasions launching into the beginnings of a verbal battle with him, only to have the wind taken out of my sails by his accepting my point of view. Then, in the meeting one day, as one of his long-winded excuses was gaining momentum, accompanied by the usual chorus of sighs and groans from everyone else, he suddenly stopped and, with a shrug, announced, "Okay, I admit it. I did it." There was a stunned silence for a moment and then the meeting broke into spontaneous, rapturous applause. It was the first time in three years he had ever admitted to anything.

He began to make friends. His tic also disappeared. His sense of being personally aggrieved faded. Perhaps this also had something to do with his relationship with his sister. At first he was jealous of her relationship with their mother. Now she is jealous of his being at Summerhill. These days when new staff meet him for the first time they find it hard to believe the stories we tell of his first few years at Summerhill. It would be dishonest to imply that he is a completely reformed character. He still occasionally steals, but it is rare and has nothing of the compulsive nature of his earlier endeavors. In the meetings he will still argue a point into obscurity rather than acknowledge that he has exhausted it. There is a playful, good-natured quality to his reasoning, though, and he has lost the harsh edge that he came to us with.

Socially, he continues to be annoying, but only mildly so. He will poke fun at other people, especially when they are working together in a group on some creative project. He doesn't participate in group activities himself, but generally prefers more solitary pursuits, such as fishing or fiddling around with bikes. Recently though, for the first time, he played a small part in the end-of-term play, throwing himself into his role with zest, to the delight of the audience who applauded and cheered.

He rarely expresses soft emotions or vulnerability and will mock them in other people. Of all our older kids at the moment, he is the only one who will do this. We had a small boy recently who was new to the school and was very homesick for a short while. Where everyone else was very sensitive to him, this boy jeered at his tears. His peers, as usual, quickly reprimanded him. There are occasional and surprising flashes of tenderness though. They might reveal themselves in small moments, such as helping a younger child in something, cuddling a baby, or his doting devotion to a beloved girl. Some time ago, when I was seeing a group of kids off on the train at end of term, he surprised me by leaning out the carriage window and quickly kissing me goodbye. I felt very touched by this sudden, spontaneous expression of affection.

Aside from the odd, irritating moment now and again he is not really such a nuisance anymore. He largely goes about his own business quietly and happily, without interfering with anyone else. After a long time of complaining that he would never learn anything at Summerhill, but needed to be pushed, he has starting attending classes of his own accord, and is doing very well. I have often wondered what he would be like now if he had gone to a conventional school. I think we would be looking at a hardened delinquent. He would have spent the last five years at loggerheads with a system that had no idea of how to respond to his needs. It would have pushed him all over the place, punishing him for not conforming to its expectations. It would have compounded his resentments and condemned him for his irritating manner, calling it "badness," rather than "unhappiness," not acknowledging the more complex conflicts that lay beneath the surface.

It is very pleasurable to see someone change in the way that this boy has. He came to us as a bundle of conflicts, but he has, at least on some levels, made peace with himself. His mother's openness and willingness to work at making things better between them has been an important factor in this change. She supported his life at the school and was even prepared to learn from it. I have seen similar changes in other kids too, and they stand out in stark contrast to those children who have to continually struggle with disapproving parents. Approval is a deep human need, it is essential to our well-being. Many people spend their whole lives driving themselves, vainly seeking the approval they never had from their parents. Approval does not mean a lack of setting reasonable limits, but accepting the child fully for who he or she is, rather than by the measure of artificial expectations. Freedom and approval are inseparable. Only when children feel accepted for who they are are they free to live their lives without anxiety. By the same token, only when they are free to express their inner lives without fear of ridicule or censure do they feel truly approved of.

Non-Compulsory Lessons

It has always surprised me that so many visitors want to see lessons. I have never understood what the attraction is. The uniqueness of Summerhill lies in its community life, its self-government, and freedom of expression—not in its lessons.

There are no special teaching methods employed at Summerhill. In fact, lessons are often taught quite traditionally. Teachers bring their own styles with them and are free to teach as they like. Nobody tells them how they should teach. If there are any particular qualities that Summerhill children reveal in their class work I have not heard of them. It is in the emotional side of life that Summerhill stands apart, not in the academic. The only important difference in Summerhill lessons is that they are not compulsory.

I was once asked by a school inspector, "What do you do about the problem of children who do not go to lessons?"

"It isn't a problem," I replied. "If the children don't go to lessons, it's because they have more important things to do."

She could not follow my logic. She could not conceive that children could have anything more important to do than sit in a classroom all day and be taught. The idea of children not attending lessons being anything other than a problem was completely foreign to her.

As lessons are only ever attended voluntarily, we have no truancy. The experience of playing truant and that of not having to attend lessons are very different. The truant experiences freedom as something sneaky and defiant. It is played out behind the backs of the adult world and in reaction to its enforced authority.

At Summerhill the kids feel approved of whether they go to lessons or not. They experience freedom as natural. It is their right, and is respected by the community they belong to. They make their own choices. To be dictated to would seem alien to them. To fear adults and to have to live out their pleasures hidden from them would be unthinkable. This might not be the case when they first arrive, but it soon becomes so as they acclimatize themselves to life at Summerhill.

There has been a lot of talk in the media about the problem of truancy, but nothing has been said about the problem of children who passively accept the regime of the classroom without challenging it. Nothing is said about it because it is not seen as a problem. Yet a quick recap of human history, especially that of the twentieth century, is all it takes to remind us that passive acceptance and unquestioning obedience have paved the way for far greater evils than the occasional rebel has ever done. Compulsive education turns out compulsive individuals, individuals who willingly allow others to mold their destinies.

Experiments conducted in America by Stanley Milgram* illustrate the problem with frightening clarity. Volunteers were invited into a psychological laboratory where they were

---

* Stanley Milgram. *Obedience To Authority,* New York: Harper & Row, 1974.

required to give electric shocks to someone in the next room. The volunteers were able to see this other person, who was strapped to a chair, through a window. They were told that they were conducting an investigation into the effect of punishment on learning and their role was to administer ever increasing electric shocks to this person every time he answered a question incorrectly. What they did not know was that the other person was really an actor and, in fact, no electricity was actually being administered.

They were egged on by the experimenter to increase the voltage, even though the actor screamed and twisted, as if in agony, each time they did so. Despite expressions of great unease by many of the participants, 65% continued to administer the maximum shock of 450 volts as the experimenter reassured them that it was all right to do so. This was despite the perceived distress of the actor and the labels on the switches, which included the warning "Danger: Severe Shock."

In a variation on this theme the actor warned that he had a slight heart problem and at 150 volts pleaded to be released. But even then twenty-six out of forty of the volunteers continued to administer the 450-volt maximum shock. When interviewed afterwards the resounding response was "I was just doing what I was told."

These experiments clearly reveal a dulling of individual conscience, which is complacently relinquished to the authority of the "expert." So it has been throughout history, as the heretics were burned and the gas taps of Auschwitz were turned on. So it continues today in everyday life in a thousand and one different guises.

The mother who lets her baby be taken away from her to fit in with hospital routines even though her instincts are screaming out to hold him and caress him. The parents who groom their children in insincere politeness, and punish them for "bad manners," not because they have any real feeling for such things, but because they are afraid of what the neighbors might think. The patients who silently suffer the side effects of medically prescribed drugs, without having ever asked, "What else is possible?" The worker in the nuclear power station who is satisfied to be exposed to "safe" levels of radiation, despite the fact that the children of dozens of other workers exposed to similar levels have contracted leukemia. "We're only doing what we're told," we implore. "Who are we to question the experts?"

I am not suggesting that the child who plays truant would operate any differently in these circumstances, or that truancy is the better choice. What I am asking is this: Why is so much attention given to the problem of truancy, which is just one symptom of the real problem? The real problem is the school, not the child. It is the school that makes a truant of the child, just as it is the school that makes a sheep of the child, and a misery out of so many children's lives. Why does this single common denominator that underlies both rebellion on the one hand and resignation on the other, as well as a great deal of unhappiness in both these situations, remain so widely unquestioned?

Some time ago I received a letter from a twelve-year-old Japanese boy whose mother had withdrawn him from Summerhill and put him back into school in Japan. He wrote, "It's hell for me every day." Not "I don't like it," or "It's really boring," but "It's hell."

A few days later I received a letter from his mother. She wrote that her son was "extremely happy" and that he "very much enjoys his new school." Like the volunteers in Stanley Milgram's experiment, we accept the word of the "educational expert" who tells us, "This is the right way" or "That is the wrong thing to do," even when it means turning a blind eye to the obvious unhappiness of our children. For their part, the experts, the authorities, do not want to acknowledge the problem of passive obedience, for it is precisely that which makes them the authorities. Authority does not like to be challenged.

Becoming Cut Off From Ourselves

The compulsive classroom truly is hell for many children. Let us consider what we demand of children when we interrupt the natural flow of their life energy and send them off to school. It is something that as adults we all too easily forget. We forget how we once felt. We forget how we once held our breath, bit our lips, tightened our legs, and squirmed in our seats as we tried to still the life that pulsed within us. We forget the deep, unfathomable yearning as we sat by the window, watching the world that moved beyond the glass, cut off, remote, unreachable. We forget the ache to escape, to merge once more with what was meaningful to us; the meandering of our own thoughts and feelings, which found their fullness in play, fantasy, friendships and a genuine desire to learn about life. We forget the almost tangible sense of boredom that seemed to bear down on us so heavily we almost moaned aloud. We forget the leadeness of our legs beneath the desk, which we had to shake into life every now and then to prevent "pins and needles." We forget the delicious sensuality, the tingling tension in our abdomens and genitals, which grew in intensity as we moved from childhood into adolescence, and which we tried to squeeze out of existence as it became an unbearable longing, an overwhelming distraction to the teacher's voice. We forget how we learned to breath shallowly, clamp our jaws shut, drift off in our eyes, and cut ourselves off from own beings as we attempted to follow what the teacher was telling us. We forget how we once belonged to ourselves, how we were once full of ourselves, until it was turned back on us as a jibe and accusation.

Compulsive education is a process of forgetting—of forgetting who we really are. We are no longer full of ourselves. We are full of other people's ideas of who we should be. We are contracted against our own feelings of excitement, split off from our own deepest impulses, fragmented, estranged, and anxious. We have learned how to follow another's voice, while deafening ourselves to our own. Resentful scowls, apathetic slouching, dreamy distraction, anxious concentration, sighs of boredom; it is all there in the expressions and attitudes of the children of the compulsive classroom. How different this is from the bright-eyed alertness, expressiveness, and joyful liveliness of children absorbed in play, or in learning that is of their own motivation.

The capacity to learn, and an emotional involvement in the subject matter being learned cannot be separated. As a child I enjoyed reading very much, and often visited the local library. I was particularly interested in the natural world, and spent hours reading up on the rain forests of South America and the African bush. I studied maps, learning all I could about the terrain, the wildlife, the local tribes. I drew up boundaries to imaginary nature reserves and fantasized a life in which I was a game warden. I remember vividly reading of the Okapi, a rare relative to the giraffe, that lived in the then Belgian Congo. I remember where Mount Kilimanjaro and Lake Victoria are. I remember that the tall, lithe Masai tribe of Kenya survive on a diet that consists largely of cow's blood and milk, and that they are able to extract the blood from a vein in the cows neck without killing it. These things fascinated and excited me as a child, and I still remember them vividly. Yet I can barely remember what a quadratic equation is, and have no idea when the Battle of Waterloo was.

The Adult-Eration of Childhood

For much of the time the only emotional involvement of children in compulsory education is anxiety, the anxiety of being found out. They are not afraid of not knowing, only of it being found out that they do not know. The concerns of the child are more centered around ways of pacifying the teacher, or avoiding the teacher's attention, than actually learning.

When I was at school we quickly focused our attentions not on what the teachers were saying, but the way in which they managed the classroom. We learned, with great intuitive insight, to understand the psychology of each of our teachers, and how we might best respond to them, be it to find the path of least resistance, or to exploit them for our own entertainment.

There was one teacher who nearly always ignored raised hands when he asked a question, and picked instead on the most puzzled-looking or blank-faced kid in the class to provide the answer. The more perceptive kids waved their hands in the air, hissing with rapt enthusiasm, "Sir, Sir!" as if they were about to burst with understanding and knowledge. Such deceit was rarely challenged, and if it was we were usually able to bluff our way out by mumbling or vague stabs in the direction of the question.

We had different tactics for every teacher. With another one it was far better to twist the face into an expression of intellectual angst, as if the answer was just around the corner, than to overplay your hand. Either way, it was all a matter of bluff, and behind the façade there was an almost blank disinterest in the subject matter.

Our French teacher used to turn different shades of crimson, eventually bursting into a purple frenzy, as he became progressively enraged by our childish taunts. We invented an imaginary color chart to correspond with his emotional states, reading him like a barometer, and taking bets on how far we could push him before he boiled over. So we broke up the day's boredom a little by amusing ourselves at this teachers expense. Our cruelty was not the cruelty of youth per se, but the cruelty of young, caged animals. Where compassion might otherwise have stepped in earlier, we were hard-hearted and relentless.

Our Chemistry teacher, known affectionately to us as "shiner" on account of his gleaming bald head, was rather old and deaf. So, at the beginning of every class, there was a rush to fill the back rows. There you could talk with your friends as much as you liked, with little fear of his noticing. At the beginning of one class he began by shouting out to the back row, "Can you hear me back there?" The temptation was too great.

"Pardon?" came back the chorus from the kids at the back.

"Can you hear me?" he repeated even louder.

"Pardon?" returned the chorus.

We managed to squeeze a few more minutes of entertainment out of the situation before it suddenly dawned on him that he was being taken for a ride.

Such tactics are used every day by kids in the compulsive classroom to add a little spice to their otherwise dull days. They are not "bad," just bored and frustrated, and that is not their fault. Imagine a kitten playing with a ball of string. It dances around in leaps and bounds, its body an instrument of its own excitement. Impulse and action are unified in this joyful dance of life. There is no fearful hesitation, no anxious contraction to fragment this unity. Anticipation and gratification roll into one, a single expression of quivering pleasure. If I were to take this kitten and tie its paws together people would be outraged. Its distress would be obvious. Its unity and grace would be destroyed. Yet this is exactly what we do every day to our own young when we send them off to schools that see them only as the citizens of tomorrow and not as the citizens of today.

One sunny afternoon I sat at my window watching a small group of boys moving across the Summerhill grounds. There was something about the way they moved that drew my attention. Every now and again there was an interaction between two or more of the boys, then for a while they would each be absorbed in their own thoughts, fanning out away from each other, independent and yet somehow linked to the others. They stopped beneath a tree. No one spoke, but a couple of the boys began to climb, while the others poked around with sticks at the base of the tree. After a few minutes there was an exchange of words, and the boys in the tree came down and the group set off again, disappearing out of view around the corner.

There was something about this little scene that I found very pleasing, and I tried to fathom what it was. It was in the overall movement of the group. It reminded me of the way a flock of birds will all suddenly move in a certain direction, as if some secret signal has just been given. Or the way that incoming waves converge and spread out as the tide creeps up the beach. There was something natural about it, something integrated and logical, while at the same time aimless and random.

It struck me how different this movement was from the way children move when they become organized by adults. They become stiff and awkward. We organize them into straight lines. We constrict their mobility. We put them behind desks and into uniforms. We impose our own unnaturalness upon them. We do this in the name of education. Adulteration would be more accurate. We literally adult-erate our children with our rigid ways of thinking and living, robbing them of their naturalness and spontaneous responsiveness.

From the moment a child is born it begins to explore its world. At first it simply absorbs its environment through its senses. Later it begins to reach out for things. It learns to coordinate its movements, to crawl, stand, and walk. It meets endless frustrations on the way, but it perseveres. It becomes more interactive, copying gestures and facial expressions. It learns to structure words from formless sounds, and to give them meaning. It asks questions, not just now and then, but all the time. "What's this?" "Why? Why? Why?" It wants to understand, to know the world. Its curiosity is insatiable. There is an incredibly powerful yearning to learn and be sociable. Somewhere along the line this continuum is interrupted. The desire to know has died at the hands of what we call "educating the child" and natural sociability has been throttled by enforced insincerity.

Children naturally live at the edges of their abilities, whether it is climbing a tree or learning to read. But when we begin to push them and mold them into unnatural situations, to learn what they are not ready to learn, we cause children to shrink from their parameters, to become defensive, instead of actively involved. We then call it laziness, when we have destroyed their excitement in life and learning.

Most adults would have the common sense not to force children into learning to climb trees when they are unwilling, but unfortunately the same logic is not applied in the academic realm. But the results are identical. The children panic and freeze. They become stuck and cannot move. So we push and prompt and eventually they move. We congratulate ourselves. They have learned something today, we tell ourselves. The lives of many children are lived in this precarious, humiliating position. They are stuck in academic trees, with adults telling them, sometimes yelling at them, to do this and to try that.

Looking After the Emotions

Most of the youngest children who come to Summerhill go to lessons quite happily. They have not had enough time in the compulsive classroom to have had their quest for knowledge undermined. When they do not come it is because they are happily playing somewhere else. For those children who come a little later, or have had specific unhappy incidents with teachers, the story may be a little different. They experience the freedom to not attend lessons not just as a choice, but as a great relief. At last they are down from the tree and on solid ground again. They may not attend lessons for several terms, even several years. They need time to feel their feet again, to regain their confidence and the drive to learn what they will need to know. It is a healing time. A time in which old humiliations and frustrations are put aside.

Getting back into the classroom may happen spontaneously and quickly, or it may be a somewhat slow and faltering process. Perhaps for several terms running children will start to attend lessons, but will then drop out. It could be that they have not quite found the confidence yet, or it could be that there are still more appealing things to do outside the classroom. After a while, though, most kids get bored with just playing or hanging around with their friends all day and they are quite aware that they will need certain skills and qualifications to do what they want in life after they leave Summerhill. So a more serious attempt is made to attend lessons.

A thirteen-year-old boy, who had been at Summerhill for three years and had not attended a single lesson could barely read and write. A friend of mine who was visiting the school asked me, "Don't you think he should at least learn to read and write? In this case shouldn't reading and writing be compulsory?"

"But he couldn't read and write when he came to us," I told her, "despite having been in compulsory education all those years before. He has a lot of problems in his emotional life to sort out first. He'll learn when he is ready, and only he can decide when that is."

I remember asking this same question of certain children when I first came to Summerhill, and staff members who had been here awhile giving me similar answers. Time proved them correct, and having seen this happen many times now I felt certain in my faith. A few terms later the boy began going to English and science lessons of his own free will. He enjoyed these periods of structured work, learning to read and write along the way, and quickly became excited by his own progress.

Unhappy children are not able to concentrate on their work. They struggle to listen to the teacher's explanations, but unwarranted thoughts well up and cloud their minds. The intellect and the emotions cannot be divided into two separate worlds that have no bearing upon each other. I find this even now in my own work. If I am reading a book, but am bothered by something that has happened earlier, perhaps an unpleasant interaction with someone, I find myself reading the same line again and again without taking it in. It has made me wonder how far intelligence can be regarded as something fixed and static. Some days I am quite receptive, my eyes charged with excitement as they weave their way down the page, my senses sharpened as I become absorbed in a discussion. Other days I am dull and stupid, and wander around in a state of permanent distraction. It is an ever-changing quality of contact with the world around me. As an adult I have the freedom to put the book down, or end a discussion and get on with something else. It is true that I often have to do things I don't want to, but I can usually arrange them in such a way that my own needs are not totally negated. The compulsive classroom does not afford children such an option. They have to battle with their thoughts and feelings, to quash them, so that they can concentrate on what someone else has deemed is important. Every now and again these quashed emotions may suddenly burst out in an uncontrollable explosion of hysteria or aggression, or they may become fixed in the child's character as sulkiness, sullenness, and moodiness—the artifacts of adolescence.

The children at Summerhill largely work through their unhappiness, as they are able to live out their emotions. They do not have to wage war against their own thoughts and feelings behind a desk, but can express them in their everyday life, in play, relationships, and outbursts of excitability. Just as expression relieves distress ("I feel better now I've got that off my chest"), so distress builds up when expression is immobilized. An eight-year-old boy comes to us, his jaw hard and tight with anger, his shoulders drawn up and tense. He has already been thrown out of several other schools, as his behavior in the classroom has been so disruptive. Yet reports from an educational psychologist say he has above-average intelligence. He is erratic, excitable, and clumsy in his movements. He has been diagnosed as hyperactive, and a report from one of his previous schools has described him as "willfully disobedient." Any references to his obvious unhappiness contained in the reports from both the schools and the educational psychologist are only made in regard to how it hinders his academic work, and what can be done about that. There is no hint in these reports that his happiness for its own sake is of value, or that academic matters might take second place for a while.

Over the next couple of years at Summerhill there are lots of meeting cases about him, all relatively unimportant, but irritating matters. Gradually his jaw has begun to soften and his shoulders relax. He has become more sure of himself, and is able to play with his peers without being such a continual nuisance to them all the time. He enjoys reading and can write quite well, but as yet has hardly set foot in class. But when he does, he will do so feeling more at peace with himself, and will not be plagued by distractions buzzing around his head like flies.

It is also the case that a flight into academic work can serve to escape uncomfortable emotions. Hence the stereotype of the unfeeling, coldly logical, dome-headed intellectual. Talking with such people is like being hit over the head with an encyclopedia. A boy we had at the school a few years ago went to every lesson available. He sucked up facts like a vacuum cleaner, and used every opportunity to show off his superior knowledge. Yet his factual prowess remained in vacuum. It was not integrated into any sense of pleasurable drive to really understand or be in contact with the world. It was just there to be aired whenever possible to impress people. He would easily have been the darling of the compulsive classroom. However, when he was in situations where his fact rapping did not impress, his façade quickly faded and he revealed another side of himself, a miserable, unconfident, self-loathing side that would never have been addressed in the compulsive classroom. Unhappiness only ever gets addressed if it interferes with academic work, as the reports mentioned above made clear. So it is that thousands of school children are able to live their lives in quiet misery without anyone's really noticing.

This boy found it very difficult to mix with his peers. He could not engage himself as an equal, but was always indulging in games of one-ups-manship. He was not well liked, and was easily provoked into grand displays of hysterics at the slightest gesture of aggression, be it a grimace, an insult, a mild threat, or a shove. This drew out the sadistic impulses of every potential bully. I even felt the urge myself to give him a well-aimed kick in the rear when he was at his most whiny and sanctimonious. He drove the community's patience to the brink with his continual ombudsman and meeting cases, which were mostly about trivial matters that anyone else would have let pass. Yet he was a big boy and was very sadistic himself in a sly and sneaky way, his eyes gleaming when he had stirred up trouble for someone else or hurt them, usually by stamping on their feet. He was just beginning to improve, and to find better ways of relating to his peers, when his parents moved to another country, taking him with them.

Academic knowledge and intelligence are two different things. The contestants in quiz shows such as *Brain of Britain* or *Mastermind* are not exercising intelligence, only reiterating facts, whereas a car mechanic, or a potter, may use their hands intelligently. Nor can happiness be learned. I remember seeing a Woody Allen film, in which the character he plays is told by his doctor that he only has so long to live, only to learn later that he had been given the wrong results and was, in fact, quite healthy. But this brush with death leaves him feeling totally dissatisfied with his old way of life, which now seems empty and without meaning to him. He tries to find new meaning in life, becoming first a Catholic and then a Hari

Krishna, but they don't do the trick for him. Eventually he immerses himself in a huge library, a great academic edifice, and studies the works of all the great philosophers, only to conclude that they don't have the answer either. Dejected and despairing he wanders into a cinema where a Marx Brothers film is showing. Watching the film he becomes absorbed in the clowning antics of the actors and begins to laugh. For the first time since his death sentence was lifted he forgets about finding a meaning for it all and just lives. Later he realizes he has found the answer he has been looking for all the time in this simple moment of enjoyment.

If it is not to further an enjoyment of life, I wonder what function education has? A Summerhill boy returning to his home in Germany for the holidays was asked by an old friend of his why he was reading a book.

"Because I enjoy it," he said.

"Ah," his friend replied, "you wouldn't if you went to the Gymnasium.* By the end of the day you'd be so sick of books you'd never want to see another book again."

It seems pointless to push children into learning to read and write if it destroys their desire to do so. We are surrounded by words all the time. There are written signs and information almost every way we turn in life. As children develop and expand out to the world they will naturally want to learn how to decode these messages that everyone else can understand. This will lead onto other things as they see adults and older children reading magazines and books around them. But in forcing the issue we divorce knowledge from enjoyment, it becomes something abstract to the pleasure-seeking child, something to be avoided and escaped from.

When children are ready and motivated to learn, like the infant learning to walk, they will tolerate the often boring and frustrating first steps that are needed to master a subject. So-called "progressive" educators have put a great deal of

---

* The German high school.

emphasis on liberalizing the compulsive classroom, making it more informal, and devising teaching methods that are more creative and interesting than teaching by rote. Within the realm of the classroom this truly is progressive, but in the wider realm of the child's life it is still compulsive. It is still the wolf of the authoritarian adult in the sheep's clothing of liberalism. The simple fact that the children are compelled to go to class in the first place is evidence enough of this. When children begin attending lessons voluntarily, they do so because they want to learn. I have several times heard Summerhill teachers complain that when they tried to make the lessons more exciting the kids told them to get on with it and stop playing around. They had had enough of play and were ready to concentrate on learning now.

We were recently visited by Her Majesty's Inspectors of schools. They observed a group of small kids playing in a sand pit. Here was a missed opportunity, they told us. Instead of the kids wasting their time playing, someone could be teaching them about coastal erosion, or weights and measures. This compulsion to make everything children do into a

Bike repairs and renovations are a popular pastime. *(Photo by Tomo Usuada.)*

"learning experience" is simply disrespectful. I wonder how we would feel as adults if, whenever we "wasted our time" enjoying a good meal, someone gave us a lecture on nutrition, or whenever we "idled our lives away" making love, it was turned into a human biology lesson. It is just as ludicrous. Whether we introduce teaching into play or play into teaching we are doing the same thing. We are cheating children. We are introducing our concerns in the pretense of respecting theirs.

The freedom to play at Summerhill is often confused with the Montessori approach to teaching through play. At Montessori schools special apparatus is used to teach children specific things. There is no fantasy or emotional content. Play is guided by adults with particular teaching goals. Playing at Summerhill is playing for its own sake. Although adults may sometimes participate in the children's games, we do not interfere in them, just as we would not expect anyone to interfere in our private affairs. It is nobody else's business if someone wants to fight off imaginary space invaders all day, or skateboard up and down the Carriage path, any more than it's anybody's business if I decide to do some gardening or read a book. Indeed, joining in the kids' interests now and then can be a pleasant reminder of what fun they have. A thrilling moment for me was during a game of gang warfare when the gang of House Kids I was part of ambushed the San Houseparent, who was in the opposing gang, at morning break. It was exhilarating, as we all turned at the same time to unleash a cacophony of caps, sending her scuttling under the table for cover. After all, isn't this what grown ups are living out in their imaginations when they watch a western or gangster movie on television?

A friend of mine from my London days very much objected to kids playing with toy guns. He thought they should be banned, or if not, there should be photographs displayed throughout the school showing the victims of real warfare. His argument was that kids should learn the consequences of what a real gun can do. I vividly remember as a kid the joys of playing with cap guns. The anticipation of a cops and robbers stakeout. The loud bangs. But it was a fantasy world, with its own landscapes, its own shadowy figures and hidden menaces. Real suffering both frightened and appalled me. The kids at Summerhill seem quite able to make the same distinction. They will happily watch Arnold Schwarzenegger blast away twenty stunt-men an hour, but a news report that depicts real violence, or a film which depicts violence in a more realistic context, for example a racist lynching, will disturb and upset them. To interfere with children's play in order to draw a moral is to rob them of their fantasy. If there is a certain element of aggression acted out in these games, all the better—for it is harmlessly discharged, instead of building up and finding a more destructive expression in a real-life situation. The most violent child I ever met at Summerhill was a twelve-year-old boy whose parents were both pacifists.

But I have strayed from academic lessons into moral ones. The two are inevitably intermixed in the compulsive classroom, as the teacher has to maintain discipline, but at Summerhill they have no bearing on each other. Summerhill teachers do not have the stress of trying to keep order, as anyone who goes to their classes does so because they want to learn. It would be absurd for them to disrupt what they feel to be theirs. Very occasionally one of the younger kids may create a bit of a disturbance in one of the primary classrooms, but this is dealt with like any other personal infringement—in the meeting. It is usually enough just to say, "If you do that again I'll bring you up," and this could just as well come from one of the other kids as from the teacher.

Having voluntary lessons can pose other problems for some teachers though. One teacher found it very difficult when children did not turn up to his classes. He would often put a lot of effort into preparing a lesson only to have no one come. It made him feel despondent and without purpose.

Working in the art room. *(Photo by Tomo Usuada.)*

The danger that a teacher may drift into in such a situation is to project his or her own feelings onto the children, seeing them as being despondent and purposeless. Their own creative processes may involve periods of boredom, but there will be a lot happening outside the classroom that is of immense importance to the children themselves. The teachers do not have the option of not attending lessons themselves, and it can be very frustrating to be tied to a classroom with no one to teach. In reality this does not happen very often, and most of the classrooms are centers of busy concentration. But there may be some terms when a particular class is not very well attended, and the teacher is left feeling a bit lost.

The principle that children will learn what they need to, when they need to, is also at work outside the classroom. Having children from so many different countries living together, they quickly make inroads into each others' languages as they begin to communicate. An eleven-year-old French girl could speak no English. Unfortunately, the only space available at the time was in a room with only Japanese girls. Very soon she could converse quite easily with her roommates in simple Japanese, though she hardly spoke a word of English. Later she was settled in a room with mainly English girls, and was quickly speaking English fluently. All this happened within the space of a year, and with no formal teaching. An American boy, also eleven, asked one of his Japanese friends to teach him Japanese. They worked hard together, and within a couple of months he had grasped a rudimentary understanding of both spoken and written Japanese.

Much of what is taught in schools has no real meaning or practical interest to the children. Most of it they will forget by the time they have left school. What is of value to them could have been learned in a fraction of the time, and without force-feeding.

Teaching has always seemed to me a strange profession. A teacher is someone who digests other people's work to regurgitate it to yet someone else. They are the middlemen of knowledge. They pass things on. How many teachers have ever done their own original research, or created their own works? Very few, I imagine. It is not a profession very likely to attract original thinkers. In their school reports the teachers of Charlotte and Emily Brontë accused them of a lack of imagination and a poor grasp of grammar. Yet the works of the Brontës are still being read today, while their teachers are long forgotten.

There are, of course, many teachers who are genuinely inspired by their subjects, and who have a deep regard for their pupils. But they are not the majority. If they were, our schools would be different places, our education system would have different values. After teaching at Summerhill many teachers decide not to go back into conventional education. They find it too stifling. The compulsive classroom is the kingdom of the compulsive adult. It is the small pool where the teacher is the big fish. The Summerhill teacher is just another member of the community, but as such can be far more real and human.

Lessons On Offer

At the beginning of every term there is "sign up." This is when all the teachers are available in the lounge to explain what courses they will be offering. The kids wander around seeing what there is and asking questions. They will usually have given some thought to what they want to do beforehand, and already have made their minds up. Over the next few days a timetable will be drawn up to cater to everyone's needs, making sure there are no clashes between subjects. The youngest kids are automatically put in Class 1, and Class 2 caters to the middle age-range, which includes most of the House Kids. These are both primary classes, teaching a broad range of basic skills. Class 1 is usually well attended, whereas the Class 2 age group are mostly interested in playing, rather than learning.

Kids move on up from Class 2 to the sign-up system when they are about twelve. By the time they are thirteen or fourteen most kids will be signing up for some courses. It would be possible for someone to spend their whole time at Summerhill without going to a single lesson, but it would be unlikely. I have heard of this happening occasionally in the past, but I have not known it to happen since I have been here. I know of one ex-Summerhillian who only taught himself to read and write after leaving Summerhill, but later went on to manage a company in which most of the employ-

ees had university degrees, and some had Ph.D.s. The principle that children will learn what they need to, when they are
ready to, can also be extended into adult life. But the story
would have probably been very different if he had spent his
school years battling a system that finally convinced him he
was too stupid to learn.

Whereas in Class 1 and 2 kids can drop in and out as they
wish, when they sign up for courses they are expected to
attend fairly regularly. They are free to drop out if they wish,
but they cannot come and go at random, as this would mean
the rest of the class would have to wait for them to catch up.
Most of the courses will be geared towards taking the GCSE
examinations. When kids do start to go to class of their own
free will they often catch up quickly. The drive to learn is
there, and not diluted by the desires of an unfulfilled childhood, as with so many young people as they embark upon
their exam years.

This is borne out by the experience of so many ex-
Summerhillians when they leave the school. They often find
their peers rather immature, still acting on impulses that they
have lived out years ago. One ex-Summerhillian told me how
he had been surprised that as soon as his college lecturer left
the room, having set the class some work to do, the rest of the
class erupted into a frenzy of fooling around. It did not occur
to him that just because the lecturer had left he should behave
any differently.

Summerhill classes are smaller than most. There are
often only four or five kids to a class, and some kids get
individual tutoring if needed. As there are no academic
criteria with regard to accepting kids to the school, there is a
wide range of needs to be met. The teachers arrange the
classes to try to cater to everyone's best interests, so there is a
great deal of flexibility, rather than strict demarcations according to age. Lessons, then, tend to have an atmosphere more
like that of a homeschooler's living room than of the conventional classroom with its thirty or forty kids sitting in rows.

Most of the teachers are qualified in their profession, though not all. Nor have the best teachers necessarily been the qualified ones. There is a fairly high turnover of staff. Many stay only a couple of years, though there is always a core that has been here longer. There are many reasons that people come and go so quickly. Despite what might seem like ideal teaching conditions to the state teacher who has to every day face a large class of kids who don't really want to be there, many adults find Summerhill a very difficult place to live. The low wages are one factor. The school has no income other than the fees paid by parents, and these are kept as low as possible. So both wages and living conditions are fairly basic. Lack of privacy is another. It can be difficult to maintain a private life while still being part of the community, and few of the teachers can afford a base outside of Summerhill. There is no hierarchy among the staff, so no way of bettering yourself, at least as far as the career ladder goes.

Most teachers who are attracted to Summerhill have no intention of making a career of the place. It is something they want to experience for a while, not devote themselves to. This is not necessarily a bad state of affairs, for while the more long-term staff provide stability, the others are continually bringing new blood and fresh ideas into the community. The fact that many teachers decide not to go back into conventional education after they leave would seem to suggest that they found their experience of Summerhill more challenging to their ideas about children than they expected. There are exceptions though. One teacher who was at Summerhill for just a year was never really able to get down from her authoritarian high horse. One day, when she came back to visit, she told a few of the kids how the headmaster of her new school made her boss the kids around, and how much she hated having to play that role. After she had gone the kids looked at each with amazed expressions.

"She was just like that when she was here!" said one, voicing what everyone else was thinking.

When they leave Summerhill most of the kids go on to some form of further education. Comparatively, they tend to take fewer GCSEs than kids in the conventional system. They have other pressures though—they have a community to run and meetings to attend. It is the older kids who act as Beddies Officers, ombudsman, and chairperson, and who run for committees and organize events. There is a thriving social life that they belong to, friends, who are like brothers and sisters to them, who they may only have a few more terms together with. It is often noisy, with other kids playing around and shouting to each other. Summerhill is not a very easy place to study.

Most kids will take more GCSEs after leaving Summerhill, quickly catching up with their peers academically. Just recently Zoë prepared, for our school inspectors, a list of what ex-Summerhillians, who had left in the past few years, were studying. This included marine biology, medicine, astrophysics, music, dance, agriculture, psychology, catering, carpentry, art, business studies, and boat-building, to name a few. One was managing a West End restaurant. Another had set up business with a friend printing and selling greeting cards. Some were doing shop work or manual work. Each was finding his or her own way in the world. The picture certainly wasn't one of people who couldn't cope or were disadvantaged by not having been pushed to go to lessons.

Academic work can be quickly caught up on, but an unhappy childhood can never be reclaimed. Who we are, our way of seeing the world, our beliefs about our place in life, our emotional tempos, evolve out of our childhood experiences. In the compulsive classroom we contract against ourselves, we diminish our own natures in order to survive. Perhaps the hardest thing for us to accept once we have been through this system is that it was unnecessary. As the saying goes, it rubs salt in the wound. For more than seventy five years Summerhill has operated on the principle of voluntary lessons, demonstrating that its students are able to make their way in the world without being compelled to attend class.

It is little wonder then that most people do not want to face up to the possibility of a non-coercive way of educating children, but defend the compulsive classroom with so much vigor. Living with children in this way I have had to grieve for something of my own childhood that I had never really questioned before. It has not been easy. Things that I accepted as normal before, which were the way things were simply because that's the way things are, are no longer normal. I know now that things don't have to be that way. It makes the hurt harder to bear. But it also makes the world a brighter and more hopeful place to live in. A world in which life does not need to be dictated by external compulsion, but can shape itself around its own inner needs and impulses. A world in which human happiness does not have to take second place, but can be the starting point from which all other concerns unfold.

7

Swearing, Bad Manners, and Unmade Beds

The high street of a small Suffolk town. Four girls, probably in their mid-teens, saunter along in the afternoon sun. They wear the uniforms of the local high school, which give them an aura of being rather prim and proper. As if to belie this image they wave around cigarettes in a show of pseudo-casualness. They talk and laugh loudly, self-consciously peppering their speech with swear words. There is a swagger to their walk. They are putting on an act for the afternoon shoppers, as if to say, "Look at us—see how free we are?" Another scene. A café, rather demure, trying to be quaint. A waitress wanders in and out serving the customers, who are mainly families or elderly couples. One table is taken up by adolescent boys whose blazers and badges belong to a nearby Catholic school. One boy, in the guise of talking to his friends, is delivering a speech to the rest of the customers. He is trying to impress by being as obscene as he can. His friends, nervous and embarrassed, tell him to keep his voice down, but he continues to hold forth, leaning back in his chair, his hands gesticulating defiantly. His whole expression is one of, "Look how outrageous I am—aren't I shocking?" Similar scenarios could be found on the doorstep of almost every school in the country.

Swearing and Obscenity

Summerhill kids, with the possible exception of kids who are new to the school, would not behave in such a way. Swearing is not something forbidden and naughty to them, nor do they feel the need to try to shock adults. Such behavior would seem infantile and boring. There are no laws restricting the use of swear words within Summerhill, and swearing is common place. "Fuck offs" and "oh shits" are used expressively, but not defiantly. Even if they were meant to shock, no one would notice anyway. Something is only shocking if people are shocked by it. Kids swear at all schools, only they do so behind the adults' backs. It is a secret language that unites them.

Children love forbidden fruit and swearing is all the sweeter when it is banned. When someone makes reference to "the F word," as if it was something too monstrous to actually utter, they are giving it an almost religious status. I remember as a kid thinking, "Oh, they mean 'fuck'" and thinking it silly that it was all right to say "truck," it was all right to say "funk," but it wasn't okay to say "fuck." After all, it was just another word.

Many adults apply a double standard, swearing themselves, but forbidding their children. The other day I was in a hospital waiting room. A mother with two young boys was complaining loudly about how long they had been waiting. Every other word was "fucking." Yet when one of the boys let go a swear word she turned on him, telling him not to "talk dirty," and threatening to slap him. I don't know if he understood why his mother could swear and he could not, but it was beyond me.

When a child swears in front of an adult in Summerhill no one takes any notice. In other schools it becomes a matter of discipline. A young state school teacher who was visiting Summerhill, told me, "If one of the kids swears I have to send them to the headmaster. They're used to seeing the teacher as an authority figure, and if I don't impose authority they see me as weak and run riot. It's stupid. I don't care if the kids swear or not, but I can't say that. The system doesn't allow it."

The Summerhill adult does not have to play this game. The adults swear just as readily as the kids, when it comes to letting off steam. Swearing only becomes a big deal when people make it a big deal. One houseparent whose strict upbringing made it difficult for her to come to terms with many aspects of the school put a notice on her door with a list of words that she didn't want spoken in her room. This inevitably led to groups of small children standing outside her door chanting these words like a religious litany. This is what happens in all schools, except the fear of punishment makes it a more furtive affair.

Personally, I do not use the word "fuck" to describe sexual intercourse. It does not come naturally to me, but reminds me too much of the macho posturing of the "Did you fuck her last night?" variety. It implies an unfeeling attitude, a mechanical act. There is something harsh about it. But few of the kids would know how I feel about this. If it came up in conversation I would not hide my viewpoint, but nor would I make a crusade of it. It is not really a question of words anyway, but the feelings that fuel them. The House Kids will talk of "fucking" in this way because it is still something abstract to them, but the older kids, whose sexual feelings have matured and deepened, rarely use the term in this way. No one has told them they shouldn't, it has just become inappropriate as their emotions have developed.

There is a law that no one can swear downtown. It is generally adhered to. A small boy once brought a case against me for swearing downtown, but it was dropped as it was just something I let slip and there was no one else around to hear it. It is always the way in such cases that circumstances are taken into account, and the laws are never applied rigidly. On another occasion another member of staff and I took a group of small kids to a local craft workshop for children.

One boy, who was new to the school, kept exclaiming, "Oh fuck!" very loudly as the modeling clay he was molding kept falling apart. Each time it was echoed by the exasperated tones of a woman's voice from across the garden, objecting to such language being used in front of her own children. The other Summerhill kids and I kept reminding him that he could swear as much as he liked in Summerhill, but not outside. A few minutes later he would forget, and let rip again. There was a case in the meeting about him, and it was explained again that although he could swear in Summerhill, when he went out he had to remember that many people took offense to swearing, which is why we had a law about it. As he was new he was not fined. It did not take him long to grasp how things worked, and he was careful not to swear downtown again.

The kids do sometimes forget where they are and swear downtown, or in the hearing of disapproving relatives, but usually they are very astute about such things. When I got married we had a party at the school. My father came along and I picked him up from the train station. I warned him beforehand that the language could be a bit ripe. However, when we arrived it struck me as quite strange how little swearing there was.

What I did not know was that, in my absence at the Saturday night meeting, Zoë had suggested that it might not be appropriate to swear in front of my father, as he was not used to children swearing so freely and it might make him feel uncomfortable. With very few slips, the whole community curtailed its language to make him feel at home.

Perhaps it is because their own values are respected that they respect other people's values. I am often asked by kids what the fuss is all about. Why is it okay to say, "Oh damn it," but not "Oh fuck it?" I don't know. I imagine it's more a question of what the neighbors might think than anything else. It didn't used to be acceptable to say "damn it," but now it is, and the English language doesn't seem to have suffered for it. When I was a kid we couldn't say "bloody" as in, "How much bloody longer are you going to be?" But we could say "bloody" if we had a bloody nose or knee. I could never see the sense in it, and still can't. My religious grandmother chased my brother and me around the house with her walking stick after hearing us say, "Gawd blimee!" which we had copied from the television.

"You're asking God to blind you," she cried. "It's a wicked thing to say." If we swore we were sternly told not to use "that sort of language." Yet we were often told that we were "little buggers." Only later did I learn what a bugger actually was!

The first words that most non-English speaking kids learn when they come to Summerhill are the swear words. They seek them out and savor them as if they were the crown jewels of the spoken language. Equally, the English kids are eager to learn how to swear in other languages. So, when watching a film recently, which had some snatches of German dialogue in it, the only word that I recognized was "*scheisse*" (oh shit). The kids enjoy exchanging insults in different languages, seeing who can come up with the worst one. Japanese is a very polite language. The worst insults that the Japanese kids could come up were "*baka*" (stupid) and "*butu*" (pig). So they invented their own Summerhillian Japanese insults, such as "*unchi-atama*," which literally translates as "shithead," but apparently doesn't really make grammatical sense in Japanese.

The freedom to swear does not give people free rein to

Children can say what they
like and dress as they wish.
(Photo by Tomo Usuada.)

be abusive though. A friendly swap of insults is one thing, but
if someone really takes offense at something then the other
person should stop, or an ombudsman can be called, or a
meeting case brought against them. Last term a girl brought
up one of the boys who was calling her a "slag." The meeting
was united in supporting her, and it was passed that if he did
so again he would be fined. Anything that anyone finds
offensive can be brought to the meeting. A boy hated being
called "Plum," a nickname that he had been given because he
always wore purple. It was carried in the meeting that no one
should call him it anymore, and the next week he brought up
three people for doing so and they were fined. The name-
calling stopped after that.

What causes offense is very individual. It is this criterion
that we use at Summerhill, rather than blanket bans on certain
words. Swearing is censored in most schools, yet the teachers
are free to call the children stupid and to humiliate them in a
variety of ways in front of their classmates. This would be
called license in Summerhill. The justification for banning
some words is that they are considered obscene. Like beauty,
though, obscenity is in the eye of the beholder.

Often a kid will interrupt a game being played in my

room to announce, "Hang on a minute—I'm just going to have a shit." It is said naturally, and without thought. It is a simple descriptive statement of what is happening.

Kids speak freely among themselves about what are only, after all, natural bodily functions. But the inhibited adult does not feel this natural ease with his or her own body, and cannot refer to its processes directly without feeling shame. Instead he or she denounces such directness as obscene. This is particularly true in the sexual sphere, where deeply pleasurable sensations and the surrender to natural movements are involved. Only as a mechanical act, as something distant and coldly scientific, does sex become a respectable subject. It is not, of course, true to say that kids are not inhibited too, quickly picking up their parents' attitudes in early infancy, but generally they live in a much more easy-going atmosphere than we adults do. I find myself being just as candid and unconscious as the kids when there are only kids around. But when I am in adult company such openness does not come naturally to me. To pretend otherwise would be forced and exhibitionist.

At Summerhill the titillation of breaking the rules is replaced with honesty and good-natured fun.
(Photo by Tomo Usuada.)

The way in which many people use so-called obscene words are harsh and are obscene, because this is the underlying feeling. Kids, in whom such words do not reflect feelings of self-contempt and shame, can use the same words and they are simply descriptive. Sending certain words to limbo does not cure us of obscenity, it just helps to reinforce our inhibitions. Conversely, it is in our inhibitions that true obscenity finds its genesis, be it the unfeeling obscenity of the sexual lout, who is all bravado and no tenderness, or the unconscious obscenity of the sexual moralist who sees dirt everywhere, except where it really is—in his own mind. Both are divorced from the deeper emotional content of their expressions.

One argument against swearing and "obscene" language is that it leads to a dropping of standards. Quite what standards they are I do not know. Are we talking about standards of conduct? A local farmer I know swears like a trooper, but he is a warm-hearted, courteous man who always has something friendly to say. The neighbor of a friend in a nearby village works voluntarily in a Christian charity shop. She would never let a swear word cross her lips, but she spreads malicious gossip like the plague, deliberately whipping up conflict between people.

Perhaps we are talking about standards of English. Of all the ex-Summerhillians I have ever met, I have not met one who swears in any profusion. They may swear occasionally, but they do not do so unnecessarily, or in an exhibitionistic way. They are usually very articulate people whose use of language is as proficient as anyone else's.

Compulsive swearing, like any other form of compulsive behavior, is not attractive. When people litter their language with swear words without discrimination or meaning it makes them sound stupid and belligerent. The words are often used mechanically, and without real expression. The tone of voice is usually monotonous. What function swearing has in such instances I do not know, but I suspect that it is the very censorship of such words that leads to their misuse in this way. I suspect that it allows the speaker to express a general air of contempt and discontent with the world, without really allowing these feelings to break through. Hence, he or she begins to sound like a stuck record. This is often put down to a lazy use of language, but that does not account for why it is swear words that are used so repeatedly and not other words. It is emotional inhibition that is at work here, not laziness.

Natural Politeness

Compulsive manners are no more attractive than compulsive swearing, and I do not understand why adults take such a delight in instilling such unnatural, stiff behavior in their children. It is as if the child were born a natural degenerate who needed to be saved from its own nature. On the one hand, swearing is considered bad, and it is assumed that the child will lapse into this "badness" without the proper training. On the other hand, manners are considered good, but it is not assumed that the child will lapse naturally into "goodness." Goodness has to be enforced. The child must be trained to be good. It is the unconscious notion of original sin that still lingers in our attitude towards children.

Children are trained to say "please" and "thank you" like a parrot is taught to say "hello" and "who's a pretty boy then?" It is just as meaningful in either case. If I give something to a child, I enjoy the child's spontaneous delight, a real response that is a pleasure to us both. We are both absorbed in the exchange. The absorption is interrupted and disturbed when someone butts in to tell the child to say "thank you." The child suddenly feels he or she has done something wrong, has not responded correctly. Delight turns to discomfort, and the real smile is replaced by a false one, as he or she utters the obligatory words. It is over in a moment, but it has spoiled something real and meaningful that had flowed between us.

There is no harm in teaching children that "please" and "thank you" are normal social responses. It would be strange not to familiarize children with the wider culture they belong to. But they should be free to adopt these responses in their own time, and not be made to feel guilty if they forget.

I do not expect gratitude from children if I give them something or do something for them, nor do I want it, unless it comes of its own accord. The expectation of gratitude rests on the premise that children are in our debt. If we cannot give freely to children, that is our failing, not theirs. To feel constantly indebted is to feel inferior. The prostitute is ostracized for putting a price on love, yet when parental love carries a price, and a far higher one, nobody disapproves. However many times parents may say to children, "I love you," as long as that love has to be earned by insincerity and little shows of gratitude, the children will not feel truly loved for who they are.

We make no attempt to encourage manners at Summerhill, yet our older kids are some of the most polite people I know. I do not mean polite in the formal "please," "thank you," and "excuse me" way (though they can certainly switch this on when they want to), but in a genuinely courteous and concerned way that runs much deeper. My partner, Gunn, who is Norwegian, finds my English manners rather excessive at times. She quickly becomes irritated by the number of times I say "thank you" when we go shopping. But this has nothing to do with true manners. It is just social etiquette, which varies from country to country. True manners, though, are a matter of being aware of other people and responsive to their feelings, not parroted phrases. The former requires an active emotional alertness, the latter is just social debris.

Table manners are largely unnecessary. How people hold a knife or fork is their own business. As long as it gets the food from their plates and into their mouths, what does it matter? One boy, who has been at Summerhill for almost four years, eats only with a spoon. I do not know why, but it is his choice, and somewhere there must be a reason for it. Children have no interest in the correct ways of holding a knife or fork, but at Summerhill they are quick to tell others to shut their mouths when they are chewing with their mouths open. One boy would always talk with his mouth full, and end up spraying everyone else at the table. The other kids complained bitterly, and he was brought up several times at the meeting. The kids only make an issue of what disturbs them in their own enjoyment. They are not concerned whether something is considered "correct" or not. Often in such everyday matters, kids reveal that they have an instinctive understanding of the difference between what Neill called freedom and license, which adults often cannot grasp with their heady analysis of things.

Food and Emotional Nourishment

An awful lot of fuss is made about eating and food. It is an area of great conflict in many homes. For a long time I have been very interested in the relationship between nutrition and health. After the mother of a friend of mine became ill with

Eating can't be reduced to nutritional concerns alone. It is also an emotional event. *(Photo by Matthew Appleton.)*

cancer, I began to look into the ways that diet could help prevent and relieve disease. Since my late teens I have been a vegetarian and am a dab hand at whole-food cooking. When I lived in London, meal times were often social events, shared with friends and going on late into the evening. For a year or so I ate only organic foods, cutting out alcohol, tea, coffee, and all dairy products. I felt very healthy, and enjoyed my food thoroughly.

But eating cannot be reduced to nutritional concerns alone, it is also an emotional event, and it is this emotional aspect that is often overlooked in the discussion of diet and eating. Eating should be pleasurable. Pleasure is emotional nourishment. Food that is forced on children is experienced as a form of punishment. Food no longer has pleasurable associations, but is caught up in a power conflict.

A girl in her early teens sits at the table, a full plate of food in front of her. She does not feel like eating. Ten minutes earlier there had been an argument between her and her mother. She wanted to skip the evening meal, which was running a little later than usual, so she could keep an appointment with her boyfriend. Her mother refused to let her go without eating first.

"You never let me do anything," she accuses her mother. "You treat me like a baby."

"Don't you speak to your mother like that," demands her father, entering the scene. "She's been slaving over a hot stove for you, you could at least show a bit of gratitude."

The air is now charged with anger and resentment as they sit around the table. Gratitude is the last thing the girl feels. Her younger sister sniggers. Perhaps it is just nerves. She feels like slapping her sister's face though. But she cannot move. She feels frozen and numb. Her mouth is dry and her throat tight. Her belly keeps lurching into her chest in leaps of impotent anger. The knife and fork in her hand feel too heavy to lift.

"Stop sulking, and start eating," says her father, with a

stern frown. Her mother eats silently, her face a stony mask of martyrdom.

"I'm not hungry," the girl replies.

"You're not leaving this table until you've finished," says her father, glaring across the table at her.

Slowly she starts to eat. She tastes nothing but bitterness. She has to force her food down and fight the waves of silent anger that ripple upward from her solar plexus. She feels like the food will choke her as she forces it down her throat, which is already constricted against crying out in rage. It settles in her stomach like stone. She feels nauseated. She thinks she might throw up. It is not just the food, but the swallowed emotion that seems to brew within her, to bubble up as if it might suddenly erupt.

Later she hides in the bathroom and thrusts her fingers into the back of her throat. She feels the rush of half-digested food and swallowed anger. She tastes bile, but nothing solid comes up. Her throat feels too tight. Something seems to catch there. Tears well up in her eyes, but even they do not want to come. It is too late now. Her face floats in the bottom of the toilet, looking back up at her. She spits into it. She thinks she is ugly, and despises herself. Ugliness eats away inside her.

This is a fictional account, but the feelings are very real. Meal times are often loaded with such feelings for children and adolescents. It may begin with minor nagging to wash hands and hold the knife and fork properly. It can then continue with how the food is eaten. The child who is eager to get back to play gulps the food down. The child who is unhappy and preoccupied picks at the food. Either may be told to "eat properly," to slow down or hurry up as if there were some regulation speed at which food should be eaten. Then there is the urging to finish up everything on the plate. After the child has finished he or she may be forced to wait until everyone else has finished before leaving the table. Meal times easily become tense affairs and a misery for children.

No one really enjoys their food in such a climate of conflict, but there is a deeper element to what is happening here. The family sitting around the table together at meal times has a ritualistic quality to it. It is symbolic of family unity. The tragedy is that the symbolic often takes over from and undermines the possibility of real harmony. The great effort that is put into maintaining the symbol is not just wasted, it is counter-productive. Many mothers will feel rejected when their children do not seem to enjoy the meals they have produced. Many fathers feel threatened when the unity of the family seems uncertain. The family table is the symbolic battlefield of such tensions.

The urgency of the child who wants to get back to play is no mere whim, it is deeply felt, and there is no rational reason to impede it. Gulping food down does far less harm to the digestion than frustration does. Forcing a child to eat when she or he has no appetite is deeply disturbing to the child. From the moment the newborn fixes onto the breast, food is identified with love.

Physical and emotional nourishment are inexorably bound together. To withdraw food is to withdraw love. To force feed is to force love, and love that is forced upon someone is not real love at all, it is power. There is a qualitative difference, and children feel it. A loving gesture is one thing, an abusive intrusion is another.

The ritual of not leaving the table until everyone has finished is like a prison sentence to children. It may only be a matter of minutes, but such minutes hang heavily in childhood. There are enough frustrations in life that children have to cope with, without our inventing more. From the moment they sit down at the dinner table many children feel a sense of being trapped. They feel uncomfortable and unsure of themselves. Food is not so much a source of nourishment to them as a source of anxiety, and this ambiguity is felt not just as an ambiguity about food, but as an ambiguity towards love.

Eating disorders are not occasional; they are epidemic.

Compulsive feeding inevitably leads to compulsive eating habits. We have the extremes of obesity, anorexia, and bulimia, along with a host of minor eating disorders that are so commonplace they are accepted as normal. This is particularly true of women. I have met few women who do not experience some form of conflict over food. The media emphasis on dieting no doubt has a hand in some of this, especially with its perpetual assault on the female form. But without the ground for these conflicts being created in childhood, I doubt they would be as widespread and as damaging as they are.

Something that has surprised me is the number of kids we have been told were allergic to this or that food, only to find, after a few weeks, they are eating it along with all the other kids, and with no ill-effect. I cannot account for this, but can only presume it to be an emotional change, for there is nothing special about Summerhill food.

Food is served from the kitchen hatch. The menu is written up on a blackboard and people can choose whatever they want. Meat or fish are served most days, but there is always a vegetarian alternative. If people only want potatoes, or pudding, nobody forces them to eat anything else. There is a very understandable nutritional concern here, but the kids are rarely ill, and grow up to be healthy, strapping young men and women. It would seem that they instinctively find the balance in their own nutritional needs, eating what their bodies tell them to, when they tell them. I know of a doctor whose five-year-old son has lived on a diet of nothing but pasta, potatoes, and fruit juice since he came off the breast. Although the parents have been concerned, they thought it better not to force him to eat food that he didn't want to. Yet he is a healthy, vivacious boy and tests have revealed no deficiencies. There is more to the question of nutrition than meets the eye.

The younger kids, who go to first lunch and supper, tend to eat very quickly, rushing off to play again as soon as possible. The older kids usually take longer, but it is nearly always the adults who take longest eating. Leisurely eating is an adult affair. At Summerhill everyone eats at their own pace and no one suffers for it, though the kitchen staff sometimes get a little impatient with the last few adults who are still eating and talking long after everyone else has gone.

There are no laws directly concerned with meals, though there are laws relating to queuing and the dining room. There is a law, for example, that you cannot throw food. The occasional colorful splatter of ketchup and stalactite of mashed potato that can be spotted on the ceiling reveal that this law is not always kept. There is also a law that first-lunch kids cannot go downtown before one o'clock. This was passed after a small group of first lunch kids starting missing their lunch and heading downtown to buy sweets instead, which meant that a lot of food was being cooked and then thrown away. But there are no laws actually concerning the consumption of chocolate or sweets. What extra sugar the kids get from eating sweets they quickly burn up in vigorous play.

Because food is such an emotive issue, it is sometimes difficult to distinguish which of our attitudes are rational and which are irrational. During my first few terms I had the recurrent dream that when I got to the kitchen hatch (which has since been enlarged and so is less claustrophobic) and put my head through, it turned into a guillotine. The kitchen staff, sitting around the table knitting, took one look at me and gave me the thumbs down. Luckily I always awoke before losing my head.

I think this dream was provoked by having to give up control over what and when I ate. This is an inevitable part of community life. I have neither the money nor the time to cook for myself in term time, and the kitchen has to cater for a broad range of tastes, so it cannot please everyone all the time. Today I am more relaxed about eating. Although I still sometimes miss being able to eat when and what I like, I recognize that it is not just a matter of food. There is also an association between food and being controlled which is a ghost of my own childhood anxiety. So when a parent says their child eats only raw vegetables and nuts, I am not surprised a few days later when the child begins to devour chips and cola. I am all for healthy eating, but healthy eating also means enjoying what we eat.

The Controlling Adult

The controlling attitudes that adults have towards children are largely the result of their own fearful projections. We try to control in children what we dimly sense as most threatening within ourselves. So the father who was forced to go to school as a boy and still resents work, projects his own unconscious rebellious attitude towards learning onto his children.

"They need to be pushed," he says, "if they're ever going to get on in the world."

The mother who was made passive in her youth mistakes the lively, expressive qualities of her children for her own unexpressed hate and contempt.

"They need to know who's boss," she declares.

The school and the nursery continue this process, working against the child's natural capacity for self-regulation and instilling the same irrational anxieties that we have, so even the children themselves begin to feel that they need to be controlled. We are rarely more unconscious than in our dealings with children.

This is not just idle theory. It has come from years of living with and observing children who are able to live their lives largely free of adult irrationality. Children with overprotective parents inevitably spend their first few weeks at Summerhill bumping into things, falling over and generally injuring themselves. They are uncoordinated, clumsy, and have lost their trust in their own abilities to function coherently. In time their confidence returns and they are off in the woods, climbing trees, and running around, as nimble and agile as nature intended. Overprotectiveness usually hides sadism. The anxiety that overprotective adults feel arises from their own sadistic impulses to hurt the child, which have been consciously denied and lie dormant. One afternoon I was walking behind a mother in a park in South London. Her young daughter skipped ahead of her.

"Don't run, you'll fall over and hurt yourself," hissed the mother through clenched teeth. Of course the girl did. Such warnings nearly always become self-fulfilling prophecies.

"Ha!" cried her mother triumphantly, dragging her crying daughter roughly to her feet. "I told you, didn't I?"

A protective instinct is vital in any animal if it is to care for its young adequately. It would not be freedom to let an unattended toddler play on a busy street, that would be blatantly irresponsible. But over-anxiety only creates anxious children. I was standing by a narrow stream watching a mother duck and her ducklings. It was particularly narrow where I was standing, and as they approached the mother duck darted behind her babes and pushed them hurriedly past me. Once they were past she gracefully glided ahead again, aware of her young, who followed in her wake, but no longer anxious. If she had continued to frantically push and hurry her young even though there was no threat anymore it would have seemed very strange. But this is how the human adult behaves towards its young much of the time. We are neurotic creatures, frantically pushing and controlling our children, though there is no real need to do so.

Why do we nag children to wash their hands before meals? Summerhill kids rarely wash their hands before eating, yet it does them no harm. There is very little sickness at the school. I always feel rather embarrassed when our school inspectors ask to see the medical records that we houseparents keep. They are mostly blank, though I record all illnesses and accidents. Issues of cleanliness and tidiness are mainly concerned with character training, rather than having any real, useful function. It is as if children have to be saved from themselves—an inherent savagery that the child will succumb to if the hands aren't washed properly.

I do not interfere with the washing and bathing habits of the House Kids, and they are quite able to regulate themselves in these matters. The San Kids seem to enjoy regular, organized bath times, but the House Kids are more independent. Most wash, bathe, and brush their teeth quite regularly. Some skip baths for several weeks on end, but it does not affect their health or well being at all. On occasions I have had kids who have hardly washed or changed their clothes at all throughout the eleven weeks of term. Yet, a few years later, they are bathing regularly, combing their hair, and generally taking pride in their appearance, quite of their own accord. There has been no need at all to bully them into it.

If personal hygiene does become a health issue then I deal with it as such. It does not happen very often though. I may stress the importance of looking after teeth to someone who is neglecting them. But most of the kids are very conscientious about brushing their teeth and need no reminding. A few times kids have asked me to come and get them when I brush my teeth in the mornings and evenings, so they do not forget, and it quickly becomes part of the daily routine. Athlete's foot has sometimes been a problem, especially with kids who wear trainers all day. In such instances I give the appropriate treatment, and recommend regular foot baths, and airing of the feet. The body has a way of telling us when things are wrong. By letting the body be our guide, instead of imposing rigid and unnecessary routines, we take the route of natural hygiene, rather than compulsive cleanliness, which only ends up making kids feel as if their bodies are dirty and shameful.

When someone's personal hygiene has an affect on other people, it then ceases to be just a personal matter. Sometimes kids will complain about one of their roommates who hasn't bathed or changed his or her socks for a while, and is starting to smell. If they don't do something about it, an ombudsman can be called, or a meeting case brought against them. But it is surprising how long some kids can go without bathing and still not smell, while others quickly turn into walking compost heaps. Where washing has been a big issue at home, kids may develop an aversion to it, or become finicky about it themselves. This will often have deeper roots in a strict regime of toilet training when the child was an infant. One young Japanese boy at the school is very finicky and compulsive about cleanliness, and he is a picture of neatness. But his humor is very anal and he makes a great exhibition of farting. Often when he and his sister have been in my room on their own and I come in, they start giggling together, and looking guilty. Then he will point to a potato-chip package lying on the floor, or a place on my bed where the duvet is slightly disheveled, and say, "We've made a mess," and they will both run out squealing with delight. Entering into the spirit of things I adopt an exaggerated stance of offended dignity and their squeals of delight grow even louder. It is a game that I enjoy as much as they do.

One young girl took this symbolic gesture of defiance a step further and began defecating in the baths and on the bathroom floors. One of the kids brought a meeting case against her. It was passed that she should not shit on the floor or in the bath, as it inconvenienced other people, but could do so out in the bushes if she wanted. After the meeting she ran up to her houseparent and with a sigh of relief said, "I'm so happy, I thought they were going to kill me." I imagine that at home she had been severely scolded or punished for soiling herself. Her defecating in public places had a clear message. It was inviting punishment, and at the same time, pleading for acceptance. It was a gauntlet thrown down to the world, a challenge to find out if it was an accepting world or a rejecting one. The meeting did not make a huge fuss about it, and it was a step towards making it less of an issue for her. These sorts of problems cloud the inner lives of many children when adults impose their own complexes about cleanliness on them.

Tidiness, likewise, tends to raise undue adult concern. When I first came to Summerhill there was a law that everybody had to make their beds in the morning. How or why it got passed I don't know, but it seemed to me to go against the grain of what Summerhill was about. After all, it affected nobody else whether the bed was made or not. I proposed the law be dropped, and my proposal was carried. Since then I took it upon myself to make the beds for the House Kids most days, so that when they climbed into bed, the sheets would be smoothed out and comfortable. The truth is, though, that the kids generally don't notice, and some have even asked me not to make their beds—a wish I, of course, respect.

My point is this: bed making and general tidiness are adult concerns that children have no interest in. The House Kids are, on the whole, very messy in their rooms. No one tells them to tidy up, unless they make such a mess that it interferes with the cleaners who come in and vacuum the rooms each morning. They are not free to create a mess in my room though, and I ask them to clear up after themselves if they do. We live a happy co-existence. I do not impose my values on them. They do not impose their values on me. I occasionally get annoyed because my room has been left messy, and just last term there were several meeting cases about one room that was always so messy the cleaners couldn't get on with their work. But these instances do not develop into huge conflicts. They are sorted out in the meetings. They become the landmarks by which we define the difference between freedom and license.

The House Kids' rooms used to be bleak, primitive affairs, with metal-framed bunk beds and rather dilapidated second-hand chests of drawers. It suited their needs perfectly.

They were able to jump around as much as they liked without fear of breaking anything. The bare floors and tatty furniture did not bother them in the slightest. In fact, it cried out "freedom" to them. Freedom from having to worry about messing up the carpet, knocking over ornaments, or maintaining an oppressive regime of order and tidiness. Recently, mainly as a response to demands from our schools' inspectors, the school has begun to work its way through these rooms, redecorating them, replacing the old beds with built-in wooden bunks, and adding carpets, built-in cupboards, shelves, and desks. The danger is that the school compromises, that it loses what is functional for children simply to appeal to adult aesthetics, and in doing so reproduces the sense of claustrophobic "niceness" that inhibits children's freedom everywhere. The pressure is there to do so, but the new rooms seem to have struck a reasonable balance. The beds are solid affairs, built to withstand a lot of horseplay and leaping around. The carpets are hard-wearing industrial ones.

Summerhill is designed to fit around kids, not the other way around. Mostly children are expected to fit into adult environments as if they were part of the furniture. The child who is best suited to these expectations is cute and docile, a one-dimensional caricature, lacking the vigor and expressiveness of real children. Images in magazines and on television often paint the same unrealistic picture. The pastel-colored nursery with a contented-looking baby gurgling away. The chirpy boy who sets off happily for school, glowing with warmth after a hearty breakfast. The soft-spoken girl who is eternally fascinated by how soft her mothers hands are after doing the washing up. Few homes are built around the real needs of children, but around unrealistic expectations that children are then expected to conform to. Already one of our new rooms had a large hole in the wall where one of the boys, holding onto the bunk above, tried to swing into bed, but ended up crashing through a plasterboard panel instead. It was an accident and was patched up without any fuss. These things happen. We do not try to make kids feel bad about themselves when such inevitable accidents occur. To do so is to make the environment a constant source of potential danger in which the child is afraid to move.

Spirituality and Religion

Visitors sometimes ask if Summerhill has much in common with Steiner schools, which put a great deal of emphasis on the natural development of the child. The answer is no. The principles at work in Summerhill are completely different than those of Steiner education. The child at Summerhill lives according to his or her own nature. The Steiner child lives according to Steiner's concept of the child's nature. Steiner schools aim to educate the whole child, not just the intellect. But this is not the same as letting the whole child express itself. Following certain stages of development, as defined by Steiner, the child's expression is guided and controlled by adults, often to a greater degree than in conventional schools. At any particular stage, for example, the child may only be allowed to use certain colors and shapes, which are considered to be in harmony with the child's spiritual development at that stage. A lot of emphasis is put on the child's spiritual development.

Religion is not practiced at Summerhill, nor does the school have a "spiritual" philosophy of any sort. Neill's belief that the "bad" child is really just an unhappy child has been borne out by over seventy five years of freedom and self-government at Summerhill. "Goodness," then, is not something that needs to be taught, but arises naturally when unhappiness is eliminated. I have never really understood what is meant by the word "spiritual," but more often than not, it seems to imply a reaching out to some higher principle outside and beyond nature. Nature is cast as a lower order to be conquered and manipulated, to be worked against and raised above. If, instead, spirituality referred to the living principle within nature, then children could only ever be regarded as spiritual creatures, for in children we encounter our nature at its most alive and spontaneous. We talk of people as being "spirited" when they are animated by life, and "spiritual" when they renounce life. Somewhere along the line it looks as if the concept of spirit has been removed from life, where once it was an expression of the embodiment of life. Children do not have to renounce life to be happy, contented people who are at one with themselves and their world. Only when life has become filled with anxieties is there any relief in renouncing life's pleasures.

Christ said, "Become ye like little children." But across the world, where children would spontaneously and naturally play with each other and make friends, organized religion has forged barriers of hate. Catholics on one side, Protestants on the other. Christians here, Muslims there. Islamic faith versus heathen disbelief. Children are told not to talk to each other. At first they do not understand. It is not in their nature to understand such stupidity. But, in time, they too learn to hate in the name of their God. The stories they have heard make them fearful and suspicious. The violence they have witnessed hardens them and makes them cruel. The outer conflict echoes the inner conflict, in which religion also has had a hand. The loving impulse of the body has been reduced to shameful torment. When it does finally break through it is laden with hateful and sadistic expressions, devoid now of the tender yearning that has long ago become a source of anxiety and frustration. The soft and sensual nature of the child that yields to life is no more. In its place emerges the harsh fervor of the faithful that turns from pleasure and preaches pain and sacrifice.

This is religion at its most extreme, but it is also expressive of how all religion, to some degree, interferes with the natural "goodness" of the child, and creates its own devils.

Religion seeks to improve the child. Throughout the religious world is the notion that there is an inherent flaw in human nature, or an original sin, which needs to be addressed. Such beliefs are inevitably anti-child. A religion that did not rest on the concept of the inherent flaw would have a very different attitude towards children. It would celebrate the child as an expression of nature. It would recognize and respect the expression of nature in the child. It would not try to improve on the perfection of nature, but would seek to protect and nourish it. It would not banish love to the heavens, or to the abstraction of the spirit, but would welcome its embodiment on earth and the expressions of that embodiment, not just between married couples, but between children and adolescents also. The great conceit of religion is that it thinks it knows better than nature. But the cathedrals, churches, mosques, and temples of religion fade into insignificance beneath the stars and among the mountains, forests, rivers, and oceans of nature. Here in this wider stream of life the child is already perfect. Only in the minds of men and women who have denied nature within themselves does the child need to be improved.

We may, of course, have "spiritual" feelings without being religious in any formal sense of the word. We might experience these as a sense of wonderment, a feeling of melting, of being at one with things. If so, then we do not need to interfere with children. They are closer to these feelings than we are, until we get in the way and disrupt them. They do not need beautiful words, prayer, meditation, or chants to get them there. These feelings arise naturally. We only have to cultivate them in ourselves if our natural capacity to experience them spontaneously and straightforwardly has been injured. Then such feelings become clouded by mysticism. They are experienced as transcendental, and beyond the realm of everyday life. But it is only because we have been cut off from them in our everyday lives for so long that they appear to us as anything other than a natural joy in living.

This leaning towards "higher things" is expressed culturally too. Children's tastes are cultivated so that they can
"appreciate the better things in life." My mother used to make
me sit down and listen to classical music for half an hour
every week. It gave me a prejudice against classical music that
I have never completely overcome. When, many years later,
I did begin to enjoy the occasional symphony or aria, it was
despite my mother's efforts, not because of them. Culture is
largely snobbery. When I began listening to avant-garde jazz I
thought myself sophisticated, and sold most of the pop
records of my youth. Later I regretted this, and began collect-
ing them again. Watching the rapt expressions of the kids
singing and dancing along to their favorite songs in Gram, I
have no doubt they are experiencing as much pleasure and
emotional fulfillment as anyone who might be listening to a
Beethoven symphony or a Wagner overture.

Music is an important part of adolescent identity. When I
was a teenager, as soon as I came home the first thing I did
was put on a record. Closing the door of my room I sang
along with the words and danced around to the music,
shaking off the tensions of the day. Music helped me survive
my adolescence. I cannot imagine what I would have done
without it. As soon as the music started I was in my world, not
that of my parents or teachers. My senses swam in the sound.
My emotions found a voice as I sang along, supported by the
voice of the singer. Teenagers make heroes of singers and
musicians because they address the emotions. It is the emotional life of the adolescent that is so urgent, so overwhelming.
Teachers often become the villains of adolescence because
they address only the intellect, and neglect the emotions.
Music is most often the only voice that adolescents can find
for their deeper feelings. To dismiss the music as "rubbish,"
as so many parents do, is to dismiss that person's inner life as
rubbish. Whatever type of music we listen to, it serves a need
in us. It is whether that need is being adequately served or not
that is important, not what form the music takes.

The same applies to art and literature. It is better that children enjoy reading the Beano or the Dandy than be forced to read a Shakespeare play they hate. It is better because one child is happy and the other is miserable. We talk of "improving the mind," but forget the emotions. The result is that the child ends up hating Shakespeare, and never reads him again. How many adults continue to read the literature they were force-fed as kids? Very few. Hence the literary diet of the masses consists mainly of the daily tabloids, not the books of their schooldays. Was there ever such a self-defeating idea as compulsory education?

As a kid I used to love reading super-hero comics, such as Batman and Superman. Shortly after I started at Summerhill I began to have the same dream again and again. In it I was browsing around a second-hand bookshop, when I came across a pile of these old super-hero comics. All at once I began to feel the excitement that I felt as a child. There was a delicious sense of pleasurable anticipation. I felt a thrill of excitement run through my body like an electric current. It made me feel whole, integrated, and totally absorbed in the moment. Then, a split second later, like the cracking of a whip, a voice reprimanded me, telling me that I was grown up now, and should put such childish pleasures behind me. When I awoke from this dream I always felt a great sense of loss.

Over the years this dream has come back many times, and I know now that it is telling me when I am working too hard and not taking enough time to enjoy life. As soon as I do, the dream disappears again. I am not particularly inter-ested in dreams, but because this one has recurred so many times I have listened to it more closely. What is most striking to me is the vivid sense of excitement and elation that I feel throughout my body. I have the feeling of belonging to myself. When the voice tells me that I should forget such childish pleasure I lose that feeling. I feel split, no longer at one with myself. My sense of self, the embodiment of my excitement, dims and dies away. Comics as a symbol of simple childhood joy does not surprise me, as I derived enormous pleasure from them as a child. That such feelings were stirred up by coming to Summerhill does not surprise me either. Here children do not have to disown themselves. Childish pleasures do not have to be subjugated to the improvement of the mind, but can mature at their own pace.

Only when we grow up in our own time do we ever really grow up. Childhood excitement can be stifled, but it does not go away. It is just diverted, and comes out in other ways, which become rooted in our personalities when the frustration is long term. It may be tightly held and felt as anxiety, so that the child develops an anxious attitude towards life. It may be felt as an inner emptiness, and the nagging thought that somehow life could and should be more than this. Sometimes it kicks against the limitations, bursting out in anti-social and self-abusive ways—delinquency, violence, drug abuse, self-mutilation, even suicide. Each of us has our own individual pattern of thwarted childhood excitement written deep into our being. It can come out in many different ways, some at odds with the wider society, some echoing the attitudes and values of that society. Much of what we do in adult life though, has a great deal of unexpressed infantile and childhood content.

What I have attempted to do, in this chapter, is describe a handful of different situations in which the lives of children come into conflict with the expectations of adults. The underlying expectation that runs through the core of most of these issues is that the child is basically "bad" and has to be "civilized." The notion that we are born in sin still runs deep, even if it isn't expressed as directly as that these days. Even Freud, who discovered the harm that we do to children by suppressing their natural impulses, later conjured up the theory of a "death instinct," yet again casting the young Homo sapiens as a brute with innate destructive tendencies that had to be sublimated.

Yet, as I have demonstrated above, our experience at Summerhill does not bear this out. The children do not reveal innate destructive tendencies, but innate sociability. Also, when they are unhindered by constant adult interference, they show a great capacity to know what is best for them. The concept of sin was fashioned out of a human nature that had already been twisted out of shape by unyielding cultural mores. The instinctive destructiveness of the psychoanalysts has arisen from studying neurotic adults and unhappy children full of hate and conflict, not children who have been brought up to trust in their own natures and feel at one with themselves. However far we go socially, politically, technologically, or whatever, as long as our knowledge of ourselves is based on this false premise we will make no real progress in our lives. Without a deep understanding of who we are, and the underlying emotional structure of our attitudes and actions, we will continue to repeat the same mistakes again and again, like stuck records, both in our personal lives and historically.

All this may seem a long way from the everyday issues of swearing, manners, tidiness, eating habits, etc. If each of these issues existed in a vacuum, then certainly they would be of little importance. It would be nonsense to suggest that any child suffers greatly, or develops terrible inhibitions, from being told not to use "bad language" or to make his or her own bed. Indeed, there are times when such requests are quite reasonable. These are trivial matters in themselves, but they do not exist in a vacuum. They arise out of and reveal to us glimpses of what is a much deeper conflict. They are symptomatic of our society's deep distrust of the child's nature. At their deepest level they exist as a distrust of nature itself, of the living continuum of which we are all a part, and yet seek so hard to detach ourselves from.

Emotions and Armoring

For many years Neill conducted what he called "private lessons," which were known among the Summerhill community as "P.L.s." They were not actually lessons at all, but therapy sessions in which Neill would take one of the kids aside for an informal chat, probing into whatever he thought might be troubling him or her. They were aimed at those kids who seemed to be having particular problems adjusting to the freedom of Summerhill, or who were going through a rough patch with their family or their peers. Later in life Neill fairly much abandoned P.L.s, declaring that the kids who had not had P.L.s made every bit as much progress as those who did. He put this down to the freedom of Summerhill, which, in itself, seemed to cure many kids of their unhappiness and anti-social tendencies.

Many people who are drawn to the idea of children's freedom have a strong political interest. When they visit Summerhill they ask questions about hierarchies and administration. They are concerned that the kids do not vote on the hiring and firing of staff, or that the meetings work on a majority vote, rather than consensus. What is often overlooked is the emotional aspect of freedom at Summerhill.

Free to play all day. *(Photo by Matthew Appleton.)*

Kids, when they come to visit the school, have little interest in such questions. Their eyes light up as they watch groups of kids running around playing games, unsupervised by adults, motivated only by the sheer pleasure of doing so. In their minds they compare this with the school they have just come from, where everyone is in class, hunched over exercise books, being overseen by a teacher who perhaps humiliates them or patronizes them with soft-spoken niceties. They delight in hearing swear words abound, without anyone making a great fuss about it. Here is a place they feel they can be themselves.

The easy-going relationship between kids and staff, boys and girls, may be both attractive and puzzling. They are used to having their defenses up, and the spontaneous interactions and gestures of affection that pass between people take them by surprise. For many a schoolchild such are the things that dreams are made of, and only dreams.

When a prospective parent and child come to see the school, I or one of the other houseparents will show them around and talk to them. The sort of questions that kids usually ask are things such as, "Can I really not go to lessons?" "What time would I have to go to bed?" "Can I wear whatever I want?" "Can I go downtown if I want?" "Can I bring my computer to school?"

The school is not all freedom, and sometimes there may be restrictions that community life necessitates, which home life does not. Some kids may be able to go to bed when they like at home. There are laws concerning the times when computers can be used, and TVs watched. There are the downtown laws, which may be tighter than the limitations set down at home. Sometimes these revelations elicit a weary sigh, or a groan, but they are quickly forgotten, especially when I mention that any of these laws can be challenged in the meeting.

The freedom that the kids embrace when they come to Summerhill is not necessarily the same as the abstract theoret-

ical freedom that many adults are concerned with. So, I have
never heard any of the kids ask why the hiring and firing of
staff shouldn't go through the meetings, or why are there so
many locks around the school. These are chiefly adult concerns, and the children are not excluded from them, they are
free of them. If they were interested they could easily challenge these areas of school life, as they question so many
others.

Children tend to think more functionally than adults.
They deal more in practicalities, and events that have emotional content for them, rather than abstract theories. For
example, when there was a spate of breakings in one term.
Playing devil's advocate, I told a bunch of kids, "I'm fed up
with this. I'm going to propose that we get rid of all the locks
in the school, and be done with it." Their response was one of
horror.

"Oh no," I was told. "Everything will get wrecked."

What restrictions there are serve such practical functions.
They are not there to mold the child, and children instinctively feel the difference between that which is functional and
that which is moralistic, or unnecessarily intrusive.

This is not to say that these laws do not get broken
sometimes, but that part of the coming to terms with restrictions is the realization of their practicality, and that they are
not just some whim of adult irrationality. The kids, then, can
live very rich, emotional lives. Perhaps for the first time in
their lives they can be themselves. They can rage, they can
scream and kick things, they can sob their hearts out, they can
laugh and play, they can dance with joy. No one will tell them
to go to their room to cool down or to stop being silly and
settle down.

They may be brought up at meeting for breaking something that wasn't theirs while they were "in a moody," but they
will not be made to feel that they were wrong or "bad" for
feeling what they did. The climate is one of emotional freedom.

Emotional Expression
and the Growth of Reason

All children, at some time, have unpleasant and traumatic experiences. It is not so much the trauma itself that does lasting harm to the child, but the inability to express the emotions associated with the trauma. Children are often encouraged, or even frightened into keeping quiet about traumatic experiences they have had with adults or other children.

It need not just be severe traumatic events, such as sexual or physical abuse, but also long-term, chronic trauma, which has become woven into the fabric of everyday life. It is children for whom school is an everyday misery, but who have no outlet for their frustration and unhappiness other than occasional emotional outbursts, that they do not understand themselves who are considered at fault, not the system. The children whose parents are deeply unhappy and are forever arguing. The children whose parents buy them expensive presents, but never show any genuine loving feelings. The children whose most tender, loving feelings have been frozen with guilt, after being told they are "dirty." These "lesser" traumas all take their toll as well.

When a young child experiences displeasure he or she expresses it directly. I have seen this most vividly in my daughter, Eva, who is now fifteen months old. If she wants me to pick her up and cuddle her she will wail until I do so. If I stop her from playing with something that may be dangerous, or that I am afraid she will break, she is furious with me and stamps her feet and bursts into tears of rage. From my perspective it is quite reasonable that I cannot hold her right now, or let her pull my cassettes to pieces. But from her perspective it is just as right that she should be able to enjoy these things, and, in that moment, I have turned right to wrong by interrupting her pleasure. She is not being "naughty" or "selfish," she is just expressing what is real to her. Both perspectives are valid, and it is right that she should be able to express her frustration at my interference, just as it is necessary for me to sometimes say "no."

As children grow they learn to accept more and more limitations. They become more reasonable. But even with the ten- to thirteen-year-olds I am houseparent for, I find appealing to reason only goes so far and there are times when I have to say, "Look, just stop it, okay?"

It is not the logic of my argument that convinces them, but the seriousness of my voice. This past term I have had an on-going battle with a small group of House boys who have insisted on rolling about on my bed play-fighting the minute my back is turned. Having several times left the room for a couple of minutes and returned to find my bedclothes scattered over the floor, I got more and more upset.

"We'll make it again after," they offered.

"But I don't want it messed up in the first place," I implored. "It's my bed! If I can't even call my bed my own, what am I left with?"

The bed, as symbolic of my own need for personal space, meant nothing to them. Realizing though that it was genuinely upsetting me, they tried to avoid messing the bed up. But the minute that a spontaneous wrestling match developed, all was forgotten in the joy of the moment and the combatants would be throwing each other all over the bed, sending my bedclothes this way and that. I became so exasperated that I took to throwing everyone out and locking my room every time I went out.

I am often visited in my room by the older kids. It amuses me how often they sit watching the House Kids at play, and my interactions with them, and say, "We weren't like that when we were House Kids were we?"

"Oh yes you were," I reply, amazed at their wide-eyed amnesia. The fact is that they are seeing life through different eyes. They are seeing how unconscious the House Kids are of the havoc they wreak. But they didn't have an inkling of this when they were House Kids themselves.

This development towards awareness and consideration of others was not something that needed to be forced, but occurred naturally, without moralizing or discipline, which only serve to inspire guilt and anxiety, not genuine thoughtfulness for others. To return to fifteen-month-old Eva. She expresses her emotions very strongly and is a powerful force to be reckoned with. When she is frustrated or unhappy she lets Gunn, her mother, and me know. It is her only route to satisfaction. She does not always get her own way—not because there is a battle of wills between us, but because it is sometimes just not possible. There are sometimes practical considerations, such as a train to catch, or an appointment to be kept. In so far as it is possible to meet her needs her mother and I do so. When we cannot we take her protest seriously.

It is a fact of life that children sometimes have to accept frustration. But the idea that it is good for them, and that they should "learn who's boss," or that "they cannot always get their own way" is tragic. It only leads to unnecessary frustration and conflict. This form of morality does not nurture emotional growth; it stunts it. When new kids come to Summerhill they let go of much of the false compliance they had adopted over the years, and often return to more infantile mannerisms for a time. This is clearly more pronounced in kids who have been especially "well trained," and far less so in those kids who have reached a more mature level of reasoning of their own accord. There is also a similar disparity between the twelve-year-old who is new to Summerhill, and the twelve-year-old who has been at the school since she or he was six or seven.

An occasion when I was particularly struck by this was one evening when I was play-fighting with three of the San Kids, the youngest kids in the school. Two came from fairly conventional homes, and were quite new to the school. The third, who was a good two years younger than the others, came from a family where there was far more freedom, and had been a day kid for some time. While we played the two older kids often slipped into somewhat sadistic and aggressive play. The younger boy, however, frequently told the others, "Hey guys, be careful," and checked with me that I didn't mind what was happening.

Where direct emotional responses to frustration are continually quashed in children, they will inevitably come out later in other ways, such as sadism and unwarranted aggression or temper tantrums. Emotional expression is a form of release for the child, a way of letting go of tension. It is the child's only defense against an otherwise overpowering world. When that expression is inhibited the child is frozen and helpless. When the emotional holding is associated with either chronic frustration or trauma it becomes a deeply embedded tension, fixed not only in the psyche, but also in the muscles and organs of the body.

Let us consider for a moment what we are asking a deeply sobbing child to do when we tell him to pull himself together and stop crying. The child cannot simply turn off the tears, and wish away the anguish he is feeling. The sobbing is an expression of his pain, it moves in waves from the core of his being to the surface. The emotion is a discharge of his pain. To stop this discharge he must contract against it. He holds his breath and bites his lip. His eyes look away, avoiding contact, hardening against any expression of softness or vulnerability. The throat constricts and the jaw tightens against the trembling that is passing up into the lips and chin. Hands clench into fists, arms are thrust down rigidly at the side. The whole body stiffens, passing from rhythmic shudders into immobility. The severity of this reaction will relate to the severity of the external pressure to quiet down. It is a fearful response. The fear of punishment or humiliation is greater than the natural urge for relief from the present anguish. If this pattern of closing down emotional expression occurs enough times or with enough intensity, it takes shape within the total personality. The child loses the ability to cry freely or fully, loses contact with his inner softness, and becomes hardened physically and emotionally.

When we cry fully we literally heave emotion. We are left breathing deeply. We feel spent. There is a sense of release, of resolution. Our bodies feel soft and alive. In reality most of us have lost this capacity to cry fully, and rarely feel that sense of resolution. Instead, we have learned to "grin and bear it," to hide behind a smile and pretend everything is all right. It is a protective mechanism that we are stuck with, long after it has served its original purpose. Mostly we are not even aware of it, except as a sense of inner emptiness or tension.

I used the male gender to describe this process deliberately, as the taboo against boys' crying is greater than against girls'. Inevitably, in many instances, this leads on to outbreaks of irrational anger and violence, as tension that might have found release in crying can only be discharged in more harsh expressions. It is by no means a purely masculine problem though. A girl who arrived at Summerhill when she was ten had suffered a lot of physical abuse when very young and had been moved from home to home many times before finally settling with a family. Her bullying and breaking of rules was a problem to the community for many of the six years she was with us. In the meetings, when confronted with what she was doing, she simply shrugged and grinned inanely. Her expression was one of "do your worst, I can take everything that the world throws at me." Unfortunately, it only served to infuriate most people. Gradually she became more able to accept and express her vulnerability as the need to be so self-protective subsided, but it didn't come easily to her.

In a different situation we may find someone who is easily moved to tears, but is unable to express anger. This is often a more feminine trait, as it is generally more acceptable for girls to break down in tears than to show anger. Anger is swallowed and then sublimated, being partially discharged in a flood of tears. This in turn will often bring about reassurance and comfort, whereas the initial anger, which may well have been very deserving, was met with deep hostility and rejection. The process of contraction and holding is still there. On the surface she becomes passive and compliant, but she develops a mean, spiteful streak that is sneaky and furtive. Again, this form of defense is by no means confined to girls, and I have seen plenty of boys who shrink away from natural aggression with great shows of distress, while happily indulging in bouts of venomous spite.

Armoring in Babies and Infants

Children express their emotions very freely, discharging tension and regaining their equilibrium again quickly, until their capacity to do so is disturbed. The primary factor in this disturbance is their relationship with their parents, but other external factors such as friends, neighbors, relatives, and schooling, also have an influence. Earliest eye contact between mother and child has a deep impact. The newborn feels safe and relaxed looking up into eyes that glow softly with love. But a hateful, rejecting look will make the child contract and shrink away from this unwelcoming world. It may leave children with the deeply embedded feeling that the world is an unsafe place in which they are not wanted and do not belong.

An infant discovers his or her genitals. There is a lovely tingling feeling that concentrates there. S/he explores it. Hands touch. Fingers stroke. It makes the child feel warm and happy inside. Suddenly there is somebody there. Somebody big. Angry eyes. Angry voice. Nose wrinkled in disgust.

"Don't do that—it's dirty!" The great anger invades the pleasurable world of the child, and it turns to fear. The child becomes conscious of what s/he is doing. Everything was right, but now everything is wrong. It must be wrong. The startled child freezes. Holds breath. Tightens muscles. Stiffens. That deadens the feeling. It deadens the fear.

The next time the child feels those pleasurable sensations in the genitals, s/he will contract against them, drawing back the pelvis and squeezing thighs tightly together to kill the feeling. The child will feel anxious. Hold breath. Bite lip. Stiffen. The same scenario anticipated. Ingrained. It has become part of who the child is. Soon she or he will not even be conscious of it.

If the invading adult was a neighbor, or a distant relative, but the parents are supportive of the child, the trauma will have less impact than if the attack came from the parents themselves. There is no comfort at all for children whose parents turn upon them. But if the parents are not the antagonists, and can offer warmth and safety to the child, s/he can release the emotions of the trauma and feel safe with the experience of genital pleasure again. A lot of reassurance is needed, such as, "You see, Mr. Smith was brought up to feel bad about those nice feelings, so he feels bad when anybody else feels them. But you and I know it's silly to feel bad about that lovely feeling, don't we?" Perhaps Mr. Smith, or Aunt Polly, or whoever, can be told to mind their own business in the future as well.

Most of us have some memory of an occasion as a child, when we were full of the wonder of life, or absorbed in some pleasurable activity, and it was suddenly ruined by a harsh reaction from an adult. A friend of mine described how she once discovered what she felt to be the most beautiful flower in the world in her back garden. She felt elated, almost intoxicated by its beauty, and rushed in to tell her mother to come and have a look at it. But her mother just snapped at her, telling her to go away and not be so silly. She felt totally devastated. We remember such things with feelings of sadness and anger. But the deeper traumas we do not remember. They are too overwhelming. We have contracted against feeling them and driven them from our minds.

Shortly after I began working at Summerhill I was chatting with an old acquaintance of mine from London, and I began talking about my new life, describing the kids and the principles by which the school runs. He suddenly became very irritated and snapped, "Well, I was lucky. I had a very happy childhood." The tone of his voice belied his words, as did his posture and physical attitude. His whole body expressed trauma, frozen fear, like that of a small boy helplessly overshadowed by an adult world that was disapproving and condemning. He was tight-jawed, with a grimace of a smile, and his shoulders were permanently drawn up, as if someone were about to slap the back of his head. His breathing was shallow, and his voice inexpressive and monotonous. He avoided eye contact when he or anyone else became emotional, and his eyes had a wide-open, staring quality, expressive of fear. They darted anxiously from side to side as he spoke. The way he moved was stiff and mechanical, without a hint of spontaneity. He dismissed my descriptions of Summerhill life with a haughty and contemptuous sneer.

The emotionally deadened adult finds it difficult to tolerate the emotional liveliness of children. In so far as his own emotional life has been crushed, he will not comprehend the validity or reality of those emotions in others. He will just feel his own inner emptiness, and attribute the emotional expression of the child to "acting up," or some other negative quality. In other instances the child's strong expressions may provoke a feeling of deep anxiety. This may happen when the adult has some awareness of these emotions in himself, but has difficulty expressing them. Because of these emotional blocks, parents tend to create similar or related problems in the lives of their own children. None of us are completely free of this process. I have found such limitations in myself, particularly in my relationship with Eva. Her strong shows of anger have sometimes touched an underlying anxiety in me, and her capacity to shift from anger to sheer bliss in seconds has often left me feeling bereft and resentful. Although some of this can be put down to present-day stresses and strains, I am aware also that there is something from my own early days that makes this difficult for me. The best I can do is try to be aware of when I am being irrational and find other ways of dealing with it than taking it out on Eva. I am also lucky that Gunn and I are often able to spot these irrational elements in each other, and act upon them before they become too much of a problem. It can be quite painful to recognize these things in ourselves, though.

Wilhelm Reich

Wilhelm Reich was the first to make the connection between emotional trauma and the contraction of the body. He was a close friend of Neill's from 1937, when they met in Norway, until Reich's death in 1957. Neill found in Reich's work a deeper understanding of the processes he was observing at Summerhill, while Reich regarded Summerhill as a living example of his own ideas about the nature of children.

Reich was an psychoanalyst, a student of Freud, although he later split with the psychoanalytic movement, as his insistence on tackling social issues, such as homelessness, abortion, contraception, and the status of women, as well as his studies of sexuality, rankled with the conservative psychoanalysts. His analytic work too was very controversial. During his analysis of patients Reich noticed that while some people's conditions improved as unconscious memories began to surface, others could relate endless traumas from the past and make no progress at all. If psychoanalytic theory was correct, and the uncovering of unconscious material itself would cure patients of their neuroses, then all these people should be getting better. With this problem in mind, Reich began to observe that it was those patients who re-experienced the emotions connected with the memory who made progress, and it was this emotional discharge, not the remembering, that made all the difference.

He also noticed that following such emotional release, not only did the patients improve psychologically, but they also showed physiological change. Rigid postures relaxed. Voices lost their affectation. Movement became less wooden. Skin and muscle tone improved. Eye contact was more lively and expressive. Respiration deepened. The whole body became more mobile. Patients also reported pleasurable sensations in their bodies that they had never felt before, or at least did not remember feeling. These were especially strong in the region of the pelvis and in the genitals, although these sensations were often interspersed with bouts of intense anxiety.

While making these observations Reich also began to change his therapeutic techniques. Abandoning the passive role of the psychoanalyst he took a more confrontational approach, directing his attention to making the patients aware of how they resisted the expression of certain emotions by adopting more artificial and superficial ways of life. He called this "character armor," as it is expressed in the whole character of the person, not just in isolated symptoms, and its function is, quite literally, to "armor" the individual, both from hostility and disapproval in the outside world, and from anxiety-laden impulses within. This armor reveals itself in many ways, for example, exaggerated politeness, macho swagger, contemptuous indifference, over-intellectualization, false modesty, and fawning insincerity. The pattern of armoring depends on many factors, such as which emotions are being stifled, the form in which the repression has been experienced, and at which stages of childhood the trauma was absorbed.

As Reich became more aware of the physiological changes his patients were experiencing during this character analysis, he began to work directly on the chronic contractions of the musculature, as well as on the "character" of the patient. This often released a great deal of held-back emotion.

Reich called this the "muscular armor." Armoring, then, exists simultaneously in the psyche and in the body as the twin expressions of a unitary process.

Neill noted that many of his most troublesome and hateful pupils had "stiff stomachs." I have observed the same thing, and come to recognize that a rigid abdomen in a newcomer is a sure sign of trouble to come. But armoring is much more complex and varied than just stiff stomachs. Many layers of emotion are held, with muscle groups throughout the body working functionally to prevent their expression. When the armor is loosened the most meek, passive person may begin to express murderous hate, or a tough know-it-all may reveal a deeply rooted vulnerability. But as Reich discovered, at the core of all these conflicting emotions we have an inborn capacity to live full, happy lives. He saw great changes in the attitudes of his patients. As hateful, spiteful feelings subsided, his patients demonstrated an instinctive sense of decency and sociability and became able to regulate their own needs quite amicably without recourse to rigid codes of conduct and externally imposed morality.

This obviously echoes our experience with children at Summerhill. We see in them a natural inclination to re-establish this self-regulating core, once the inhibitions on their emotional lives have been removed. The degree to which any individual child is able to do so varies enormously, depending on the depth of trauma he or she experienced before arriving, and what his or her relationship with home is like. But every child seems to make some movement in this direction, however small.

In an earlier chapter I described a boy wanting a baby bottle after seeing Zoë feed a young goat with one. Over the next couple of weeks lots of kids began to demand baby bottles. I ended up going down to the local chemist almost every day, much to the bewilderment of the shop assistants, who exchanged questioning looks, but never asked me directly what I was doing with all the bottles. Visitors to our meetings at this time were rather taken aback to see even big, hulking sixteen-year-olds sitting around blissfully sucking away on their baby bottles. Although this became a bit of a trend at that time, there are still often a handful of San and House Kids who take great pleasure using baby bottles.

Clearly the enjoyment of sucking is an infantile need, and in so far as it has not been satisfied early in life it will reassert itself later in various guises. The breast is not just a source of nutrition for the infant, but also provides pleasure and reassurance. The mouth at this stage is a highly erogenous area. Later in life the genitals will take over as the primary source of sexual pleasure. This shift in focus of erotic excitement, which occurs in infancy, is often disturbed in modern society. Negative maternal emotions during breastfeeding, premature weaning, timetable feeding, compulsive toilet training, parental disgust over natural body functions, and negative attitudes towards masturbation may all serve to frustrate natural development. Where needs have been unsatisfied they may remain fixated at that point. Hence eating is felt by many people to be more satisfactory than sex. This is particularly true of sweet things, which, with their similarity to the sweetness of breast milk, are eaten for comfort. Also, in the face of negative adult attitudes, sexual excitement may be diverted from its natural flow towards the genitals and become fixated at the anus. Anal eroticism arises in response to genital guilt and parental over-concern about bowel movements, which expresses itself in enforced toilet training, often accompanied with bribes, threats, and nervous fussiness. Oral and anal eroticism also tend to meet adult disapproval, but having nowhere else to go, become secret pleasures. When children feel free to express themselves these attitudes and impulses begin to surface.

It is hard to imagine an older child enjoying a baby bottle in the conventional school environment. He or she would be called a baby, ridiculed, and teased. I have heard very little comment on the matter at Summerhill. The kids seem quite happy to accept another kid's having a baby bottle. This level of acceptance I can only attribute to the kids feeling accepted themselves. Schooling in general does little to improve, or even address, the emotional lives of children. It is a hardening process, reinforcing what armor kids already have.

The atmosphere of acceptance can also touch the adults at Summerhill. Many express previously inhibited feelings and find that they can be more fully themselves than they had been before. I experienced this myself. I had always found it difficult to express anger, feeling acutely anxious afterwards if it ever broke through. This led to an overall diminishing of my ability to push for what I wanted in life. An interest in eastern religion had enabled me to convince myself that I was going with the flow of things, where in reality I was left most of the time with a brooding sense of resentment and helplessness. As a child I had been afraid of adult anger. It seemed unpredictable and dangerous to me. So, I told myself, after getting the job at Summerhill, I would be careful not to get angry with any of the kids. It did not last long though.

There was one small boy who was obsessed with trying to jab me in the genitals. One day he jabbed me particularly hard, and I flared up with anger, shouting at him to stop doing that. Far from being scared, for the next few days the kids made a game out of coming up to me, pulling the most extreme grimaces and announcing, "That's what you look like when you're in a moody." It made me realize then that kids are not scared of anger, only of the way in which adults use it. My anger was neither the malicious or authoritarian anger that many adults use to overwhelm kids, but a clearly expressed reaction to being hurt. If the kids weren't scared though, I was devastated. As they gleefully did their impressions of me "in a moody" I felt as if I had revealed to them something awful in me. It was the same anxiety I always felt after anger broke through.

Gradually, though, I realized that although the kids were making fun of me, there was also something accepting about the way they did it. They were ready to show these sides of themselves to me, and to each other, so why shouldn't I? It was as if they were saying, "Look, you're just like the rest of us really, don't be so high and mighty." Slowly I found it easier to trust my anger and to express it clearly when provoked, without feeling so miserable afterwards.

Anger is often regarded as a very negative emotion. It is here that the dynamic role of armoring gives us a deeper insight into the way we express and perceive emotion. If the self-regulating core of our being is not disturbed in infancy and childhood, our responses to the world are direct and rational. As emotion is evoked it is discharged, maintaining a balanced emotional equilibrium. However, when armoring sets in due to parental and societal influences, emotion is held back and the emotional equilibrium is thrown into disarray. In so far as we have been unable to release the tension of a frustration or trauma, it becomes internalized and prevents us from returning to the relaxed flexibility we felt before.

This is not to say that any outburst of emotion is a sign that all is well. Far from it. Emotion may often break through in inappropriate and irrational ways. But this is a function of the armor, which diverts the energy of the emotion from its original course, either sublimating it into more unnatural expressions or allowing it to build up so that every now and then it breaks through in a harsh and distorted manner. Emotional health is not just a matter of expression, but of integration; a balanced emotional equilibrium.

My experience with the kids made me feel more relaxed about myself, but it only went so far. This prompted me to seek help, and I started to see a therapist practicing Reich's Orgone Therapy.* The sense of acceptance that I felt from the kids is similar, I imagine, to what the kids themselves feel at Summerhill. I need the skills of a well-trained therapist to

---

* Reich described a specific biological energy that he named "orgone," which is synonymous with the concept of a life energy as described in other cultures, such as "ki" in Japan, "chi" in China, or "prana" in India.

take me that bit further along the line I want to go, but children are not so stuck in their ways. Their armoring is generally more flexible than that of adults, and they have a greater capacity to let go and adapt to new situations. The soft, responsive self-regulating core of their nature re-asserts itself when the emotional climate is right.

This isn't to say that everyone who goes to Summerhill will turn out to be completely well balanced and un-neurotic. Even though children are very adaptable, our basic emotional structure is fairly much fixed by the age of four or five. From then on the way we experience and deal with life will, to a large degree, depend on the manner in which we have had to armor ourselves in these first few years. But certainly the armor softens and becomes more mobile when children are in an environment where they are able to express themselves and feel accepted, as opposed to the inhibiting environment of conventional schooling and adult-oriented homes, which serve only to build upon whatever armoring already exists.

Expansion and Contraction

Adolescence is another critical time in the life of the growing child. With a maturing of the sexual impulse and the increasing urgency for genital gratification, there is another strong push from within to express this mounting sexual excitement. If this increase in highly charged excitement is denied expression, it leads to a further hardening of the armor in response to the extra strain put on it. This accounts for much of the chaotic behavior seen in adolescents; mood swings, clumsiness, day dreaming, listlessness, depression, resentment, rebelliousness, bellicosity, delinquency. The adolescent literally expands out to the world, glowing with excitement. But meeting both the inhibitions of an uncomprehending outer world and the inner inhibitions of the already established armor, s/he contracts against this high sexual charge. What otherwise might be experienced as a natural pattern of tension-charge-discharge-relaxation* becomes a chaotic battleground of conflicting emotions, in which adolescents feel themselves to be pulled one way and then pushed another. After a few years of this turmoil the young person usually becomes emotionally resigned and the armor is deeply rooted as a limited repertoire of fixed attitudes and expressions. Childhood liveliness and spontaneity have given way to a more dull and deadened existence.

This is not a question of an orgasm a day will keep the doctor away, though. It is not a matter of sexual experience or performance. In fact, sexual sophistication has gone a long way in replacing sexual morality as a way of avoiding the emotional depths of sexuality. It is the capacity to feel deeply that is diminished by our armoring. It is diminished in infancy, and then again when it re-asserts itself in adolescence. The joyful, loving impulse of the body that carries us toward the gratification of our deepest emotional needs is reduced to a temptation to be avoided, an itch to be scratched, or a pressure to be relieved.

It is this strengthening of the armor in adolescence that makes it so much more difficult for adults to remain in contact with their original self-regulatory nature. Between infancy and adolescence, although many basic traits are already fixed, children are still usually much more in touch with their feelings than adults are. This allows them to discharge much of their tension spontaneously in uninhibited fantasy and play, as well as in strong expressions of emotion. So by the time most Summerhill kids reach adolescence they are far better equipped emotionally to deal with the increase of sexual excitement, and to avoid succumbing to further armor-

---

* Reich called this four-beat pattern of tension-charge-discharge-relaxation the "orgasm formula" as he found the orgasm to be the major release reflex for excitement that has not been otherwise discharged. The release of pent-up excitement proved fundamental to the overall well-being of the organism. Indeed, the re-establishment of this natural biological pulsation became the goal of Reich's therapy.

ing, than they would be if their emotional lives had been restricted by the regulations of "good" behavior that conventional schooling expects of its children. While most schools experience adolescence as being quite a disruptive period, the adolescents at Summerhill are its most stabilizing influence.

Although, as Neill pointed out, it was the freedom, and not his private lessons in particular, that improved the lives of the children, a little bit of emotional first aid can help now and then when one of the kids is feeling a bit stuck. Nobody does regular P.L.s as such these days, but occasionally Zoë or one of the staff may take one of the kids aside for a little chat to see how they are doing or give them a new perspective on a problem they might be experiencing. A little while back a couple of Japanese boys were feeling rather down after being given a hard time in a special meeting. The meeting had been called because they had been disregarding many of the laws for most of the term and the community was fed up with them. Noticing their dejected looks, Zoë wandered over to lighten their mood a little, and let them know that although the meeting was tough on them it didn't mean that people wouldn't like them anymore. Later I met one of these boys in the corridor. He beamed smiles at me.

"Zoë is not like a Japanese headmistress, you know," he told me. "She likes things that kids like. She likes having fun—and sweets." He waved a sweet that Zoë had given him under my nose. "Zoë is not like a Japanese headmistress. I didn't know that."

Another time a couple of our more troublesome boys set fire to a post box downtown. The police apprehended them, and when they were returned to school a special meeting was called. The community is especially sensitive to trouble that occurs downtown, and gave the two boys a real grilling. Afterwards they looked very edgy. I felt rather sorry for them. They had already been given a hard time by the police, and now by the meeting. I tracked them down to their room, and stuck my head around the door.

"Go away," I was told belligerently.

"I just wondered if you'd like come out to the woods with me," I said. "I thought we could build a fire out there." They brightened instantly, and we set off to the woods, where we made a small fire and roasted some marshmallows. The police were due to come and interview them again, and just as we were coming back out of the woods a police car was drawing up outside the school.

"We've just been in the woods making a fire with Matthew," one of the boys announced enthusiastically to the policeman, as he climbed out of the car. I smiled weakly. Summerhill logic isn't always easy to explain to outsiders.

Neill would sometimes reward children for stealing. His view was that, in many cases, children became compulsive thieves because no one had ever given to them freely. So by rewarding them, they felt loved and approved of and the compulsion to steal disappeared. Such "tricks" cannot be applied systematically. It is the underlying emotion that is being addressed, not the "crime," and the adult has to be able to sense this. Neill noted that his American pupils who populated the school in the sixties were too sophisticated and aware of psychology for such gestures to have much effect. We haven't had many American kids in the past few years, but of the few we have had the same has been largely true.

In my first term a bag of peanuts was stolen from my room. It was not difficult to work out who had stolen it—a group of girls in the room next to mine. Fresh to Summerhill and ready to apply my "Neillian psychology," I presented them with another bag of peanuts the following day. Most of the girls seemed suitably bewildered by my gift, but as I left the room I heard one of the girls, an American newcomer, proclaim, "Oooh, it's just like the book."

I can only think of a few times when I have given rewards like this, but it can sometimes help in shifting a mood. One of the House Kids, a small Japanese boy, was riding round and round in circles on his bike looking very depressed. I asked one of his friends what was wrong with him. It turned out that he was feeling very guilty on two counts. The first was that he had spent most of the afternoon hiding from his violin teacher. His mother had arranged for an outside tutor to come into the school and give him special lessons, which he hated, but felt pressured to attend. The second was because he had accidentally given me a black eye while play-fighting with me the evening before. Several times I had told him not to worry about it, that I realized it was an accident, but he still felt bad about it. Remembering those awful moments of paralyzing guilt with which my own childhood was punctuated, I wandered over to him and thrust a fifty-pence piece in his hand.

"That's for not going to your violin lessons," I told him. I pushed another fifty pence into his palm. "That's for giving me a black eye." The cloud lifted and his face opened. I could never side with the moralist who believes that unhappiness and suffering make children into better people.

In this instance the reward was a concrete symbol of approval, and broke the spell of guilt, which verbal reassurance had failed to do. Ironically rewards for "good behavior" often serve to negate this deep sense of feeling approved of. The child who has acted out of genuine desire and then is rewarded feels his or her achievement has been usurped. A price has been put on the deed. What was pleasurable and selfless becomes self-conscious and confused with the wider arena of reward and punishment by which the adult world manipulates the world of children. In this context, punishment and reward are just different sides of the same coin. If the child is acting insincerely just to win the adult's approval, then that insincerity is reinforced, and the child's feelings of hypocrisy and guilt are intensified. Many kids when they first come to Summerhill are stuck in this mode of relating to adults. They do and say what they think is expected of them until they realize that the adults do not deal in this currency. Only then do they begin to be themselves.

Unrepressed, flying high, and expanding out to the world with excitement and energy. *[Photo by Tomo Usuada.]*

Where there is emotional inhibition there is usually guilt, and many children's lives are riddled with guilt. Guilt is an emanation of the armor, arising from the tension between the impulse to express a prohibited emotion and the internalized taboo that prevents its expression. Armoring may also arise from expressing the tabooed feeling and then contracting with anxiety. This is why guilt feels so paralyzing; it is the subjective sensation of emotional immobility. Sadly, many adults believe that instilling a sense of guilt, and playing on it, is the way to teach children right from wrong. But it only teaches compliance and self-hatred. Right and wrong are just the codified abstractions of compulsive morality—they have nothing to do with real human needs or feelings. Nor did genuine love or altruism ever grow out of fear and self-loathing. The need for these moralistic manacles has only ever arisen when the primary capacity for sociability and self-regulation was nullified in the first place, and harsh secondary expressions have begun to break through. Even then, it is only an ignorance of the armoring process, and its underlying emotional strata, that have made it necessary to govern human life by fear, rather than love.

The confusing of superficial compliance with love and approval makes it very difficult for most children to admit they are angry with their parents. They feel that they are in the wrong for having these feelings, that they are somehow betraying their parents. I have often had to explain to a distressed child that such feelings are quite natural, and that it doesn't mean you don't love somebody just because you feel angry with them.

One evening after lights out, a few days before the end of term, I heard the sound of crying coming from one of the bedrooms. I opened the door a little and looked in. A small figure was sitting up in bed sniffling. It was the Japanese boy whose mother had arranged violin lessons for him. I went over and sat on the edge of the bed.

"What's wrong?" I asked.

He buried his head in my chest, and sobbed silently. I held him for awhile and let him cry. When I asked him again what was wrong he told me that his mother, who was a teacher in Japan, had set him homework to do during the term and threatened not to let him return to Summerhill if he didn't do it. Like any other lively child of his age faced with the excitement of playing with friends all day, he had put off doing this work until another day, and now it was too late. I asked him how he felt about his mother's threat.

"I feel bad," he said between sobs.

"What do you feel like saying to your mum when she says these things to you?" I asked.

"I don't know," he replied, looking away.

I picked up a pillow. "Okay," I said. "Let's pretend this is your mum. Now you can say anything you want to her, all right?" He nodded. "Right...she's telling you that you've got to do your homework, and if you don't she'll take you away from Summerhill, away from all your friends. What are you going to tell her? Here she goes—'yap, yap, yap, yap, yap, yap, yap, yap, yap, yap, yap, yap...'"

Biting his lip he glanced up at the pillow. "Shut up," he mumbled.

"She can't hear you," I said. "She's too busy yapping."

"Shut up," he said a little louder.

"Still can't hear."

Squaring up to the pillow and fixing his eyes on it, he shouted at it to shut up and swung his fist at it. The pillow let out a high-pitched squeal and tumbled backwards. Then it was back again. "'Yap, yap, yap, yap, yap, yap, yap, yap, yap, yap, yap.'" He pummeled it with his fists until it finally shut up. Beforehand he had looked dejected and defeated. Now his eyes shone, and a mischievous grin replaced the bitten lip.

The moralist will be horrified by such things, and accuse me of encouraging children to hate their parents. But all I have done is encourage what is already there to express itself. The discharge of anger and the approval that the child feels does not build on tension, but relieves it. It clears the air. The relationship between kids and their parents usually improves, not worsens after such feelings are safely vented. From the standpoint of the moralist such feelings are simply "bad," and so the child should be trained to deny them, or he or she will become "bad" too. But knowledge of armoring and the capacity for self-regulation in children leads us to a different conclusion. Anger is neither "good" nor "bad," it is either there or not there. If it is there, it is better that it comes out in a safe and supportive environment than be turned back in on itself where it will fester and eat its way deeper into the life of the child.

After a long holiday I am often surprised at how physically small many of the kids are. My memory of them from the term before is of being much bigger. But this impression is not completely false. What I am remembering is the personality of the child, and when children are free to express themselves they truly have big personalities. When I first see them again at the beginning of a new term it is after a break in our interaction, so my first impression is of physical stature only. They soon regain their emotional largeness again, though. Armoring holds us back from living fully. It keeps us little. We shrink from life, instead of expanding out to it. Children radiate personality until they are forced to contract against it and stiffen against their own nature. Most adults have never really grown up—they have been ground down. The cultivation of bad conscience in children makes emotional bonsai of them. Children reach out for life, love, and happiness, like the sapling that stretches out to the sun. It is in their nature to do so. This reaching out only becomes a "breaking out" when there is something to break out of.

The Sexual
Continuum

It is said that from the mouths of babes and sucklings comes great wisdom. But this is only a partial truth. It could equally well be said from the mouths of babes and sucklings comes the same old nonsense that their parents spout. Before I came to Summerhill I had a flat in South London. My bedroom window looked down on a raised area of tarmac and cracked concrete where the neighborhood kids played. Returning home one evening I nodded to two small boys, whom I vaguely knew, as they wandered around this miniature plateau scuffing their feet and looking bored.

"My little brother just let his willy hang out," said the older boy, with the sly and sneaky look of one who enjoys telling tales. "That's dirty, isn't it?"

"No," I answered, "a bit draughty maybe, but there's nothing dirty about it."

Reflecting on this exchange later on, I thought it sad that here was yet another generation being brought up to believe their genitals were dirty, that there was something wrong in taking pleasure or showing an interest in their own bodies. The older boy could only have been five or six, yet already he had adopted this anxiety about sexuality. It pains me to look at fifteen-month-old Eva, and to know that one day she will have to encounter this craziness in the wider world. For the moment she is blissfully ignorant of such unhealthy attitudes. Her body is soft and mobile. The notion that any part of her body or its pleasurable sensations are "dirty" or undesirable has not invaded her consciousness yet. Nor would such self-loathing occur naturally. But she will meet such contempt one day, and it will be a shock to her, however much Gunn and I try to protect her from it.

Most, if not all, children inherit some sexual anxiety, be it from parents, peers, or from the distorted attitudes of society at large. Far from being approved of, the sexual expression of children and adolescents is met with suspicion, embarrassment, incomprehension, anger, jealousy, and fear. Where approval does seem to be forthcoming it is often inappropriately thrust upon children as an ideological expectation, instead of their sexuality being allowed to develop naturally in its own time. Left to their own devices children and adolescents are naturally sexually interested in and active with each other.

Maybe I am stating the obvious here, but I seem to meet so many people who become blankly uncomprehending when "childhood" and "sexuality" are mentioned in the same sentence. It is the sort of expression I would expect if I presented someone with baked beans and jelly on the same plate—the expression that somehow these don't go together.

Then there is the so-called "latency period," as postulated by Freud, and still prevalent in psychoanalytic and child development theory. The latency period is presumed to exist between infancy and puberty, as a time in which children are sexually disinterested and inactive. That a lull does occur about this time in children's sexuality is probably generally true, but only within cultures where there is a certain amount of sexual anxiety.

In societies where children's sexuality is naturally approved of by the community as a whole, such as the Muria of India and the Trobriand Islanders, the latency period does not make an appearance, and the children remain joyfully sexual throughout. Although these societies are the exception to the rule as far as twentieth century "civilization" goes, they are well documented,* which begs the question as to why, if the latency period is inherent in human nature, does it not occur universally. My experience of Summerhill also reflects the observations by anthropologists, in that the latency period is less prominent than in society at large.

Even infantile sexuality, despite the very obvious sexual expressions of infants, is very often denied. One father I know found it shocking that his young son might have sexual feelings and did not think it even possible for the boy to experience an erection. That this child had managed to hide or deny this side of himself so well reflects the anxiety that he must have felt in his father's presence.

Although adolescent sexuality is not denied in content, its expression is largely disapproved of. The feelings are considered natural, but it is not usually considered appropriate to act on them. It is like expecting a rose bush to bud one year, but not bloom until the next. Nature has its own rhythms, which we cannot expect to conform to our cranky notions without expecting problems.

Adolescent sexuality is not the taboo subject it used to be. So even though we cannot openly allow our adolescent boys and girls under sixteen to sleep together at Summerhill, we can acknowledge that, like adolescents everywhere, they do have sexual relationships. This change in societal attitudes towards adolescent sexuality has partly been prompted by the number of teenage pregnancies that have occurred over the past few decades, resulting in many quarters in a begrudging acceptance of a problem that will not go away, rather than a genuine enlightenment and approval of adolescent sexuality. (At which point it is interesting to note that in seventy five

---

* Bronislaw Malinowski. *The Sexual Life of Savages*, Routledge & Keegan Paul, London, 1929. Verrier Elwin. *The Muria and Their Ghotul*, Oxford University Press, Bombay, 1942.

years of sex approval and co-educational boarding Summerhill has not yet had a single pregnancy among its pupils.)

The expected role of the educator in the overall scheme of things seems to be to make sure that the students are not left to their own devices, but kept in a permanent state of distraction. Children are kept busy learning about life from books, while their own life impulses are largely put on hold. Most schools forbid physical expressions of affection or petting between the sexes. School uniforms, which are forced on older children in particular, are designed to detract from any hint of sensuality. Instead, at a time in life when most young animals are preening themselves and strutting around displaying the bright colors of their unfolding youth, the young Anglo-Saxon Homo sapiens is reduced to shades of gray anonymity. These imposed regulations further reinforce the feeling that sexuality is something dirty, naughty, or embarrassing.

Sexual anxiety becomes very deeply rooted in some children. One eleven-year-old boy told me how, when he had a bath, the warm water gave him an erection. He would then be tempted to masturbate, but when he fondled his penis he began to feel "dizzy," and stopped. This anxiety was reflected in his personality as a whole. He shrank from situations that excited him. He could not expand out to life around him. (It could be said he had a flaccid personality.) His mannerisms were tense and fearful.

Sexuality is often talked about as if it were a sphere of being separate from the rest of our life. Such segregation is mystical and unfounded. Sexuality is an expression of the living process, and in so far as it is disturbed the whole living process is disturbed. The way we think, feel, and function in our everyday lives are all disturbed if our sexuality is disturbed, and vice versa. These are all functions of a unitary living process, not separate items all operating independently in their own particular realm. Sexual energy and life energy are one and the same.

It is no wonder that children develop mystical attitudes towards sexuality, shrouded as it is in the other-worldliness of the unspoken and "adults only." Some while ago I was leafing through a popular children's version of Rudyard Kipling's *The Jungle Book*. The young Mowgli was pictured romping naked through the jungle, but in every illustration his genitals were discretely hidden by a conveniently placed branch, or penciled out with a hazy shadow. The illustrator could not have found a more effective way of drawing attention to the genitals, while at the same time removing them from the wholeness of the person and endowing them with the quality of something that should not be acknowledged, and yet was mysteriously enticing.

Children become caught in this double bind that we present to them. Their own nature becomes something sneaky to snigger about behind the backs of adults. It is ironic that while adults often won't talk openly about sexual feelings in front of children because they think children can't handle such things, children often behave the same way towards adults for the same reasons. Children feel whole and at one with themselves until they begin to sense that certain feelings and expressions are not approved of. Then they begin to feel bad about themselves and the softness and sensuality of their own nature becomes a source of anxiety to them. The simple straightforwardness of the child is warped—literally, as the pelvis is pulled back and muscles tighten to diminish excitement in the genitals. Guileless spontaneity recedes, a general evasiveness in the presence of adults appearing in its place. This evasiveness will later become an evasiveness of all deep feeling and express itself in all areas of life. Life is sexual. Sexuality is the motivating force around which the living in nature organizes itself, from the melodious streaming of a blackbird's throat to the up-river surge of the salmon, from the pollen-laden work of the bumblebee to the jousting between stags. Beyond our cultural pretensions, our own arts and endeavors are not so different.

Many influences act upon children to reinforce a negative attitude towards pleasurable sexual feelings, and gradually undermine children's ease with themselves. It is a damaging process that is not acknowledged. This is not surprising, as the whole name of the game is evasiveness, with the child playing a participating role by armoring against his or her own feelings, and presenting to the adult world the face that world wants to see. Although children initially feel this to be alien to their own nature, it soon becomes incorporated into their sense of who they are, so that by the time we become adults we do not even recognize this warping, either in ourselves or in children as we inflict it upon them. When feeling good about oneself has become a matter of external approval, instead of inner ease and satisfaction, it inevitably becomes passed on down through the generations, as each generation is unable to feel or empathize with the full emotional life of its as-yet unspoiled young.

Just as sexuality does not exist in isolation, so the approval of sexuality is not an isolated aspect of Summerhill life, but comes of its own accord with the approval of the child as a whole. The freedom to be sexual is also the freedom to not attend lessons, to play all day, to wear and say what you like, to have a voice in the school meetings. Sexual expression is just part of the children being more of who they really are. Nothing is pushed or imposed on them, but the environment is one in which the children may develop as they will without interference.

Young children coming into Summerhill sense the relaxed attitude towards sexuality. It is something talked about openly by both adults and children, not in a contrived or intrusive way, but as a normal part of our lives. When the older boys and girls form relationships they are said to be "paired up." This is given a certain status in the community, and whether it lasts only a day or for years, it is respected as a special bond. These couples express their tenderness openly, wandering around arm in arm, kissing and cuddling without embarrassment or self-consciousness. Adult couples are also open in their affections.

In the summer term the school's outdoor swimming pool is open and both adults and children swim without clothes. There is no pressure to do so, but it is a choice, and one that many people enjoy. Last summer I particularly remember one boy, his face beaming, after swimming naked for the first time.

"That was really lovely," he cried, hopping from one foot to another. "It feels so free!" For children, who will already have been bombarded by many media images of or allusions to nakedness, this will often be their first experience of being naked themselves around other people and of being around people they know who are naked. In this context nakedness is secondary to the personalities of the other people, as opposed to being the major focus of attention. People's bodies are expressions of who they are, not of abstract and impersonal appetites. Sexuality does not exist in fragmented isolation, but is integrated into the wider picture of social life.

Childhood Sexuality

The youngest kids, the San Kids, who are aged mostly between seven and ten, live in rooms in which the sexes are mixed. At this age the boys and girls are generally happy to play together with little or no discrimination, although there may be some who strongly prefer the company of their own sex. The bathrooms have locks on them, so that anyone who wants to change their clothes or bathe in privacy can do so, but others prefer to turn bath time into playtime, hopping between baths and splashing each other.

Love affairs among the San Kids are expressed fairly openly. They may play at being paired up in emulation of the older kids, and give each other gifts as tokens of their adoration, but this is mainly done within the confines of their own age group, and not expressed in the wider community as with the older kids. There is a certain shyness and vulnerability that these younger kids have about their feelings, and it only takes a bit of teasing by one or two of the House Kids for them to clam up. Erotic interests between these kids are lived out in exploring the differences between the sexes both verbally and in sex play, involving looking, touching, and role playing. I only know about this because when they are older they often confide in me about their time in the San. The adults in Summerhill do not snoop and pry into the affairs of the kids. Their privacy is respected.

I remember from my own childhood a love affair when I was about nine years old with a girl in my class. We played together like I would with one of my male friends, but the relationship evoked a strong sensuality and softness in me that I found deeply exciting. I can't remember who issued the challenge of "I'll show you mine if you'll show me yours," but issued it was and I remember disappearing into the bushes at the local park to explore each other's anatomy. These were precious but secretive moments.

Boys together, and girls together, also sometimes explore their sexuality in a mutual admiration of their respective genders. There is much anxiety these days about same-sex sex play. Parents fear that it means their children will become homosexual. But same-sex sex play in itself does not lead to adult homosexuality. If it did there would be more homosexuals in our society than heterosexuals! It only becomes fixed as a homosexual attitude if the child has excessive anxiety around heterosexual feelings, which make same-sex relationships the safer bet. This may be the result of sexual repression or of pushing the child into heterosexual relations before she or he is ready. Even then there are inevitably other factors, such as earlier infantile conflicts and possibly pre-birth predisposition. But sexual experimentation with the same sex is something that many children enjoy and grow out of quite naturally.

As their houseparent, I obviously tend to have more everyday contact with the House Kids than I do with the San Kids. Many kids are too old to be in the San when they first come to Summerhill, and so start their lives in the House. These kids are approximately ten to thirteen years old. Coming in at an older age than the San Kids, they have been in the conventional system for longer and have adopted more of its negative attitudes towards sexuality. Although these attitudes will have been largely formed at home, and at an earlier age, the influence of peers and the insidiously anti-sexual environment of the school should not be underestimated. In the House the distance and disdain between the sexes is more apparent than in the San. How much of this is influenced by the influx of new kids at this stage and how much it would happen anyway, I don't know. But I suspect it is relevant.

It is a legal requirement at this age that boys and girls do not share the same bedrooms. But it is also something they want themselves. The House Kids tend to socialize and play largely in same-sex groups, and the boys and girls often treat each other with a certain amount of distaste. But this is mostly of a flippant and humorous nature, and masks a deeper interest. They are much more focused on sexuality as a central issue than the younger kids are. There is a lot of sexual humor. I have heard jokes told that would make a rugby team blush. Humor in children is not the same as humor in adults, though. Children use humor to explore their feelings, to delve into taboo areas and taste forbidden fruit, whereas when adults joke in a similar vein the humor tends to reflect fixed attitudes and a harsh, pornographic contempt of sexuality. Children who are new to the school will sometimes laugh at a joke just because it is "rude," without really understanding why it's meant to be funny. "Rudeness" is an adult concept that wears off in time at Summerhill, and the same child a few terms later will be saying, "That's stupid" to the same joke. When adults say to children something is rude, or they shouldn't tell such jokes, they simply increase its value on the stock market of shock status. Left alone these things fade of their own accord. The older Carriage Kids are a lot less interested in sexual jokes than the House Kids.

Sexuality is also talked about a lot among the House Kids. Masturbation is a common subject. For some new kids it is something they thought only they did, and it is a relief to find that other people do it too. Others have not tried it yet, and their friends explain to them how to do it. They also ask questions of the adults, often personal, intimate questions about the adults' own sexual experiences. Their interest in sex is not just a mechanical one, as is presented in the anatomy and physiology lectures of formal sex education. They are more interested in the sensations and emotions involved. As adults we may choose to answer these questions or tell the kids these are aspects of our lives we would prefer to keep to ourselves. But they are never made to feel that there is anything wrong in asking.

Children may also be guarded about their own sexuality. Some people believe that a "healthy" child is one who is totally open about his or her sexuality, who has no reservations about nudity, who talks about sexual feelings as if talking about the weather, and is always sexually active. That there should be such a thing as natural modesty seems quite appropriate to me. I have seen this in children who are quite at ease with themselves, just as I have known children who are sexually precocious and acting a part they do not feel. Sexuality is the vehicle of our strongest excitement and our most tender feelings. When we surrender to sexual feelings we surrender to the depths of our nature. To turn this over to the public arena is to diminish this intensity and become superficial. Even in those societies in which sexuality is quite naturally approved of there are built-in provisions for privacy and intimacy.

In our own culture, where negative attitudes abound, it is even more logical to be instinctively protective, which should be distinguished from being repressed. While sexuality has a

high profile in society today, it is still laden with anxiety. To
be totally open to this would be foolish. Recently one of the
House boys confided to a friend that he was sweet on one of
the girls. This "friend," a boy who is especially prone to
malicious gossip and taunting others, immediately ran around
telling everyone else. He took particular delight in gathering a
crowd and telling the girl concerned. The girl, to save her own
blushes, was extremely derisive of her admirer, leaving him
feeling totally flattened.

The tail end of this drama was enacted in my room, where
the boy ended up hiding under my bed to escape the jeering
of his "friend" and the other kids he had stirred up with his
virulent excitement. I stepped in at this point and asked the
"friend" why he was making such a big deal about this. He
shrugged. I asked him whether he thought there was anything
wrong in a boy having such feelings for a girl. He shrugged
again and said "no." The jeering had stopped by then. There
was a tangible sense of relief in the room, not only from the
boy who had hidden under the bed, but also from the other
children. Clearly they had felt uncomfortable with what was
happening, but were afraid that if they did not participate they
might themselves become targets.

Despite these difficulties, the children do express their
sexual interest in each other. This can involve rather wild
larking around, with lots of pushing, grabbing, and contemptuous jeering. At other times they can be very gentle and
affectionate, snuggling up together in a corner, or grooming
each other and commenting on how nice the other looks.
Sexual play is more of a communal, exploratory affair among
the House-age kids than among the older kids, in whom
relationships become private, serious affairs. At night, after
lights out, a group of girls may sneak into one of the boys'
rooms, or vice versa. This may just be for the thrill of
breaking the bedtime laws, or for a kissing competition, or to
snuggle under the covers with a chosen partner and explore
the warmth and intimacy of such close contact. This "sneaking

out," as it is called, does not have the shameful connotation to it that the word "sneaky" often implies. It is simply a matter of getting past the Beddies Officers without being caught. This is a source of excitement in itself. The kids are quite open about their nocturnal expeditions, especially the girls, and I often get to hear which of the boys is considered to be the "best kisser!"

The incorporation of sexual curiosity into competitions and games allows children to explore their sexual feelings without being too personally vulnerable. Dare games, in which a group of kids take it in turn to dare each other to do something, or "spin the bottle," where a bottle is spun and whoever it points to must perform a deed, become safe avenues for expressing sexual interests. Not all of these tasks will be of a sexual nature, but some inevitably are. These may include, for example, kissing someone for twenty seconds, touching someone's breast or genitals, or taking off an item of clothing. These dares take the responsibility out of the hands of the individual and make them a shared responsibility, which is encapsulated by the rules of the game.

As the children begin to experience puberty their sexual interests intensify. During puberty excitement becomes more focused in the genitals. Until then children have pleasurable genital feelings that come and go, but without such strong peaks. This increased genital excitement begins to build up and a state of high sexual tension is reached. Instead of a gentle ebb and flow of genital feelings they culminate in an intense climax, followed by deep feelings of relief and relaxation. With boys the climax is accompanied by ejaculation. I have a vivid memory as a child of being pleasantly amazed by this new-found intensity while masturbating. I experienced it as a vivid quiver of extreme pleasure that convulsed my whole being, momentarily taking my breath away. The intense orgasm marks the change from childhood to adolescent sexuality. Much of the confusion that surrounds childhood sexuality stems from the notion that because children are not orgasmic in the way that adults are, they are not sexual. However, because children's sexuality does not have such intense peaks does not mean that they do not enjoy sexual feelings.

Around this time they become more interested in their looks and aware of themselves as sexual beings. The girls at this age mature far more quickly than the boys, and their infatuations are often focused more on the older boys than the boys their own age, who are still running around playing with cap guns and water pistols. The older boys have a distant, dreamlike quality to them, over which the girls sigh continuously. The boys may also have similar feelings towards the older girls, and ask for "beddies kisses" and "beddies hugs" from the female Beddies Officers. They will also sometimes cuddle up to one of the Carriage girls in the meeting or on the Carriage Bench, with blissful smiles. For their part, the Carriage Girls are quicker to indulge the House boys and coo over how sweet so-and-so is than the Carriage boys are to acknowledge the House girls. Although flattered by the attention they are getting, the boys usually pretend not to be.

It is these observations of the San and House Kids that have led me to conclude that the "latency period," with its sexual sublimation and disdain of the opposite sex, is largely a manifestation of sexual anxiety, which is generated by parental influences and then compounded by wider social forces.

This is evident by its spontaneous relaxation in the free and approving environment of Summerhill, and by its severity in individual children, such as the boy in the bath, who articulate their anxiety very clearly and whose overall emotional expressiveness is severely diminished. The latency period is also more noticeable in children from strongly repressive cultures, such as Japan. (This is discussed further in the next chapter.) What differences we would see in children who grew up with no sexual anxiety at all remains to be seen. We can only refer to our anthropological sources for this, and they indicate an even greater degree of sex play among children of this age. This is also indicated by the fact

The boys and girls are confident and at ease with each other.

(Photo by Matthew Appleton.)

that even in our culture, where sexual anxiety is prevalent, when children feel trusted and approved of as people in their own rights, the urge for sexual contact emerges of its own accord as an expression of an overall more active emotional life.

Adolescent Sexuality

When they are around thirteen the kids move up from the House into the Shack. The Shack Boys and Girls live in different buildings, which are some distance from each other. It was not planned this way, but is a matter of geographical necessity. The Shack acts as a transition between the House and the Carriages, and in many ways the Shack Kids are more like big House Kids. As such, they continue to socialize largely in same-sex groups. By now, though, relationships between the sexes are starting to take on a more private nature. There is more of a tendency to form couples than there is in the House. But these distinctions become clearer in the Carriages.

The Carriage Kids, aged mainly between fourteen and seventeen, are divided into the Boys' Carriages and the Girls' Carriages, which are adjacent to each other. When it is warm outside a lot of social activity centers around the Carriage Bench, which is between the two. The boys and girls socialize together with little differentiation. They are confident and at ease with each other. The veneer of scorn with which they regarded each other in the House has disappeared. Spontaneous displays of affection both between and among the sexes are commonplace. Like teenagers anywhere, they are more clothes-conscious than when they were younger. Music has also taken on a greater social significance. But their tastes in these things are highly individualistic, and although wider fashions and trends have an influence, there is a certain casualness and inner coherence within the Summerhill community that remains untouched by external influences.

My experience of the adolescents at Summerhill is that their attitudes towards sexuality are very sensible and responsible. When difficulties arise in relationships they will usually come and talk to someone about it, maybe an adult or one of their friends. The most common argument for encouraging and enforcing sexual abstinence in adolescents is that although they are biologically ready, they are not mature enough emotionally to handle sexual relationships. If this is the case then it is because they have been kept from developing a mature attitude towards sexuality by the infantile behavior of adults towards their sexual lives throughout. Maturity develops; it does not arrive on our doorstep one day with open arms and a suitcase full of wisdom. From the conversations I have had with Summerhill adolescents, I find them very feeling and caring in their relationships. There are conflicts, tensions, and problems, as with anyone, but they are aired and resolved, with a large number of people available to talk things over with. Their experience is a far cry from that of many adolescents for whom a quick fumble in a dark alley, or while Mum and Dad have gone out for a few hours, is their

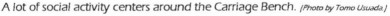

A lot of social activity centers around the Carriage Bench. *(Photo by Tomo Usuada.)*

introduction to their love lives. How is maturity meant to develop in these circumstances? How is anyone meant to evolve the capacity to feel and respond to another person's feelings when they constantly have to look over their shoulder or at the clock?

People often mock the way in which adolescents sometimes shift their affections from week to week, and cite this as a sign of emotional immaturity. An adult who has an immature or Don Juan attitude to relationships is often described as "adolescent." But this is inappropriate and unfair to adolescents. Adolescent love has all the intensity and integrity of adult emotions, and often more so, while the Don Juan is shallow, fickle, and driven by a compulsive need to prove himself sexually. The fact that the object of an adolescent's affections may change quite rapidly does not mean the feelings themselves are not deeply felt. This is part of growing up, of developing maturity, of finding out who we are and what we want from life. It is vivid and real. Such feelings should not be dismissed as fickle.

It is far more appropriate to explore these feelings and discover what we want from life at this age than later in life, when such considerations as children and homes are involved. The so-called mid-life crisis owes much to this. There is a sudden panic and feeling of not having fully explored life's potential. The experience that enables us to make rational decisions throughout our adult lives comes about more surely if we have lived life fully as children and adolescents. Instead, we are mostly thrust into adult life with little idea of who we are or what is important to us. For many people this is still true in middle life. The realization hits people hard. For some it is the signal for a desperate last fling, for others it is just another chapter in an unfulfilled life of resignation.

Relationships between the older kids are instigated by asking the other person if they want to pair up. Being paired up is to be recognized within the community as being in a couple. It has an almost official status to it, like a temporary marriage. While the relationship lasts it is taken seriously by the rest of the community. There is a sense of taboo against encroaching on or deliberately undermining this bond, although it may spontaneously dissolve and a new relationship develop. Such relationships may last weeks, months, even years, or they may last only a day or two. But however long they last they are treated with respect.

This approach to relationships is not something that has been imposed in any way by adults, but has evolved from the kids themselves, and seems to be adopted from one generation to the next as a normal and natural way of conducting a love life. There are no attempts, for example, to impose binding contracts of monogamy, or to introduce polygamous relationships. Nor is there a frenzy of wild promiscuity, which is what many adults seem to expect of adolescents who are not restrained by staunch moral codes and dark foreboding. The kids regulate their relationships in a thoughtful and responsible way.

As it stands, the school is not legally able to allow its adolescent boys and girls to sleep together, and the kids are aware of this. If boys and girls find their way to each other's rooms after bedtime, this is covered by the bedtime laws, which have been worked out in the meeting. If they get caught they can be fined by the Beddies Officers.

The Beddies Officers' role is to make sure everyone is in his or her own room at bedtime, and that people who want to sleep are not disturbed. They do not snoop into people's rooms after lights out, although they may ask to come in if there is a lot of noise. Anyone caught sneaking out may lose their pudding the next day, or be given half an hours' work fine. The severity of the fine usually depends on how noisy the person is, or whether they've already been caught once. But there is never any moral judgment or shame attached. These are practical measures by which the law of the land is upheld and no one is kept awake all night.

Once when I was lecturing in Madrid I was asked a lot of questions about how the kids handle sexual relationships, and I described fairly much what I have written here. Afterwards a man from the audience came up to me and said he was disappointed that the kids were not sexually "free." His perception of sexual freedom was of everyone leaping in and out of bed with each other. I argued that this was compulsive and contactless sex, that is sex without emotional content, and that this was not freedom from repression, but a reaction to it. Summerhill adolescents do not behave in this way towards each other, nor is sex the final goal of each and every relationship. The promotion of sexual gymnastics as sexual freedom does not appeal to them. The man from the audience was not convinced. He shook his head and walked away still disappointed.

Another argument that has cropped up from time to time is that if the kids were really sexually free there would be more homosexuality among the adolescents. I cannot see it myself. There is an openly articulated tolerance among the older kids towards homosexuality and a great deal of physical affection between friends of the same sex. Yet homosexuality does not seem to make an appearance among the older kids, and I can only presume it is not there, not that it is being repressed. On occasions there have been openly homosexual and bisexual teachers on the staff, but the kids seem neither shocked nor particularly interested by the subject. One Japanese boy went through a phase of arriving at parties with a long dress and makeup on. No one blinked an eyelid. He was not homosexual, as might have been assumed in many adolescent cultures, but if he had been I don't think anyone would have thought much of it. I know of at least two ex-Summerhillians who are homosexual and there may well be more, but the notion that more adolescents would experiment with homosexuality if it was not so strongly tabooed does not hold water. This is not to say such experimentation never happens at Summerhill, or that it should not happen, but the fact is that it does not exist as a strong interest among the older kids. Instead it is in environments where sexuality, both heterosexuality and homosexuality, is most strongly tabooed that homosexuality is most prevalent, such as in single-sex boarding schools, where the sexual urge has nowhere else to go.

Adult Attitudes Towards Childhood and Adolescent Sexuality

The authorities are slowly having to acknowledge that adolescents do have sex, whatever the law says. It is a fact that the rising numbers of teenage pregnancies are forcing them to accept. A couple of years back the Minister for Health supported the decision of a health worker to supply thirteen-year-olds with condoms in an area with a high rate of teenage pregnancies. There has also been talk of lowering the age of consent to thirteen. This is a far cry from the total avoidance of facing reality that has existed for so long. But without its being accompanied by genuine approval, there is a danger of legalizing bad conscience, rather than liberating sexual health and happiness.

The condemnation and criminalization of sex between adolescents has made it difficult for them to get much-needed advice and contraception. Even when contraception is obtained, there are far more likely to be accidents resulting in pregnancy when intercourse is hurried and anxious than when it is relaxed and there is time to make sure everything is as it should be. As it is, when things do go wrong adolescents may not know where to turn for advice, at a time when they need to discuss what choices are open to them as soon as possible. How many young girls have had to go through weeks of hell feeling there was no one to talk to? How many could have avoided this by a simple pregnancy test that might have relieved their fears? How many have gone on to injure themselves, sometimes terribly, or even died attempting do-it-yourself abortions? With the dangers now associated with AIDS, an open and responsible approach to adolescent sexuality is an even more urgent necessity.

The emotional maturity and confidence with which Summerhill adolescents handle their sexuality is, I believe, a direct outcome of the approval they felt during the inappropriately named latency period and puberty. For many kids the strong increase in sexual excitement that comes with puberty reawakens old infantile conflicts that might have been largely resolved if the latency years had been ones in which they felt comfortable with expressing their sexuality. This comes out in harsh, pornographic attitudes, excessive shyness with the opposite sex, clumsiness, embarrassment, guilt, anxiety, and social withdrawal. These difficulties are further reinforced by the general distrust that society has towards adolescents and their sexuality, and the specific problem of having no private place in which to make love without fear of intrusion.

Sexual attitudes that are developed in infancy and throughout childhood become more rigidly fixed patterns of perception and interaction during adolescence, either inhibiting or enhancing sexual happiness and emotional well-being in adulthood. The unfolding of sexuality as an undisturbed continuum throughout infancy, childhood, puberty, and adolescence has a fundamental role in this. But it is more than this. It is not just a promise for the future, but the right of children to live their lives as fully and happily as possible now.

The development of a well-balanced sexuality can also be disrupted by adults who push children into sexual expression before it comes naturally to them. (I use the word "naturally" here to mean what comes naturally to the individual child with his or her own life experiences and contacts, not in the broader terms of psycho-sexual development.) This is just another way of showing children that we have lost our trust in them. Children are already surrounded by images of sexuality that are more concerned with meeting external expectations than with internal needs. Anxious parents intensify this dilemma by intruding into their children's natural development. The promotion of premature or inappropriate sexual expressions and the approval of children's natural sexuality are not the same thing. The mother of one eleven-year-old girl sent her daughter pornographic magazines and a vibrator. She was a deeply unhappy child who was unable to be natural with anyone. Her sexuality was a source of great anxiety to her, for it was forced and brought her no pleasure, which in turn made her feel herself to be a terrible failure. A teenage girl, whose parents held very liberal views about sexuality, told me, "I get on really well with them, but I just want to get on with my life without them being around all the time." There is a vast difference between approval and intrusion, between acceptance and control. These former qualities are expressions of a trust in child nature, the latter ones of distrust, and children feel this distinction keenly.

The practice by some parents of giving girls contraceptives on their thirteenth birthday also intrudes into the child's natural development. While the intended message is one of support for the girl's independence and an acknowledgment of her budding sexuality, the effect is to pressure the girl into taking on this role of newly liberated, sexual woman. It does not allow her the chance to feel her own feelings in her own time. The teenager whose independence and sexuality is truly respected by his or her parents will feel at ease to ask for contraceptives when the time is right. The question is, whose needs are being met in these situations? Is it the child's need? If so, why isn't it coming from the child? Or is the parent's need to feel and appear "liberal" and "modern?"

The question of whose needs are really being served also applies to the way in which the problem of child sexual abuse is being tackled. At the heart of this problem there is real human suffering and children who need protection. But in our efforts to come to terms with this as a society we are in danger of creating even more suffering by making the whole issue of childhood sexuality a taboo and returning to the dark ages when any expression of sexual arousal and experimentation by children was regarded as an aberration. Children are sexual beings and will always explore their sexuality with other children. Sometimes they will try something and not like it. Sometimes they may feel anxious because they are enjoying something they have been told is "wrong" or "dirty." Other times they will be blissfully absorbed in their own pleasure. But if we turn sexuality into a no-go area for them they will never learn what they like, or be able to distinguish it from what they don't like. This does not protect children from abuse, it opens them up to it.

A further danger is that if children are not able to find outlets for their sexual interests with each other they are more likely to be drawn into inappropriate or exploitative relationships with older and more powerful people. Children's sexual needs and adults' sexual needs are different, but when both are suffering from chronic sexual frustration these may become confused. Just as adults need to be clear about this, so children who are clear about their own needs will define clearer boundaries themselves, and be more certain in defending them. The protection of children from unwanted sexual advances goes hand in hand with protecting their own sexual integrity. Searching the shelves of various book shops recently I found many books about identifying and dealing with child sexual abuse, but I could find none about identifying and dealing with children's natural sexual needs. There was, as they say, a deafening silence.

Making children anxious about all things sexual does not protect them from abuse either, it only makes it more difficult for them to open up about it when it occurs. When the whole subject of their sexuality is shrouded in silence, children are even more reluctant to tell anyone about something that has happened to them which they feel uncomfortable or unhappy about. Even the language with which children talk about sexuality among themselves is one that they are not used to using with adults. Kids may not know the proper terms for "dick" or "wank," and in society at large these are words that they snigger about out of adult earshot, not part of their dialogue with adults. So they do not even have the language to express their concerns and fears. This silence in sexual matters is not preserving "childhood innocence" it is disempowering children. People who have no voice make the easiest victims.

The vibrancy of life runs deep in children. To undermine this is itself a form of abuse. The issue of child sexual abuse has become the resting place for much adult sexual anxiety that has nothing to do with protecting children. Tight-lipped prudishness and an intolerance of lively child nature are reasserting themselves in a new guise. They have slipped in through the back door, so to speak, of what otherwise would be a very rational and serious concern. Old themes of childhood innocence and its corruption by its own internal dark forces are still being played out. Children are far more dynamic and complex beings than we give them credit for. The desire to paint them as angelic or demonic, and to control them, has always been a reflection of the desire to control our own angels and devils, which in turn were shaped out of the dynamic flux of our own childhood experiences.

We are in danger of creating a whole generation of children who will not know the joys of pleasurable touch, or sexual experimentation. The impulses of life do not go away when they are denied expression, they become something else—an intolerable yearning, anxiety, restlessness, spite, bad dreams, bed wetting—which in turn become further sources of conflict and tension. It is a sick and cynical world that does not recognize the simple joys in life and value their expressions in its children. Is there not also the danger that by denying children what is theirs they will later seek it out as adults from their own children in inappropriate and abusive ways? In short, by negating childhood sexuality today, we may well be helping to create the child abusers of tomorrow.

Children do not need to be protected against life. The task ahead lies in recognizing what belongs to life and what belongs to the distortions that arise when life has to armor against itself. All the do-gooders in the world will only add to the confusion unless they are able to put their own prejudices and anxieties to one side and see children as they really are. The answers to this dilemma do not lie with the myriad of child experts with their various theories, but with children themselves, in learning to listen to them, to decipher their expressions and feel the emotions that are behind them. As long as we force children to hide from us, to contract in our presence, we will never understand them, as we will never fully know them as they really are. We do this in a thousand different ways—in the tone of our voices, in the way we hold ourselves, in our eye contact and use of words—they all communicate something about us and our attitudes. Children pick up on these things, and are aware of them even when we aren't. They know instinctively whether they are being met as people in their own right, or whether this is just another adult who wants to mold them into their own images of what children should be.

10

The Language of Culture, the Language of Life

Ironically, Summerhill is better known in many other countries than it is in Britain. Neill's book *Summerhill* is standard reading for education and psychology students in many foreign colleges and universities, while in Britain it has been dropped from the curriculum of most teacher training colleges, and our school inspectors tell us they are not interested in our "philosophy." In Japan translations of most of Neill's twenty books are available, while none of them are in print in Britain. When giving lectures in universities and public institutions in Spain and Germany, I found myself talking to packed halls. At home Summerhill is occasionally infamous after some newspaper article or documentary has tantalized the public's taste for titillation, but as a source of serious discussion about child nature and educational processes Summerhill is largely ignored. There is something particularly British about tolerating an idea or way of life, while at the same time castrating it with complacency and ridicule.

Against this backdrop of interest from abroad Summerhill life has a strongly international flavor. This is reflected in the many different nationalities that make up the school community, and in the almost constant trickle of visitors, journalists, and film crews who come from abroad to discover Summerhill for themselves. As a member of the community, you soon become used to hearing different languages being spoken around you. In my room the other day I suddenly became aware that there was a conversation on one side of me going on in Japanese and another being conducted in German on the other side. Sometimes it is almost possible to forget that this is actually England.

Although groups of children often continue to speak to each other in their own language, they also learn English quickly and with little or no formal teaching. I was showing a German journalist around a few weeks ago, and she was very surprised to learn from a small group of German children, who spoke to her in fluent English, that they had not been able to speak it when they had arrived a couple of terms earlier. Of course, during this process there are always occasional misunderstandings, such as the Spanish boy who asked me, when I was running the Orange Peel Café, "Do you have penis?" Only after much puzzlement, to the amusement of

A film crew visits Summerhill. *(Photo by Tomo Usuada.)*

all, did he declare, "You know...salted penis."

"Ah, peanuts!" exclaimed everyone at once.

Or the Greek houseparent who, proclaiming the virtues of Greek hospitality, announced, "If you ever come to Greece I will hospitalize you."

I have always been impressed by how quickly new kids become part of the social scene, and are actively involved in playing with peers long before they are able to communicate verbally. An English girl and a German girl, who both started in the San at the beginning of this term, quickly invented their own sign language, and the English girl can now easily interpret to her friend what other people are saying. They are inseparable and play together with complete ease. Children are far more aware of the language of expression and gesture, quality of touch, and tone of voice than adults are. They detect nuances and subtleties that are often lost on adults. We become far more awkward when we cannot use words than children do, feeling ourselves adrift in uncharted seas. We have allowed the word to largely replace these more fluid and contactful expressions of communication, instead of complementing them and expanding on them. We have learned to communicate from a distance, to retain a distance that children bridge spontaneously and with a certainty we lack. They do not fear the intimacy of living communication that comes with lively eye contact, sureness of touch, mobile expressions, and expansiveness. At least not until we have educated them to fear it.

Children's play contains a universal language of its own. Its rules may vary from place to place, but it is always governed by its own built-in pleasures that children grasp intuitively as pleasure-seeking beings. They are not so concerned with the "right way" of doing things, but with the fun way. There is a mutual understanding that overcomes the limitations that different languages impose. The myth of the tower of Babel is a powerful metaphor for humanity's folly at attempting to be Godlike, in trying to live up to an idealized image, that is, rather than regulating our lives from the depths of our own nature. In trying to rise above our nature we have not become more Godly, but have lost contact with the sensations of life that make it such a vivid, all-embracing experience. As the word became the language of our detachment from our instinctive depths, so we became ever more incoherent and fragmented, both within ourselves and between each other. It is a mistake that is repeated again and again in the life of every child, as she or he is molded by an educational system in a language that is written and spoken without being felt.

The multicultural environment of Summerhill is such that when new children arrive from abroad there is usually someone, either an older or more established child or one of the staff, who will be able to talk to them in their own tongue. They will help the children settle in, and translate for them in the meetings so that they are not excluded from these more structured aspects of community life. The older kids are mostly very happy to help in this, and the meetings are often interspersed with short pauses, with the community waiting patiently while someone is translating for a new kid who is involved in that particular case. This toleration of different languages as an ever-present element of daily life reflects a deeper tolerance of differences, which the children grow up accepting as normal. Just as language poses no great problem, neither does nationality nor skin color. These are prejudices that children learn from adults. They have no innate base in children's lives.

Summerhill kids do not see each other primarily as Japanese, English, German, or American, but as playmates and personalities, brothers and sisters in the extended family of the community. The differences are acknowledged and become part of the texture of everyday life, but nobody is regarded as inferior because of her or his race. Nor is this something that the adults need to preach about. Only those who feel inferior in themselves have to make an inferior of someone else. It gives a false sense of superiority that the truly self-respecting individual has no need for. It is not incidental that racial hatred always contains strong suggestions of sexual and moral misconduct. The Nazi propagandists painted a picture of the Jew as a sexual fiend, infiltrating and polluting Aryan purity. The lynching of blacks in the American South was fueled by stories of the rape of white women and children, and the lynch victim's genitals were often mutilated or completely severed. During the people's revolution in Iran, young Islamic fundamentalists flailed themselves in the streets to cleanse themselves of sin, and cried for the death of western degenerates.

When we are able to tolerate all that we are, we are able to tolerate all that others are. There is no hidden motive to dress up others in our own dirty laundry. We see people for what they are, not as the projections of a repressed fantasy. This is not the same as the rigid morality around which much "political correctness" is woven, but a genuine self-acceptance that naturally expands out to others. At its extreme, "political correctness" is both ludicrous and patronizing. Many years ago, when I was at college, a fellow student mentioned to me that he had met Carol, a friend of mine. Knowing two Carols, one who was black and one who was white, I asked which one, this being the most obvious distinguishing feature.

"Oh," he answered, rubbing his chin musefully, "I didn't notice." I was left open-mouthed and speechless.

At Summerhill we are more down to earth. At the beginning of term we ask, "When are the Japanese arriving?" When a small group of German boys were making a nuisance of themselves in the House, one of the girls complained bitterly about "the bloody Germans." Our one Spanish boy was affectionately nicknamed "Spanish" by his closest friends, and felt no offense as it was not said offensively. Race is not something to be evaded, or tiptoed around—it is part of who we are. The children accept each other for who they are, and feel accepted themselves. A sense of personal well being is the most fertile soil for a sense of well being towards others. Race hatred takes root in the barren soil of fear and self-loathing, and all the talk in the world about political correctness does not eradicate hate, it just drives it underground until it emerges again in another form.

Over the past few years the greatest number of non-British Summerhillians have been German or Japanese. It is poignant to remember that just over half a century ago these children who now sleep in the same rooms, play together, and clasp each other in warm embraces of friendship would have been raised as bitter enemies, and later drilled to shoot and bomb each other. All because they were born to certain nations and at a certain point in history, a time in which the madness of the world had reached a particular crescendo, throwing countless lives into its bloody cauldron of frothing hate and frenzied brutality. The children of the blitz, of Dresden and Hiroshima, were children just like these. Such is the world as it is regulated by conniving politicians, rather than the openness that we bring to it as children.

I felt something of the same absurdity when I visited Berlin a year after the wall had been pulled down. As I crossed the boundary between the old East and West, now just an ugly scar of wasteland running through the city, I struggled with the fact that only a year or so earlier people were being shot for attempting to cross these same few meters. One day someone decides that if you try to cross from A to B you will forfeit your life. Another day someone decides that it's quite permissible to cross from A to B. Such is the pattern that history weaves. Yet we take these people seriously! We give them power! If small children can achieve, spontaneously and without effort, what these bristling bureaucrats with their stiff-necked dignity and long-winded speeches find such a struggle to reach, it has to be wondered why we put so much faith in them and so little in the innate humanity of children.

As an abstract sentiment or philosophical paradox this

question has become an age-old cliché. Christ anticipated it when he answered, "Become ye like little children," and it has been echoed by a thousand prophets and gurus since. But as a practical solution to be found in the raw stuff of child nature it has been largely untried, at least in more recent millennia.

Education in Japan

Each nationality brings its own characteristics into the Summerhill community, yet each gravitates towards something more essential and universal. Culture arises out of life, not the other way around. Life is the deeper, broader process. We try to impose as little as possible in Summerhill, but put our trust in this larger process as it emerges and expresses itself in the life of each child. We have our social structures and traditions like any society, but these are shaped equally by the needs of both adults and children. The children do not have to sublimate their needs and expressions to this culture, but are active in its everyday evolution. This is a way of life that most children are not used to, and it takes time to adjust, to let go of old anxieties and resentments, and to feel life rather than live it compulsively.

At various points in the school's history it has seen especially large groups of kids from one or other culture— Scandinavians, Germans, Americans, and more recently an influx of Japanese children.

The Japanese education system could not be much more different from the Summerhill approach. It is a very rigid system that emphasizes academic achievement but wholly neglects the emotional life of the child. Throughout their school years the children are taught by standardized teaching methods and repetitive drilling. Between the ages of six and twelve years old, children attend elementary school. As well as academic work they are also given social training, such as serving lunch to classmates, which is organized by rota, and moral training, which stresses the importance of manners, order, endurance, and hard work.

When they are twelve the children move onto junior high school. This is more formal. Uniforms are compulsory and are based on the German school uniforms of a hundred years ago, when Japanese educationalists, impressed by Germany's industrial growth, studied the German schools. The driving force behind this approach is to mold national character. Punctuality and dress are rigidly regulated. The emphasis is on conformity and uniformity. Buttons should be done up properly and hair must be the right length. This is overseen by the teachers and a "lifestyle committee" of older children. Any deviance from this narrow path is marked down in a personal rule book, which each child is required to carry. Too many marks and the child is called in for a talking to.

The classes are large, with children of mixed academic abilities studying together. Teaching is formal, with constant drilling and testing. All classes of the same age are expected to reach the same point in the curriculum at the same time. National and internal exams are set on a regular basis. There is a ten-minute morning break, and a forty-five minute lunch break, with classes ending at three thirty.

But school does not end there. Then the children have to clean the school. This is followed by other activities, such as sports and music, which are supposedly voluntary, but it would appear there is a great deal of pressure to attend.

It is a very competitive system, with academic success being greatly emphasized. Places in senior high school, which will later lead on to good universities, are anxiously sought after. Compulsory education ends at fifteen, but few take that option, being concerned that they will not find good employment in the future if they don't continue schooling. Because of the competition for places in senior high school, many attend *Juku* in the evening. These are private cramming schools, which focus on getting the children good grades in their exams. It will be nine thirty or ten o'clock before these finish, and then the children return home to begin their homework. This period of swotting for exams is commonly referred to as "examination hell." It is a time of great stress and misery.

School attendance extends to six days a week, with shorter holidays than those enjoyed by children in Europe or America. The academic standards are high, as are the suicide rates among teenagers, compared with Europe and America. Getting the right answer is the absolute goal. Individual opinion has no place in this scheme of things. From the viewpoint of turning out citizens for an efficiently run, highly industrialized ant-like society this system cannot be faulted. Indeed, Japan has one of the leading world economies, having reached that position after its defeat during World War Two, which left it devastated and in debt. But from the perspective of the children's emotional well being it is rather bleak.

Paradoxically, Japanese babies and infants are greatly indulged. They tend to be cuddled and breast fed far more than their Western contemporaries do. Traditionally the mother will be very attentive, and even submissive, particularly in relation to boys, allowing the child to pull her hair and slap her face without complaint. But the freedoms and indulgences of infancy are short-lived, and around the age of four or five a new regime of rigid discipline and self-reliance is suddenly introduced. All at once the child is faced with strong feelings of anxiety and rage, which it must then repress or face punishment. From now on the child must buckle down. The motive for this sudden turn of events is to train the child in self-discipline and to endure frustration. Not only does the child now learn to obey authority, but authority is imbued with all the memories of and yearning for a lost golden age. This conflict undermines any feelings of rebellion and binds the child to an authoritarian way of life.

Outlets for the intense frustration that underlie the impassive face of Japanese culture are highly structured and ritualized. It expresses itself in the hardships and passion of the endurance games, the strongly masochistic and sadistic images of film and literature, the outbursts of frenzied violence in comic books, which are far more extreme and graphic than their European and American counterparts, and the thrust and parry of the martial arts. In times of war this inner rage has erupted from its carefully controlled veneer in vivid flashes of intense cruelty.

On the other hand, Japan does not have such vast problems with crime and delinquency that many western countries have. Every so-called civilized culture has its own built-in layers of compulsion and chaotic, destructive reactions. Each takes on its own particular configuration. Every industrialized nation has its own history of atrocity in time of war and conflict. The British Empire was born from the childhood humiliations and pain of beatings that the English aristocracy stifled behind stiff upper lips in the company of their own kind, but unleashed with fury on those they considered beneath them. The early American settlers waged a campaign of genocide against the already established nations of that land, butchering the pagan natives to whom nakedness and nature did not carry the same brand of shame that had been burned into their own pious flesh during childhood. Here is a holocaust that has still not found its proper place in the pages of history.

In all of this, national character is always only ever a caricature, a one-dimensional image, which, when filled out by flesh and blood, thought and feeling, is something far more complex and vital. But it does give us a guide to the underlying structures that shape the life of the child, that point the way towards a certain type of adulthood.

Japanese Children at Summerhill

At the beginning of every term a couple of teachers meet the Japanese kids at Heathrow Airport and bring them to

Summerhill by coach. They arrive around midnight, pulling their suitcases behind them, exhausted from their trip, which has taken them halfway around the world, but also full of excitement. It is dark outside, and the grounds are full of shadows. They spill into the lounge, with its high ceiling and wooden walls, which have been chipped and battered from decades of children's play and parties. The emptiness fills with excited chatter and the squeaking of castors as their suitcases meet the floorboards. Most of the other children will have arrived earlier. Some will have gone to sleep now, but others have stayed awake to welcome their friends back. Houseparents appear to meet their charges. The children who have made this journey before shout out greetings, throwing their arms around both adults and peers in a wave of pleasure at being back again. And the new ones stand back a little, looking around. I can only imagine what they might be feeling.

As the school rarely takes children older than twelve, most of the new children will only have been to the elementary school in Japan. But their experience will still have been quite a rigid one of correct answers and correct behavior. Most of the teachers in Japan are aloof and distant, maintaining a stiff, dignified manner with the kids. What can these new kids think when they first see the freedom and intimacy that passes between the already established kids and the adults—adults who are informally dressed, smiling, laughing and playing the fool.

When he first arrived, one young boy stood stiffly, clutching a suitcase almost as large as he was in one hand and a violin case in the other. He looked lost and terrified. Another boy, who had been at Summerhill a couple of terms, tapped him on the shoulder and said something to him in Japanese. He looked even more frightened as the boy came over to me and playfully punched me on the thigh a few times. His eyes widened and his mouth dropped open as the boy merrily gesticulated in my direction and warbled on in an almost singing tone. I presume he was telling his new friend that he could even do this here, and there was nothing to be afraid of. On another occasion a new Japanese girl arrived a day early. There were no other kids around and she was very rigid and subdued with the adults she met. When I dropped a Japanese swear word into my conversation with another member of staff her eyes almost popped out of her head. Instantly she dropped something of her stiff formality and let out a little peal of laughter.

The culture shock must be tremendous. The contradiction between these two different ways of life finds its own balance. Four or five small Japanese boys were wrestling together on my bed one day in a squirming heap of tangled limbs and breathless laughter. On the other side of the room a row of shoes sat in a perfectly arranged straight line. Two images that both mocked and complemented each other.

Some of the new Japanese children are immediately playful and expressive, but most are reserved and have a silent, brooding suspicion of adults. They hold themselves stiffly, avoid eye contact, and give little away in their facial expressions. In time, though, as with the European and American kids, the façade fades. It is as though some invisible ice has thawed and human warmth has once more rekindled the mobility of life. The same desire for childish pleasures and spontaneous joy that children around the world display makes its way to the surface.

This melting may take a while, often longer than with the European or American kids. Self-government also presents something of a culture shock. The Japanese kids are generally far more reticent to use the meetings, although there are some who go on to have very strong voices. The idea of speaking in public, and in English, which they may not feel confident in, can pose some problems. But even when an older kid or ombudsman is prepared to speak on their behalf there is a strong resistance to working things out in the larger social sphere, which is not so evident among the other foreign-speaking children. Partly, I believe, this is due to inhibitions about expressing a strong opinion in front of others, particularly adults. Many of the Japanese kids also feel personally slighted when someone argues a contrary opinion, especially if the meeting votes in favor of the other person. There seems to be a feeling of humiliation at not having "won" the debate—an echo of the competitiveness of Japanese schools, with their emphasis on getting the "right answer," rather than expressing a viewpoint.

To show hurt or vulnerability is also strongly tabooed. A grazed elbow or bruised shin is often accompanied by a biting of lip and holding back of tears. This refusal to submit to feelings is a quite logical consequence of the armoring against anguish and rage that the child must adopt at the end of infancy, when discipline is suddenly imposed and emotion severely suppressed. This holding back extends to taking a problem to Tribunal or using the Ombudsman. It is seen as a sign of weakness. Instead of being dealt with openly, personal grudges are avenged by petty acts of revenge. When there were a large group of Japanese kids in the House several years ago, I was frequently having to change sheets after someone had squirted toothpaste or rubbed noodles into someone else's bed.

Such problems are far more difficult to resolve when there is a large group of new Japanese kids. Because of this, there is now a policy of not taking more than one or two new Japanese kids at a time. This gives them more of a chance to mix with kids from other cultures and integrate into the larger community, instead of congealing into homogenous non-participating groups. When we did have this problem a while back the strongest voice of protest came from the older Japanese kids, who had found their own footing in the community in dribs and drabs. They complained that it was ruining Summerhill by taking on so many Japanese kids at once. For them this was everything they had left behind, and didn't want to deal with here in Summerhill.

The problem of integrating this particular group was also exasperated by some of the Japanese parents. One of the older boys was irate after overhearing several parents at Narita Airport tell a group of younger kids, "Don't forget, we Japanese must stick together and look after our own." Such advice could only act to discourage the children from taking an active role in the self-government of the community.

Another example of this problem was when I came across several Japanese House Kids, with furrowed brows and deep sighs, struggling to figure out a book of very complex-looking mathematical problems. It puzzled me, as I was pretty sure that none of them were actually attending class at that time. When I asked them where they had got it from they nervously pretended not to understand the question, which was a common bluff that they employed when they wanted to avoid dealing with something. It did not seem to bother them that minutes later, after the awkward moment had passed, they would lapse back into English with little difficulty.

Later on, one of them explained to me that during the holidays they had been given lessons by private tutors, who set homework to be done during term time. The reason they didn't want it known at Summerhill was that they were afraid there would be a confrontation between the school and their parents, and they would be taken out. But this lack of trust in their capacity to learn in their own time could only undermine the children's trust in Summerhill, which is founded on such faith. It also destroyed their capacity to play freely without anxiety. It was a problem that not only affected those particular children, but the community as a whole, as it reinforced the separation of this group from the other children. We tackled it as diplomatically as possible in a letter addressed to all parents, emphasizing Summerhill's principle of self-regulation, and that trying to push children into academic work before they were ready would only hinder this process. It seemed to do the trick, and the tutors and homework died out.

Towards Self Regulation

The shift between authoritarian culture to a self-regulating society is a big step. It is one in which anxieties and misunderstandings are inevitable. When these shifts begin to occur within a society, similar fears and misconceptions abound. All is flux and nothing is certain. We have seen this in the attempts by some teachers and parents to liberalize British schools. The fear of harsh discipline and corporal punishment that governed children's lives for so long has been largely removed. Consequently, many children feel more free to express their discontent by opting out, or creating their own entertainment to relieve the boredom. A system that fights against life needs fear to maintain it. To remove the fear without changing the system is a half measure that is sure to fall short.

But in essence, even with the extinction of the more obvious and physical barbarities, fear still exists as a motivating force in British schools. It is a more subtle and insidious affair though—the fear of humiliation, of failing, of the future. The a priori of academic success and increased competitiveness, underscored by parental expectation, takes up the reins where the cane and the slipper left off. In some ways it is even harder to rebel against. The sources of guilt and anxiety are not so easily defined, although their effects are still clearly felt. When anger finally erupts in acts of belligerence and destruction, the old authoritarian vanguard calls for the restoration of old authoritarian disciplines, while the liberals cast aspersions on a system that they are not themselves prepared to abandon in its essential denial of the child's capacity for self-regulation. It is a vicious circle of half-truths, a visionary no-man's land.

The Japanese children, in their journey to Summerhill and the hopes of their parents that bridge the distance with them, encounter in a single leap of several hours what the British education system has failed to come to terms with in decades. Their struggles and difficulties, although uniquely their own, also reflect something of the upheaval that British parents and children have been contending with over a much longer period, and have still not resolved.

Another noticeable feature of having a large group of Japanese children in the House was that the "latency period" of sexual disinterest was far more pronounced. The boys and the girls had very little to do with each other. The boys were generally contemptuous of the girls, who remained docile and distant. Sexuality was not so openly discussed, and sexual jokes had an especially bitter bite to them. There was little in the way of sexual play between the sexes, but a guarded intimacy between the girls and a lot of larking around and genital grabbing between the boys, with both erotic and sadistic overtones. This was accompanied by an exaggerated anxiety about homosexuality, which found voice as sniggering and cries of "homo, homo," especially when two boys expressed their affection for each other by hugging or walking around with arms around each other.

These are all elements that crop up to some degree among the European kids at this age, but not so consistently and strongly as among this large Japanese group. Authoritarianism is always anti-sexuality, just as self-regulation can only arise out of an emotional life that is at one with its sexual nature. Most of these children were also ignorant of or misinformed about basic sexual functioning. One girl's mother had warned her not to kiss boys until she was an adult or she might catch a disease. She is now thirteen and her parents have never broached the subject of sex or menstruation with her. When she first began to learn about these things at Summerhill she thought people were joking.

How far children are able to go in dropping old attitudes and anxieties is very individual. If we were to build two fires next to each other, both the same size and with exactly the same materials, the flames of each would still dance differently from each other. Watching the flames, we might try to analyze the various elements that cause a flame to leap this way or that, to glow blue one second and yellow the next. We could talk about chemicals and atmospherics and arrive at some understanding of the process, but we could never predict what shape the flames would take, or how they would move. Nor could we recreate a fire that behaved exactly the same as an earlier one. By the same token, it is impossible to interpret the lives of children mechanically, though we may come to some understanding of the living processes by which they function. But these cannot be grasped by the intellect alone, any more than a fire can be frozen and dissected. We must feel the warm glow of life and follow its lively flickerings with all our senses. In every child, life dances its own individual dance, describing its own unique patterns from moment to moment. The brightness and warmth may become dampened down, the patterns may become rigidified, but where there is life there is always the possibility it will flare up now and then in unexpected, unpredictable ways.

In the conventional Japanese schools the children would live out their latency years in the emotional vacuum of an authoritarian education system, inundated with academic pressures. It would not prepare them for the intensity of puberty. Their anxieties would deepen and attitudes harden. When they are able to live out this period according to their own impulses, even when they are edged with expressions of contempt and sadism, their anxieties fade and their attitudes soften. Life begins to sparkle again.

The Japanese children clearly enjoy the freedom of Summerhill. Whether they are always able to enjoy it as fully as children from less authoritarian cultures is questionable. But it says something about their depth of experience that few of them return to Japan after leaving Summerhill, but continue their studies either in Europe or America. One eighteen-year-old who had returned to Japan the previous year told me that it was difficult to find friends with whom he could share his thoughts and feelings. Their experiences were so different. I asked him if he regretted having come to Summerhill. Without a moments hesitation he said, "No. I like myself far better than I used to. I'm far more confident now." The last I heard of him he was traveling around Japan exploring both the culture and his own feelings about who he was.

I have wondered a lot in the past whether Summerhill is ultimately the right place for Japanese children. It would be stupid to ignore the conflict that must inevitably arise between a way of life that is so rigid and emotionally restrained and one in which life moves freely. But I have yet to meet a Japanese child who has not become a happier, more confident person in Summerhill, or a Japanese ex-Summerhillian who has any regrets about having been raised more freely. The sense I get is that they have gained something special, and if that has put them slightly outside of their culture, it has also placed them more solidly within themselves.

Why Summerhill has proved so popular in Japan in the first place is a complex question. Certainly many parents are aware of the deep damage that is being done to their children by the schooling there, and want something different for them. Japanese educators are realizing that they have too much neglected the emotional side, and many visit Summerhill to try to find out what its secret is. There is no secret. It's just a matter of trusting in children's capacity to regulate their own lives, to play, work, love, and live according to their own

Free-range children radiate happiness and personality.

[Photo by Tomo Usuada.]

needs, not ours. But this is not something that can be mechanically learned; it has to be felt. Professor Shinichiro Hori, a long-time admirer of Neill and frequent visitor to Summerhill, founded a school in Japan loosely based on Summerhill principles. Called Kinokuni Children's Village, it caters to primary-age children, and does not have the scope of freedom that Summerhill has. And it has run into problems with teachers who felt they deserved more respect from the children. Children who are continually frustrated become frustrated adults to whom such petty values are important. Despite these teething troubles, Kinokuni appears to be thriving.

Last year Summerhill had its first pupil from Taiwan. There has also been interest from the media and educationalists in Korea. With the unification of Germany a few years ago, visitors from the old East have begun to make their way over. A school for street children was founded recently in Thailand, influenced by Summerhill. I was recently told of a Tibetan lama who is developing a similar school in northern India, in which there will be no religion, but the children will be allowed to grow naturally. (This is possibly the most trusting of faiths—that children do not have to be imposed upon to become "good.") There always have been and always will be people who side with what is most alive within themselves, rather than that which has been warped. Most of these people will live their lives quietly, in small, unassuming ways, raising their children to have their own thoughts and feelings. They belong to many cultures, but more importantly they belong to themselves and to life. Then there are those who march up and down, banging the drums of their own little ways. They demand respect from children, not happiness for them. Their culture is something to be conformed to, not to facilitate the fullness of life. These things are important to them, and they make a lot of noise about it. But the deeper rhythms of life are forever present, quietly getting on with the business of living and will continue to do so long after this or that way of molding young life has fallen by the wayside.

Selected Bibliography

Although this book is based mostly on personal experience, a great deal of background reading helped me to consolidate my thinking about children and Summerhill. These are just some of the books that have been important in shaping my understanding during the period A Free Range Childhood was written. Many of them are now out of print, but may be tracked down via libraries and second-hand book shops. Some of the details refer to British editions and may differ slightly to the American.

Adams, Paul; Berg, Leila; Beger, Nan; Duane, Michael; Neill, A.S.; and Ollendorf, Robert. *Children's Rights: Towards the Liberation of the Child.* Elek Books,1971. A collection of essays giving a social and historical context to the needs of children and adolescents. Full of interesting and sometimes surprising details that put the prevailing, narrow view of childhood in a wider perspective.

Bazeley, E.T. *Homer Lane and the Little Commonwealth.* New Education Book Club, 1948. Neill was very much influenced by Homer Lane, whose Little Commonwealth was a self-governing community for delinquents. This account by a houseparent at the Little Commonwealth reveals Lane's wisdom and compassion, showing how love and approval may succeed where discipline and punishment fail.

Berg, Leila. *Risinghill: Death of a Comprehensive School.* Pelican, 1968. One criticism of Summerhill is that such an approach could not work in the state system. This is the story of a school in London in which the Summerhill way was attempted and worked, until the school was closed for political reasons.

Boadella, David (ed.). *In the Wake of Reich.* Coventure, 1979. Various essays written by therapists and educators on some of the offshoots of Reich's work. These include therapeutic derivations, approaches to childbirth, and the emotional needs of babies and children.

Croall, Jonathan. *Neill of Summerhill: The Permanent Rebel.* Routledge & Kegan Paul, 1983. A biography of Neill and of life at Summerhill as it developed throughout Neill's life. Croall describes the hopes, conflicts, frustrations, and complexities that lay behind the ideal.

Croall, Jonathan (ed.). *All the Best Neill: Letters from Summerhill.* Andre Deutsch, 1983. This collection of letters by Neill was the first of his writings I ever read. The tone of the letters are at various times humorous, angry, frustrated, and pessimistic, but never lose sight of the belief in the inherent "goodness" of the child.

DeMeo, James. *Saharasia: The 4000 BCE Origins of Child Abuse, Sex-Repression, Warfare and SocialViolence in the Deserts of the Old World.* OBRL, 1998. Thoroughly researched and extremely well documented. Traces the roots of warlike and destructive human behavior to sudden climatic changes around 4000 BC. With data from a vast range of disciplines, the book shows humans to be innately sociable and peaceful. Cultures where the emotional and sexual needs of infants, children, and adolescents are met are compared with those in which they are negated. The research reveals that these two different approaches give rise to two very different modes of adult behavior. Can be obtained from Natural Energy Works, PO Box 1148, Ashland, OR 97520, USA.

Elwin, Verrier. *The Muria and their Ghotul.* Oxford University Press, 1947. Anthropological account of a non-Hindu people in India, describing their democratic children's houses, the "Ghotul," in which childhood and adolescent sexuality is approved of.

Hart, Harold (ed.) *Summerhill: For and Against.* Hart Publishing Company, 1970. Essays by educators, psychologists, and others for and against Summerhill. Most miss the mark completely, being more concerned with their own theoretical bias than the reality of Summerhill.

Keleman, Stanley. *The Human Ground: Sexuality, Self and Survival.* Center Press, 1975. Describes how we shape ourselves emotionally, mentally, and physically around our experience as we grow up.

Leboyer, Fredrick. *Birth Without Violence.* Fontana/Collins, 1974. One of the seminal books of the natural birth movement. Leboyer's poetic text is interspersed with beautiful photographs clearly depicting the difference between a violent birth and a peaceful one.

Liedloff, Jean. *The Continuum Concept.* Arkana, 1986. An approach to meeting the needs of babies and children based on the experience of living with the Yequana, a South American Indian tribe. The author became intrigued by the connection between their child-centered child-rearing practices and their ability in later life to live contentedly, free of the frustration and neurosis we "civilized" folk suffer from.

Lifton, Betty Jean. *The King of Children.* Pan, 1988. A moving account of the life of Janus Korczak, a Polish-Jewish doctor, who ran orphanages along democratic lines and was a great advocate of children's rights. Korczak eventually died with the children in his care in the gas chambers of Treblinka rather than abandon them. The quotes from Korczak's own writings are full of humanity and insight into the world of children.

Malinowski, Bronislaw. *The Sexual Life of Savages.* Routledge & Keegan Paul, 1968. An anthropological study of a Melanesian people. Their method of child-rearing, including children's democracies within the wider community and a positive attitude towards childhood and adolescent sexuality. As a people they are non-violent, sociable, and emotionally well-adjusted.

Milgram, Stanley. *Obedience to Authority*. Tavistock, 1974. Research to show how we are conditioned by authority to commit atrocities. Has important ramifications for the many ways we give up responsibility for ourselves to outside authority.

Neill, A.S. *Summerhill: A Radical Approach to Education*. Gollancz, 1962. Compiled from four of his earlier books, *Summerhill* became a best-seller in the 1960s and '70s. It was fascinating to read this while working at the school, having read it first beforehand. Although the context it was written in makes the book feel dated in places, so many of the descriptions of Summerhill life and the insights into child-nature could have been written in the present. I also noticed that as an adult at Summerhill, I was far more aware of Neill's emphasis on staff's needing to be patient while the children went through their anti-social phases than I was during the first reading!

Neill, A. S. *Freedom—Not Licence*. Hart Publishing Company, 1966. Written for an American audience after the success of *Summerhill* in the States. A question-and-answer format. Neill was not happy with it, feeling pressured rather than inspired to write it, but it's good to dip into.

Neill, A. S. *Neill! Neill! Orange Peel*. Hart Publishing Company, 1972. Neill's autobiography reveals him as both a man of his time and a visionary.

Odent, Michel. *Entering the World*. Penguin, 1984. Pioneering work at the famous Pithiviers Clinic in France. A woman- and baby-centered approach to childbirth.

Placzeck, Beverly R. (ed.). *Record of a Friendship: The Correspondence Between Wilhelm Reich and A.S. Neill*. Gollancz, 1982. Two very different personalities, but with a mutual respect for each other's work and mutual anguish at the way the world was going, with events such as the rise of fascism, the dropping of the atom bomb, and the cold war. It is fascinating to view world events through these two men's eyes and to feel their deep love of humanity animating the pages.

Prescott, James. "Body Pleasure and the Origins of Violence." Pulse of the Planet. OBRL, 1991. Excellent article researching the links between violent behavior and the negation of the body as a source of pleasure in childhood and adolescence. (Can be obtained from Natural Energy Works—see DeMeo above.)

Raknes, Ola. *Wilhelm Reich and Orgonomy*. Penguin, 1969. Clear, concise account of the scope of Reich's work by one of his colleagues, with a short biography and personal reminiscences. A good introduction to Reich's work.

Reich, Wilhelm. *The Function of the Orgasm.* Orgone Institute Press, 1948. Traces the development of Reich's work from his psychoanalytic roots, through his understanding of sexuality and the orgasm as expressions of health, to his discovery of a specific biological energy underlying both psyche and soma. Probably the best introduction to Reich's writings, as it makes clear the "red thread" that links his development from one area of research to the next. A book that I have come back to many times.

Reich, Wilhelm. *Children of the Future.* Farrar Strauss Giroux, 1978. A collection of papers about the specific problems of trying to raise healthy children in a sick society. This book proved very useful to me in helping to clarify processes that were not always clear to me. It is probably best read with a prior grounding in Reich's work.

Sharaf, Myron. *Fury on Earth.* Hutchinson & Co., 1983. The most extensive biography of Wilhelm Reich. It suffers a little at times from a tendency to psychoanalytic reductionism, but nevertheless is a very readable and moving account of a complex life story.

Walmsley, John. *Neill and Summerhill: A Man and His Work.* Penguin, 1969. A lovely book of photographs taken at Summerhill in the 1960s and interspersed with quotes by Neill, various staff and pupils, and others. Gives a real flavor of Summerhill.

Afterword: Summerhill in Court— A Historic Victory

Just before the publication of this book, the Office for Standards in Education (OFSTED) withdrew its threat of closure. This followed an appeal by the school that was heard at an Independent Schools Tribunal in the High Court. This was described on the front page of the *Daily Telegraph* (March 24, 2000) as "a historic victory after David Blunkett, the Education Secretary, dropped his demands that it [Summerhill] improve its instruction."

An impromptu community meeting was held within the court to decide whether to accept a nine-point "statement of intent" offered by the government. In an article headed "Court Deal Saves 'Freedom' School from Closure," the *Times* describes how "in extraordinary scenes at the Royal Courts of Justice, the school was allowed to take over Court 40 to hold a student council to debate Mr. Blunkett's new proposals." There really is something extraordinary about this case in which High Court proceedings are stopped and government officials are forced to wait, while a meeting of children decide whether or not to accept their proposals. Added to this, the Department for Education and Employment were ordered to contribute towards Summerhill's legal fees, which could be as high as £150,000.

A press statement issued by Summerhill on 23rd March 2000 states:

> The Summerhill school community hailed the unique agreement reached with the Secretary of State for Education after the collapse of his case against the school today. Carmen Cordwell, the chair of the children's meeting said, 'This is our charter for freedom. It gives us the space we need to live and breathe and learn into the future. After 79 years, this is the first official recognition that A.S. Neill's philosophy of education provides an acceptable alternative to compulsory lessons and the tyranny of compulsory exams. With this one bound, we are free at last.

The Court had heard that OFSTED had put Summerhill on a secret "hit list" of 61 independent schools that were listed as TBW (To Be Watched). It had inspected the school every year, most recently in 1999 with a team of eight inspectors who did not understand its democratic philosophy and did not consult its pupils, ex-pupils, or parents. OFSTED insisted that the school should change over to compulsory lessons, knowing that then it would have to close. But instead, Summerhill went to court to challenge the narrow and unimaginative thinking behind the recommendation. After it produced evidence from two teams of educational experts and from an army of distinguished ex-pupils, the Secretary of State's representative concluded in cross-examination that OFSTED's recommendation was unacceptable. The three "Notices of Complaint" served on Summerhill were annulled, and a protocol guaranteeing the school's right to continue as A.S. Neill desired was formally agreed to by the school community and the Secretary of State.

As a true measure of Summerhill's legal victory, the Government has agreed to make a contribution to the school's legal costs. This is remarkable, since the Independent Schools Tribunal has no power to award costs to a successful appellant—it is an acknowledgement of the force of

Summerhill's case, which would have become more embarrassing for OFSTED had the hearing continued.

Zoë Readhead, A.S. Neill's daughter, who administers the school, said, "This is the most wonderful triumph for us. My father always had faith in the law, and he would be delighted at how it has brought him victory and vindication over a bureaucracy which could never cope with his ideas."

In a nine-point "statement of intent," the Government concedes that Neill's philosophy must henceforth govern OFSTED's approach to the school. It will not subject the school to another full inspection for at least four years. Most dramatically for children's rights, it accepts that "the pupils' voice should be fully represented in any evaluation of the quality of education at Summerhill." It also agrees that "learning is not confined to lessons" and acknowledges the right of children not to attend them.

In opening the school's case, its counsel Mr. Geoffrey Robertson, QC, said he would call evidence to show that the school had devised a system that eliminated "the great evils of contemporary education—bullying, racism, sex abuse, and drug abuse" and that could usefully be copied by other schools. He argued that education meant equipping a child for responsible citizenship, and that Summerhill was "the happiest school in the world." He said that had Neill's friend George Bernard Shaw reviewed the evidence in the case, he would have changed his famous maxim ("Those who can, do. Those who can't, teach.") to read, "Those who can, teach. Those who can't, inspect."

Zoë Readhead said, "We have lived for a year under the OFSTED falsehood that we have mistaken idleness for liberty. Today's verdict refutes that defamation and shows that liberty and learning go hand in hand at Summerhill. We can now put all the pettiness and incomprehension to which we have been subjected behind us, and look forward to a sensible and productive relationship with OFSTED and the Department of Education."

For myself and many others who care about Summerhill and have supported it through this difficult time, there is a great sense of celebration and relief. Beyond these personal concerns, Summerhill has also fought a battle that has resulted in a historic legal precedent, which has important ramifications for children and parents in Britain. I also wonder how the children who were personally involved in the campaign and tribunal will look back on this episode of their lives. After all, how many children get to take on a government and win as part of their education? But then, this is only the Summerhill ethic acted out on a larger stage.

—Matthew Appleton
March 27, 2000

A Note About the Author

Before living at Summerhill I worked in a variety of medical and charitable environments. Working with young homeless people, often with drug and psychiatric problems, led to an interest in the childhood roots of these difficulties. After studying humanities at Bristol Polytechnic in England I spent a short but creative time singing, writing, and performing with an experimental band and performance-art group. Childhood and adolescent themes were central to many of our performances. My interest in these themes seemed to lead me naturally to Summerhill.

It was hard leaving Summerhill after being part of a vibrant and caring community for so long. I left because I felt I had given my best and had no more to give. It was time to explore other avenues. While still at Summerhill I trained in craniosacral therapy in London and in psychotherapy at the Centre for Orgonomy in Germany. Today I work in private practice combining these two disciplines. My craniosacral practice has a strong focus of working with babies and young children who have been traumatised at birth. I became interested in the traumatic effects of modern, technological birthing methods on babies while at Summerhill. I have also gone on to teach craniosacral therapy and, with colleagues, recently founded the Institute of Craniosacral Studies. My psychotherapeutic work draws much from the work of Wilhelm Reich, especially his understanding of the relationship between mind and body. I am continuing my education by studying core process psychotherapy with the Karuna Institute in England.

My wife and I split up when our daughter, Eva, was eighteen months old. Because of her young age, Eva returned to Norway with her mother, where she now lives. It is painful being separated from her, but I am happy to know she is growing up to be a happy, healthy child and see her when I can. My hope is that when she is older she will have the chance to live at Summerhill.

My home is now in Bristol, England, where I grew up and have recently returned after many years away. When I am not working I practice Aikido, enjoy walks in the country, swimming, reading, and continue to write poetry, fiction, and articles about my work. Summerhill continues to be a strong influence in my life and I visit it when I can. My most vivid dreams are always based there.

271

Praise for Matthew Appleton's
A Free Range Childhood

"Matthew Appleton's view of childhood and of Summerhill grew and developed during his time as a houseparent at the school. In this book he uses many examples and anecdotes to illustrate the feeling and depth which only somebody in his position would be able to see. The stories are full of humor and fun, and many of them take me back to my time as a Summerhill 'House kid.' Matthew was a popular member of staff, allowing Summerhill to work its magic on him and offering a great deal to the community in return. This is a personal and candid view of his time with us—it is a very enjoyable read, and it raises some important, if uncomfortable, questions about modern methods of child-rearing."   —ZOË READHEAD
Principal of Summerhill School and daughter of founder A.S. Neill

"Matthew Appleton reminds us of the importance of love, emotion, and freedom in the life of the child, discussing the findings of nearly-forgotten social pioneers, such as A.S. Neill and Wilhelm Reich, who proved that self-regulation for children really works."   —JAMES DeMEO, Ph.D.
Author of *Saharasia: The 4000 BCE Origins of Child Abuse, Sex-Repression, Warfare and Social Violence*

"In a time of crisis and confusion, *A Free Range Childhood* connects us with the ethical heart of education at its best—the deep respect for human growth in diversity, the clear recognition of childhood as a distinct time of identity-creation within community, the abiding commitment to learning and an apprenticeship in liberty as indispensable to participatory democracy."
—WILLIAM AYERS
Distinguished Professor of Education, Senior University Scholar, University of Illinois at Chicago and author of *To Teach*

"With our schools more prison-like every day and the obsession with artificial standards fast becoming a new religion, the reappearance of Summerhill on the world stage couldn't be more timely. Matthew Appleton is an able guide, thanks to a prose filled with immediacy and passion. Old Neill would be proud."
—CHRIS MERCOGLIANO
Co-director of the Albany Free School and author of *Making It Up As We Go Along: The Story of the Albany Free School*